Edmund Spenser

THE FAERIE QUEENE

Book One

Edmund Spenser

The Faerie Queene
Book One

Edited, with Introduction, by
Carol V. Kaske

Hackett Publishing Company, Inc.
Indianapolis/Cambridge

24 23 22 21 20   4 5 6 7 8 9

For further information, please address
    Hackett Publishing Company, Inc.
    P.O. Box 44937
    Indianapolis, IN 46244-0937

    www.hackettpublishing.com

Cover art: Walter Crane illustration and ornament for Book One, *The Faerie Queene*, ca. 1890.

Cover design by Abigail Coyle
Interior design by Elizabeth Wilson
Composition by Professional Book Compositors

Library of Congress Cataloging-in-Publication Data
Spenser, Edmund, 1552?–1599.
    The faerie queene / Edmund Spenser.
        v. cm.
    Contents: Book one / edited, with introduction, by Carol Kaske —
Book five / edited, with introduction, by Abraham Stoll
    Includes bibliographical references and indexes.
    ISBN 0-87220-808-7 (bk. 1) — ISBN 0-87220-807-9 (pbk. : bk. 1) —
    ISBN 0-87220-802-8 (bk. 5) — ISBN 0-87220-801-X (pbk. : bk. 5)
    1. Knights and knighthood—Poetry.   2. Epic poetry, English.   3. Virtues
—Poetry. ÂI. Kaske, Carol V., 1933–   II. Stoll, Abraham Dylan, 1969–
III. Title.
PR2358.A3K37   2006
821'.3—dc22   2005026668

ISBN-13: 978-0-87220-808-7 (cloth, bk. 1)
ISBN-13: 978-0-87220-807-0 (pbk., bk. 1)

CONTENTS

ABBREVIATIONS

Citations from other books of *The Faerie Queene* are documented in this volume in the conventional format, listing book, canto, stanza, and line number. For example, II.i.33.4 refers to Book Two, Canto One, stanza 33, line 4. Citations from Book One do not list the book number: x.1.9 refers to Book One, Canto Ten, stanza 1, line 9.

ACH	Spenser, Edmund. *The Faerie Queene.* Edited by A. C. Hamilton.
Aeneid	Virgil, *Aeneid.*
Colin Clout	Spenser, Edmund. In *Yale Edition of the Shorter Poems.*
F.E.	*'Faults escaped in the Print,'* 1590 ed.
GL	Tasso, Torquato. *Gerusalemme Liberata.*
M&P	*Edmund Spenser's Poetry,* 3rd edition. Edited by Hugh Maclean and Anne Lake Prescott.
Metamorphoses	Ovid, *Metamorphoses.*
OED	*Oxford English Dictionary.*
OF	Ariosto, Ludovico. *Orlando Furioso.*
SE	Hamilton, A. C., et al., eds. *The Spenser Encyclopedia.*
TPR	*Edmund Spenser:* The Faerie Queene. Edited by Thomas P. Roche.
Var.	*The Works of Edmund Spenser, a Variorum Edition.* Edited by Edwin Greenlaw, et al.

INTRODUCTION

1. The Place of *The Faerie Queene* in English Literature

Spenser holds a secure place in the canon—insofar as there still is a canon—just below Chaucer, Shakespeare, and Milton. This is partly because his longest work, *The Faerie Queene* (about 35,000 lines), is a fantastic and myth-imbued narrative, and one involving basic moral issues. C. S. Lewis claims he never knew anyone who "used to like *The Faerie Queene.*" By this he meant that while some people do not like it, one can never revert to distaste once one gets on Spenser's wavelength. Perhaps I should say "wavelengths," for one of his strengths is his variety of moods, modes, or tones, ranging from the pious, through the heroic and patriotic, through the sentimental, to the comic and satiric.

Spenser has been called "the poet's poet," in that his poetic effects yield to analysis (e.g., the analysis of his versification, below) and hence to imitation more easily than do, say, those of Shakespeare. Not only Keats and Tennyson, but also Milton, Shelley, Wordsworth, and Yeats went through apprenticeships to Spenser in various respects. Melville imitated him not only in his poetry but also in his prose, as did Hawthorne in *his* prose. With respect to content, Milton praised Spenser's "forests and enchantments drear / Where more is meant than meets the ear" ("Il Penseroso," 120) and rated him "a greater teacher than Scotus or Aquinas" (*Areopagitica*).

2. Versification

Another of Spenser's appeals is his versification, an achievement for which he sometimes sacrificed meaning, clarity, or conciseness. Spenser invented a distinctive and demanding but (for all its countless repetitions) satisfying stanza for *The Faerie Queene:* nine lines, mostly in pentameter, with a rhyme scheme of *ababbcbcc*. It was based on existing stanzas, such as the eight-line stanza of Ariosto and Tasso. The *b* ending recurs four times and stitches the entire stanza together. Still, when line 5 is supplied with the *b* ending (the third occurrence of *b*), the effect is destabilizing: now this *b*-rhyme is no longer appearing in an even-numbered line, as previously, but in an odd one (as the emerging quatrain of lines 5 through 8 displays the rhyme pattern of *bcbc*). Line 8, while picking up the rhyme of line 6 (*c*) and thus completing the second quatrain, now enters into an interlocking couplet with the final line 9 (also *c*). This concluding couplet gives a sense of closure, as couplets often do—one augmented by the extra (hexametric) length of line 9 (an "alexandrine"). Thus, although this last line also repeats a rhyme unexpectedly, it is not destabilizing; it wraps up the entire stanza. To avoid too much closure, though, in the first line of a stanza, a relative pronoun often refers back to the preceding stanza, or a word or phrase is repeated from it. Because of its complexity and the attachment of Spenser's name to it, the presence of this stanza in a later author's work is a sure sign of influence, direct or indirect. The Spenserian stanza was imitated by many poets, both major and minor, perhaps most successfully by Keats in "The Eve of St. Agnes" and Tennyson in "The Choric Song of the Lotos-Eaters."

3. *The Faerie Queene*, Book One

Book One, The Legend of Holiness, presents a mutually enriching amalgam of discourses because its religious allegory is abstract and often complex and debatable, whereas its story appeals to the emotions, including some of the simplest and most basic ones. To the general public, the first book of *The Faerie Queene* has furnished quotations to copy into high-school yearbooks and subjects for Mardi Gras floats and children's plays and stories. This Introduction will alternate brief essays on relevant topics with a plot-centered commentary that proceeds more or less chronologically through the poem.

4. Spenser's Religious Milieu

While romance materials like love and combat are relatively timeless, a religious theme is inevitably inflected by the surrounding culture. Since the subject of Book One is holiness (whatever that may mean, be it wholeness, sanctification, or a true faith), it is enriched by a familiarity with the religious situation at the time Spenser was writing. In the Reformation, various sects in various nations of Western Europe seceded from the once hegemonic Roman Catholic Church in order to regain the purity of the primitive church and of the Bible on which it was supposedly founded. One important disagreement was over the proportion of divine versus human causes of salvation. To oversimplify a bit, the Catholic Church said that mankind must earn heaven and even day-to-day forgiveness by exerting free will, whereas the original Protestant reformers retorted that free will is "vaine" (as in x.1: "If any strength we have, it is to ill, / But all the good is Gods, both power and eke will") and that we obtain heaven by unmerited grace caused by God's arbitrary election (ix.53; x.57). This debate will recur like a leitmotif of this Introduction. By Spenser's time, England had become Protestant and was destined to remain so, though constant vigilance was required to keep it that way. The last Catholic monarch was "bloody" Mary Tudor, who died in 1558 when Spenser was a child. Elizabeth, a moderate and evasive Protestant, ascended the throne, and she ruled throughout the rest of Spenser's life. But sixteenth-century Englishmen continued to strive with their Catholic foes at home and abroad, both with arms and with arguments. The popes had denied Elizabeth's right to the throne and absolved in advance anyone who would assassinate her. On at least two occasions, Spain tried to reconquer England for the papacy. Continually, from the 1580s on, Catholic missionaries skulked around England hoping to win converts and to give the existing Catholics spiritual support (Haigh, 201–5). Spenser's Archimago—an evil enchanter who keeps appearing in Book One and the first eight cantos of Book Two—may symbolize on the political level one such missionary, since he has a breviary and says "Hail Marys" in Latin.

The Reformation conflicts emerged within Protestantism itself regarding how many of the old ways and beliefs Englishmen should discard and how many they should retain. Factions were starting to coalesce, which in the seventeenth century would polarize in the English Civil War. Some disagreements were as follows: about foreign policy—militant anti-Catholicism versus isolationism and a live-and-let-live attitude; about worship—all the features that later came to be polarized as Low Church versus Anglican or High Church, such as plain versus ornate churches, "pastors" or "ministers" wearing plain black clothing versus "priests" wearing vestments, and preaching and Bible reading versus emphasis on the sacraments; about governance—"puritan" or, as they were more frequently called, "precisian" congregations taking considerable initiative (Collinson, 1985, 189–93), versus an established Church under bishops and a sovereign who replaced the pope as Supreme Governor of the Church; and about anthropology—divine predestination and grace versus human free will as causes of salvation.

As to the last issue, a few silent or isolated conservatives, including Queen Elizabeth and Richard Hooker, retained a certain limited trust in human agency—though none dared call it "free will," which was a rallying cry of the Catholics—and they always stipulated the help of divine grace (Lake, 192–7). This minority was stigmatized under the label of Lutherans (Collinson, 1967, 29–37). In the last quarter of Book One (x–xii), we will see Spenser suddenly preaching good deeds as the ticket to heaven and thus sharing these relatively conservative beliefs of Queen Elizabeth and her small party. Against these few was a vocal and powerful majority designated as Calvinists. Its pillars were those who had fled to Calvin's Geneva to escape Mary's persecution, but who returned upon Elizabeth's accession, bringing radical religious ideas and their own glossed translation of Scripture: the Geneva Bible, which was to become important for Spenser. In the first eight or nine cantos of Book One, Spenser attacks Roman Catholicism. This stance would seem to put him in the Calvinist, or "precisian" camp. Perhaps he reverses himself in Canto Ten in order to shake the reader out of the sin of intolerance; perhaps, as I will suggest later, the hero Redcrosse has entered a new phase of religious experience. Finally, in sixteenth-century English society, antipapal rhetoric was part of the standard political discourse of the day, like anti-Communist rhetoric in the 1950s. Almost every Englishman—however conservative his personal practices and beliefs often were—railed against "popery." One reason was that it was associated with foreign control—the pope and Philip of Spain, bloody Mary's hated consort, which royal couple may be symbolized on the political level in Canto Eight under the persons of Duessa and Orgoglio (Collinson 1985, 175, 184; Marotti, 1; Watkins, 118).

5. The Proem

The introductory section of Book One is called by scholars its Proem. Each book of *The Faerie Queene* has one. Every other proem extols the virtue that is the alleged theme of its book, called its "titular virtue"; but the first proem never mentions holiness, nor any other religious topic. It deals instead with issues affecting the entire poem: namely its genre and its place among Spenser's works, its leading characters, and its relation to the current monarch. It thereby foretells that the poem as a whole will not be as religious as is The Legend of Holiness. To take the last issue first, Spenser extols in awestruck, incantatory terms his sovereign Queen Elizabeth, asking her as another "Goddesse" to join the Muses, Cupid, Venus, and Mars in inspiring him (Proem, 4). Flattery of a ruler was characteristic of classical literature and even more so of Renaissance literature. Spenser asks one of the Muses (it is not clear which one) to bring him material on Tanaquill, another name for Gloriana, who is the Faerie Queen of the poem's title. This numinous female is the "type," in the world and time of the poem, of Queen Elizabeth in Spenser's time (Proem, 4; see ACH, note ad loc.). Surprisingly, she proves to be an elusive figure, presented, if at all, chiefly through the speeches of other characters.

6. Genre

Most of the first proem is taken up in one way or another with genre. Changes in literary terminology have obscured what Spenser is telling us about genre, both here and in the "Letter of the Authors" (now called the "Letter to Raleigh"). Yet in order to harbor the right expectations, we must know what kind of literature we have in hand.

By invoking the Muses (Proem, 2), Spenser announces his present genre to be that of the epic—or so he has usually been understood. He has progressed from the pastoral genre, "oaten reedes," in his *Shepheardes Calender* (1579) to "trumpets stearne," whatever they might metonymize. This was Virgil's career pattern, from the *Eclogues* to the *Aeneid*. Indeed, Spenser translates almost verbatim those autobiographical lines, which were then thought to constitute the beginning of the *Aeneid* and printed as such (see note ad loc.), but which are now recognized as a later interpolation. He thus announces himself to be the English Virgil. Virgil too extolled his ruler, Augustus. But the term "epic" was not much used by Elizabethan critics and never by Spenser, nor did they have any other term of comparably specific function, such as the French *chanson de geste;* they used the broader term "heroic poem." In the "Letter to Raleigh," Spenser labels the works he wants us to see as his models simply as "historical" poems, which could include Arthurian romance (see *SE*, "Heroic Poem Before Spenser" and "Heroic Poem Since Spenser"). When he says both here and in the "Letter" that his hero is Prince Arthur, and an Arthur whose principal motive is romantic love, he definitely classes his poem as being a romance as well as an epic, thus including romance with the epic as a subcategory of the heroic or historical poem. The two genres also intertwine in the genre *romanzo,* or romance-epic, which was practiced by his avowed Italian predecessors Ariosto and Tasso—avowed explicitly in the "Letter" and implicitly here by his epic proposition (statement of his subject matter) as "Fierce warres and faithfull loves" (Proem, 1.9), echoing Ariosto's similar proposition and significantly expanding Virgil's proposition, "arms and the man I sing" (see note ad loc.).

Nowadays we can see that the pervasive genre of *The Faerie Queene* is chivalric romance—adorned with some of the trappings of the epic, such as epic similes and invocations to the Muses. It is not Spenser (except perhaps in Book Two) but Milton who is the real English Virgil. The minimal recipe for a romance plot is a love interest and the testing of the hero's worth by physical combat: again, "Fierce warres and faithfull loves." The basic plot is a quest—a plot that can include combat but that also entails a variety of characters and settings as well as the education of the hero (cf. H. Cooper, 7–15). If the romance is long, as is *The Faerie Queene,* the plot can become extremely complicated by deferrals, flashbacks, and inset narratives, which are themselves short romances. Prince Arthur is the overall hero, whose quest is to find and earn the hand of

Gloriana, the queen of Faerie Land (Proem, 2; ix.6–17). Since the poem is unfinished, he never fulfills his quest, but he helps others fulfill theirs. Each book is itself an inset romance, the hero of which exhibits, sometimes imperfectly, a different virtue: Holiness, Temperance, Chastity, Friendship, Justice, and Courtesy. Redcrosse is the hero of Book One; his quest is to kill the dragon that has occasioned the imprisonment of Una's parents, Adam and Eve, the king and queen of Eden ("Letter"; vii.44; II.i.1.4–5). Within any romance, episodes often succeed one another without the "horizontal" laws of causation—those familiar from our ordinary existence, such as "action affects character and character affects action"; rather, they are caused from above and they unfold in the way someone wishes. The author may shape them into an allegory; author and reader want the entertainment of an emotional rollercoaster ending in wish fulfillment; and society wants a reenactment of its rituals in a glamorous light (Benson, 72–4; Frye, 47–50). Because the aim is entertainment, incidents partake of the erotic, the violent, the coincidental, the mysterious, and in some romances the fantastic.

Romance differs from epic in that it regards love as at least potentially ennobling: as Spenser says, "love does alwaies bring forth bounteous [i.e., virtuous] deeds" (III.i.49). The best knight and the most beautiful and virtuous lady are meant for each other (IV.v.1). Romances tend to end happily for the hero and heroine; this is the element of wish fulfillment. To merit this outcome, the protagonists do not have to be perfect. Many romance protagonists, though high minded, commit occasional sins and make occasional mistakes; they are saved in the end by repentance, luck, and mercy. In these cases, romance evokes wonder not so much at the magnitude of their virtues as at the world around them—a wonder that says, "Isn't it amazing how things work out for the best?"

The *dramatis personae* consist of young heroes and heroines—the men physically invincible and everyone good looking—older people who exist only to interact (for better or worse) with the young, and double-dyed villains. The main characters are aristocrats, however much their birth may be hidden by circumstance; people who are truly lower class are portrayed condescendingly at best. Romance oscillates between the idyllic world and the nightmare world, between the healthful, beautiful landscape or the harmonious court and the dungeon or the cave (Frye, 53, 58). The settings are temporally, spatially, or socially remote; indeed, *The Faerie Queene* is set almost exclusively in Faerie Land (Davis, 5).

Renaissance critics charged the genre romance with a looseness that was moral as well as aesthetic—too much sex and violence. Spenser shows he was aware of such charges when he strangely includes Contemplation, a seemingly reliable spokesman, who categorically condemns both combat and love (x.60, 62)—at least for the elderly. Moreover, Spenser strove to raise Book One above the limitations of romance: the quest is to kill a dragon, not a man; the heroine is pure, inspiring, and religiously symbolic; and extramarital sex is painted in the blackest of terms. This must be part of what Spenser means when he promises that his song will "moralize" his subjects, war and love (Proem, 1.9; see note ad loc.).

7. Allegory

Allegory and irony were lumped by the Middle Ages as *alieniloquium*— "otherspeech," saying one thing and meaning another; it is logical that otherspeech included irony, whether the verbal irony of a sophisticate saying the opposite of what is meant or the dramatic irony of an *ingenu* unknowingly saying something stupid, like Redcrosse's boast—"Vertue gives herself light, through darkenesse for to wade"—of which more below. Allegory is difficult to define in a general sense. It was defined by Spenser and most of his contemporaries so broadly as to include any story that has a moral, and in this sense allegory is almost omnipresent. Spenser says in his "Letter to Raleigh" that romance can and should be moralized by allegory, though he puts it the other way round: that moral precepts should be embodied in a "delightful" story. Accordingly, Una is said to symbolize Truth as her opponent Duessa symbolizes Falsehood (ii.Arg.; iii.Arg.; iii.6.5; viii.1.4; viii.49.4). Some of the actions and relations of these two antipodal women make sense only when they are seen politically and precisely as the true and the false churches, or Protestantism and Catholicism. If Duessa did not symbolize something evil, Redcrosse would be sinning only venially in transferring his affections from the supposedly promiscuous Una to her. Besides good and bad women, Book One also contains other moral oppositions: good and bad wells, cups, books, trees, garlands, dragons, castles, hermits, and fasting. While Elizabethans with their broader definition of allegory probably would have called this pattern allegorical as well, it is not necessarily so, demanding only comparison and contrast. This habit of using a given image in both a good and a bad sense Spenser found in the Bible, as it was understood from the Middle Ages to his own day, and it is an important clue to meaning throughout *The Faerie Queene.*

Such allegory as is important to understanding the plot can be appreciated without looking for symbolism of specific historical persons and events—except for Redcrosse's symbolism of Christ on the third day of his fight with the dragon. For example, Una can be read simply as a typical good woman who redeems her man. Duessa, however, as we have

seen, cannot be read simply as the typical bad woman, though she often
represents that as well, as when she faints to interrupt her lover's train of
thought. Personification is presenting an abstraction as if it were a
character. Personification-allegory (for example, the personification
Despaire) is easy to decode, since the subject is stated in the name. The
political allegory, on the other hand, requires knowledge of history;
except for that of Duessa and the controversial contrast between the dis-
course and lifestyles of Britons and Faeries, of the New Jerusalem and
Cleopolis, it is a frill, not necessary to the coherence of the plot of Book
One. Even less necessary are analogies to specific people in the real world,
as in a key-novel; fascinating though it was to Elizabethan readers, the
political level is flickering and inconsistent, generating arbitrary equa-
tions. My notes generally avoid the political and biographical allegory,
except for the anti-Catholic satire and the rare references to Queen
Elizabeth.

The Bible, on the other hand, though a vast subject, is a single, physi-
cal book and one well supplied over the centuries with interpretive tools.
Though as an educated man Spenser read his Bible and commentaries
thereon in Latin, he also used English Bibles that were essentially the same
as ours today, and one of them included a commentary in English: the
Geneva gloss. Even without much background, one can recognize or look
up in a concordance allusions and analogies to the English Bible, though
one may need to look at unfamiliar parts of it or even its apocrypha.
Redcrosse and Arthur, in their respective duels with the giant Orgoglio
(vii.7–15; viii.2–25), are conditional parallels (that is, parallels with
significant contrasts) to David and Goliath (1 Sam. 17). Such analogies
with historical personages in the Bible are called *figurae,* or types; another
instance is when Redcrosse becomes a Christ figure (on Day Three,
xi.52–3). According to the "Letter," examples—and so any stories that
could conceivably convey morals—are another kind of allegory; types
and examples represent the most concrete and subtle kinds; and some-
times, unlike personifications, they can be difficult to decode when details
do not correspond or even conspicuously contrast. Spenser hints that the
Bible is a major target of allusion when he says in the "Letter" that the
armor Una brings to Redcrosse symbolizes the armor of the Christian
man described by St. Paul in Ephesians (6.11, 14–7). If only for this piece
of information, the "Letter" must be read—even though it is often con-
fusing and sometimes at odds with the text, e.g., it makes the daunting
and misleading claim that the entire poem is a continued allegory; it
alone recounts the symbolic knighting of Redcrosse and the beginning of
his alliance with Una. The Bible is not merely a source; it forms a good

clue to the allegorical interpretation of Book One. It is rarely relevant to succeeding books of the poem, however, because they are broadly humanistic in viewpoint.

8. Sources

If the pervasive genre of the Legend of Holiness is romance, as Spenser's eighteenth-century critics perceived, then his most important subtexts or global sources are the romances. Spenser explicitly invokes within the text the Arthur story and the St. George legend (preserved most conveniently for us in *The Golden Legend,* by Jacobus de Voragine); but he treats them so freely (e.g., Arthur's original beloved was Guinevere, and the original St. George was not interested in marrying the princess) that he must have cited them mainly to lend the luster of their famous and nationally prominent names to his two heroes (St. George was the patron saint of England's elite and chivalric Order of the Garter). Medieval chivalric romances—in prose and in verse—available to Tudor readers include Malory's *Le Morte D'Arthur* (mid-fifteenth century), as well as Chaucer's *Knight's Tale* and *Squire's Tale* (late fourteenth century) and a host of others now neglected. Romances written in England in Spenser's time include the almost-contemporaneous *Arcadia* by Sidney, which was first published posthumously the same year as *The Faerie Queene,* but circulated in manuscript before then (like *The Faerie Queene,* imbued with moral idealism and occasionally rising to epic grandeur, although it is a romance more pastoral than chivalric); Lyly's *Euphues* (1578, 1580); Lodge's *Rosalynde* (1590); and the twenty romances of Robert Greene. Four English verse romances with allegorical characters who sometimes enact episodes of continuous allegory include *The Example of Virtue* by Stephen Hawes (1511) and, less similar, his *Passetyme of Pleasure* (1509), as well as two originally Burgundian allegorical romances: *The Travayled Pilgrim* (1569), translated by Stephen Bateman or Batman (1569) from the French romance *Le Chevalier délibéré* (1483), by Olivier de la Marche; and *The Voyage of the Wandering Knight* (1581), translated by William Goodyear from the French romance *Le Voyage du Chevalier errant* (1557), by Jean Cartigny. These four romances closely resemble Book One in their addiction to allegory—more closely than do the Renaissance Italian romance-epics. For example, Hawes portrays an allegorical female giving the hero the Christian's armor allegorized by St. Paul so that he can fight a symbolic dragon in order to win an allegorical princess. On the other hand it was the Italians, and not the English or the Burgundians, who were the first to dignify their romances, as both Spenser and Sidney do, with many conspicuous classical structures, motifs, and allusions. The Italians in fact incorporate even more epic elements than does Spenser, chiefly the theme of the destinies of nations decided in large-scale battles and in councils divine and human. The most famous Italian romance-epics are Ariosto's *Orlando Furioso* and Tasso's *Gerusalemme Liberata* and *Rinaldo*, all cited prominently in the "Letter" and imitated conspicuously in Books Three and Four. Tasso's *Gerusalemme* contains some allegory, and Tasso's own commentary imposed it in other places; Ariosto's poem—containing occasional moral reflections but basically fanciful and humorous—had allegory imposed upon it by its commentators. And, finally, the Book of Revelation furnishes models for the two women who compete for possession of Redcrosse's soul—both the Whore of Babylon and the true church as the Bride of Christ (Rev. 21; Canto Twelve). As for local sources, Spenser alludes piecemeal to the Bible and the classics throughout The Legend of Holiness in ways too various to mention here (for some of them, see the notes). Almost every reference to the classics in the Legend of Holiness is disparaging.

9. Romance as Biblical Allegory: Duessa versus Una

Una's rival Duessa is essential to the plot, and she is both biblical and allegorical. Duessa deviously introduces herself as a romance damsel in distress, but she eventually turns out to be the biblical figure known as the Whore of Babylon (Rev. 17–19.3)—a figure that Protestants read as a symbol of the Catholic Church of their day. From Cantos Two to Six, Redcrosse is completely deceived, whereas the sixteenth-century Protestant reader could probably identify Duessa from her initial description (ii.13). At least by Canto Seven she is readily identifiable when she appears with a golden cup, riding on a seven-headed beast as the Whore does in Rev. 17.3–5. Finally, Duessa is explicitly labeled the "scarlot Whore" in viii.29. Spenser thus enriches the love interest of romance with a conflict of creeds.

Spenser's allegorical characters are interrelated by parallel and contrast, and they often constitute aspects of Duessa. Three bad female characters are analogues, unfoldings, refractions, or conditional parallels of Duessa. Lucifera is represented as her friend; like her, she is beautiful (in her flashy way) and powerful. She contrasts with Duessa in her virginity (iv.8.5). Since she symbolizes pride in the procession of the Seven Deadly Sins (iv.16.1–2; 17.1; 18.1), we infer that she is just too proud to submit herself to a man, and therefore that her virginity reflects no special credit on her (see also Mirabella in VI.vii.27–viii.30). We infer too that she represents pride in general because of her role in the sin parade and because she manifests, on the one hand, social pride (see, for example, iv.10; 14) and, on the other hand, pride against God in bearing the religiously resonant name "Lucifera" and employing Satan as her coachman. Abessa and Corceca are not friends of Duessa, but are still refractions of her; they highlight what Protestants considered to be the faults of the Roman Catholic rank and file—nuns and the laity (Canto Three). Una too generates conditional parallels—the females that operate the House of Holiness; but this must suffice to exemplify the relatedness of Spenser's allegorical characters.

Some such heroine as Una was dictated to Spenser, first, by his choice of Duessa as the false church seducing the hero, which required a portrayal of the true church; and second, by his overall project of redeeming romance, which meant providing a positive picture of woman and of love—ideally, a heroine capable of inspiring the hero to save his soul. Una derives from and alludes to several previous figures and types of figure, such as the Woman Clothed with the Sun in Rev. 12, and the Bride in both the Song of Solomon and in Rev. 20. Her most influential and least appreciated predecessor is the biblical personification Wisdom or Sapience (as in Proverbs 7–9, also described in Spenser's *Hymne of Heavenly Beauty*, 183–259), invoked, for example, when Una says, ". . . wisedom warnes, whilest foot is in the gate, / To stay the steppe" (i.13). Sapience also dominates the deuterocanonical books Wisdom and Ecclesiasticus (now called Sirach)—books that were still included in Protestant Bibles in Spenser's day, though not today.

Besides being a literal heroine—beautiful, virtuous, and wise—Una bears two allegorical roles. When she is with Redcrosse, she exercises a private influence as his guide, the true church (as when she seeks him, e.g., iii.Arg.); or more inwardly, his own divine spark, or the indwelling Christ or Holy Spirit (as when she asserts that Redcrosse is among the "chosen" in refutation of Despaire: ix.53; see also i.13). Similarly, Wisdom is betrothed to a human individual—Solomon, the fictional speaker of the book of Wisdom (8:2, 9, 16, 18; 9). Secondly, Una exercises a public role as religious truth or the true church in the world when she is off on her own and meets various unenlightened creatures, especially when she endeavors to convert the Satyrs (Canto Six), whoever they may be. The Satyrs rescue Una from Sansloy's sexual assault. All Una's adventures are in fact dominated by a series of champions—real or pretended, superhuman, human, three-quarters human, half-human, or animal. One possible meaning of this pattern is that the true church needs believers and, if possible, champions who, like Satyrane, are at least three-quarters rational, in order to continue to exist among humankind. Una's kinship with animals and nature, while a charming and indeed a mythic touch, remains a mystery. Una can be deceived, at least temporarily, by Archimago (iii.26–40); she needs to be counseled out of her despair by Arthur (vii.38–42); despite being "borne of hevenly berth," (x.9), she has human parents—Adam and Eve (i.5; vii.43; xii.26). These three human touches force us to identify her, at least in her public role, as a human organization, a church, not truth or wisdom in the abstract. Her liability to deception (though not to sin) illustrates Christ's warning that "false Christs shall rise, and false prophets, . . . to deceive if it were possible the very elect" (Mark 13.22, Geneva version). Thus Spenser elevated the love interest of romance; he portrayed a good, redemptive, and symbolic damsel; furthermore, he added a biblical symmetry and an apocalyptic contrast by balancing her with a bad damsel symbolizing the false church.

10. Romance as Biblical Allegory: Redcrosse's Adventures

Redcrosse is not a static personification of Holiness; he is an Everyman or, more specifically, an Everyknight. Every knight aspires to prove himself. Redcrosse has more to prove because he started out as a "clownish young man," a "hick."

What theme, if any, vertically determines the sequence of Redcrosse's adventures? In the middle episodes, Spenser wants the readers to be almost as confused as is Redcrosse. But the Despaire episode (ix.21–54; x.1) finally reveals the diagnosis: that Redcrosse has all along exhibited subtle kinds of pride against God—kinds based on doctrinal errors and fostered by though not limited to Catholicism. Despaire's project is inducing knights to commit suicide, and he has recently succeeded with Sir Terwin. Let us concentrate on what is wrong with Despaire's arguments from any Christian's point of view. Catholics as well as Protestants would notice that he emphasizes God's justice to the exclusion of his forgiveness for those who repent. Despaire's rhetorical question, "Shall he thy sins up in his knowledge fold, / And guilty be of thine impietie?" (ix.47), implies the answer "No," whereas a fully Christian answer would be "Yes," in the sense that God in Christ assumed and expiated mankind's guilt by dying on the cross. By accusing Redcrosse of betraying Una with Duessa, Despaire leads Redcrosse to at least the beginning of repentance: "The knight was much enmoved with his speach, . . . Well knowing trew all, that he did reherse" (ix. 48). When Una interrupts her knight's resulting attempt at suicide, she cries, "In heavenly mercies hast thou not a part? . . . Where justice growes, there grows eke greter grace" (ix.53). In other words, "It doesn't all depend upon you." Similarly, when the poet-speaker moralizes in x.1 on the previous action (the first stanza of a canto is often devoted to such a retrospective moralization; see vii.1; viii.1; ix.1), he declares "fleshly might, / And vaine assuraunce of mortality" to be useless in avoiding sin and achieving virtue because "All the good is God's, both power and eke will." Through grace, however, we can gain the victory over "spiritual foes" that baffle "fleshly might." In this categorical statement, Spenser parts company with Catholics, who attribute something, at least, to human agency. To exaggerate slightly, Catholics say "salvation depends upon me," whereas Protestants say "salvation depends upon God." Redcrosse learns to say to himself, unheroically but truly, "It doesn't matter if I can't handle it, because everything does not depend upon me."

Armed with the doctrines and advice laid down by ix.53 and x.1, let us turn our attention backward in the story to Redcrosse's adventures in Cantos Two, Four, and Five; they are typical of romance, but we can now see that they are subtly critiqued and corrected by the Bible, especially by St. Paul. To his credit, Redcrosse often fends off the initial and obvious temptations; but he falls to subtler, more finely tuned temptations. He fends off Archimago's temptations to lust (i.45–55) and falls only to Archimago's temptation to jealousy (ii.3–9). He fends off Despaire's hedonistic motives for suicide (ix.39–41) and succumbs only to moral despair (ix.43, 45–47). Also to his credit, it is not until he falls before the giant Orgoglio in Canto Seven that he is clearly defeated in battle; it is not until he fornicates with Duessa (vii.2–7) that he is "disgraced" in terms of the monogamy demanded by chivalric love etiquette. In these middle cantos, his adventures are just slightly off-color. His separation from Una leads to these; but even before that he reveals himself to be a "man . . . that boasts of fleshly might / And vaine assuraunce of mortality" (x.1.1–2) when, warned by Una to stay out of Error's den, he replies, "Vertue gives her selfe light, through darkenesse for to wade" (i.12.9), and the poet comments, "his glistring armour made / A litle glooming light, much like a shade" (i.14.4–5). Redcrosse is saying heroically but erroneously, "Everything depends upon me, and I can handle it."

As a result of responding to challenges from Sansfoy and Sansjoy, he gets himself involved in chivalrous liaisons with women who turn out to be bad—Duessa and Lucifera. During the joust with Sansjoy (v.1–15), Redcrosse is inspired by Duessa's cry to gain the upper hand and strike the crucial blow; but she is really cheering for his opponent, or at least hedging her bets by being ambiguous. Lucifera's sinfulness is at first perceived by Redcrosse (though it is chiefly because she has slighted him): he "thought all their glory vaine in knightly vew, / And that great Princesse too exceeding prowd, / That to strange knight no better countenance allowed" (iv.15). Yet through the chivalric necessity of jousting with his challenger Sansjoy—a dubious necessity, despite the apparent endorsement of the poet-speaker (v.8.1; 9.1), since the prizes are Duessa and the shield of Sansfoy (v.1–15)—he gets drawn into Lucifera's community; for after his uncertain victory (v.13, 15), he accepts a ride in Lucifera's chariot (v.16), in which position, we recall, Lucifera is accompanied by Satan and represents pride served by the other six deadly sins. Redcrosse finally leaves Lucifera's castle on the prudential warning of the Dwarf to avoid the temporal ruin that a sight of her dungeon portends.

Conquering Sansjoy and escaping from Lucifera's obvious form of pride, without paying her usual price, leads Redcrosse into two subtler forms of pride. The first is complacency, or what the Renaissance would have called the vice of "security," or spiritual laziness: "Everything depends upon me, and I've done enough; I deserve a break." Various religious thinkers, ancient and modern, have warned that acquiring a virtue or performing a good deed can lead to spiritual pride of one sort or another. In this complacent mood, he stops for rest; he takes his armor off—an act that, in *The Faerie Queene,* usually symbolizes bad relaxation, especially in the case of this armor, which is the armor of a Christian man in Ephesians 6.11, 14–7. He drinks from the well of the lazy nymph. The nymph parallels Redcrosse at this moment, in that she "sat down to rest in middest of the race." Drinking of her well or fountain makes him lazy, thus expressing and intensifying his complacency and desire for some rest and relaxation. Duessa catches up with him, and it is in this mood that he fornicates with her (vii.2–7). Redcrosse himself, to whom "lust" was once "unwonted" (i.49.1), would have condemned this act earlier on; and it was for her alleged sexual infidelity to him that he abandoned Una (ii.5–6). Incidentally, we know that this sexual act is consummated, contrary to some recent doubts, because he is said to be "careless of his health," which implies penetration. Because his partner is Duessa, this union allegorizes joining the Roman Catholic Church and renouncing the Protestant Church, which is represented by Una.

The second form of pride is his habitual combativeness, his can-do attitude, his eagerness—usually a virtue in the romance hero—to prove his supposed abilities, which he tremulously tries to resume when challenged by Orgoglio. Orgoglio as a giant is not only a typical romance opponent but a symbol for Redcrosse's basic sin, or ruling passion—moral overconfidence, as if to say, "I am a moral giant: everything depends upon me and I can handle it." The giant exhibits "presumption of his matchlesse might" (vii.10.3); his "boasted sire" is "blustring Æolus" (vii.9.2). These traits help us to see Orgoglio as a projection of the bad side of Redcrosse, whom we have seen to represent the "man who *boasts* of fleshly *might* / And vaine *assuraunce* of mortality" (x.1, my emphasis). Because its possessor "yields" to "spiritual foes," presumably Orgoglio and Despaire, we can see that "fleshly might" in these contexts is used in the peculiarly Pauline sense of, not just the body and the passions, but even the "will" (x.1.9)—everything in mankind outside of divine grace or apart from the spirit of God (e.g., 1 Cor. 1.29; Rom. 8.9, 12, 13). There are of course many meanings to Orgoglio, but it seems to me that this Pauline meaning of flesh as one's own moral strength is primary, while those representing his earthliness and fleshliness are literal and ancillary. Spenser was not inept but perceptive to tempt Redcrosse with two kinds of pride.

Later, Arthur vanquishes the giant as a romance hero should and as David did Goliath (1 Sam. 17), creating a contrast of bad and good giant-fighters. The knights differ principally in regard to their armor and especially their shields. Redcrosse has laid aside his armor, which includes his shield, glossed by Ephesians as the shield of faith (6.16; see "Letter"); and Orgoglio attacks him "ere he could get his shield." Now, David took off the armor donated by King Saul, including the shield, when going to meet his giant; but he did so because of his faith, faith in the protection of God (1 Sam. 17.39, 45–6). That which substituted for armor in David's case is symbolized by armor in Redcrosse's. This symbolism is continued when Arthur's armor, especially his shield, is described at laudatory length; ascribed to it are some of the same miracles later said to be wrought by Fidelia, or faith (x.20), so it seems to be related to faith, perhaps as its miraculous result (see note ad loc.). This shield is crucial: it saves Arthur from Duessa's seven-headed beast and, finally, from Orgoglio himself (viii.18, 19, 20, and 21, mentioned once in each stanza).

Despite this humiliating defeat and humbling rescue, in the Despaire episode, Redcrosse still exhibits his can-do attitude when he cries "hence shall I never rest, / Till I that treachours art have heard and tryde" (ix.32); he needs to be and will be humbled again. Medieval and Renaissance readers saw moral presumption and moral despair as related (Torczon); they represent the happy moments and the sad moments of someone who thinks everything depends upon him. As we have seen above, the way to stop these vicious mood swings is a wise passiveness—a dependence on God's grace both for forgiveness after failure (ix.53) and for help toward success (x.1.6–7). In retrospect, then, the rights and wrongs of Redcrosse's adventures in these temporarily ambiguous middle cantos can be sorted out.

In the House of Holiness in Canto Ten, presented as the normative opposite of Lucifera's House of Pride, most of the speakers after x.1 are surprisingly Catholic; they tell Redcrosse what he must do to get to heaven: penance (x.27) and good deeds (x.34, 51). This apparent about-face remains an interpretive problem. We gather that the Calvinist Manifesto of ix.53 (in essence, "God decides who is going to heaven, and you are one of them") and x.1 (in essence, "No human being has the power or the will to do anything good, so when you seemed to do some, it was only God working through you") applies only to Redcrosse's adventures so far, exemplifying how and how not to set up a proper relationship with God. Apparently, once one is in a state of grace, as Redcrosse now is, the Catholic ethic of self-help is correct. At a deeper level, Spenser may have planned such a reversal in order to eliminate intolerance and reunite the two denominations, or at least to counter the Romanist charge that Protestants neglect their neighbor's welfare and focus only on the inner life and on sin. Whatever Spenser's intention, at least we can infer from the Catholic coloring of almost everything, except the first stanza in Canto Ten, that the anti-Catholic satire is over; religious issues will be ones that Catholics and Protestants have in common—the conquest of evil and Satan. And sure enough, there is no indubitable anti-Catholic satire in the rest of the book except possibly Archimago's attempt to reclaim Redcrosse for Duessa (xii.24–36). A Christian's good works are declared meritorious (x.33.9; 34.9; 38.5–6; 51.3–4), as only the Catholics believe they are; moreover it is not Fidelia (faith) or Speranza (hope), but Charissa (charity) and her deputy Mercy who "to heaven [teach] him the ready path" (33.9; 34.9; 51.3–4; see also *Amoretti*, 68.13–4; and *Hymne of Heavenly Love*, 169–217). Conversely, the poet-speaker warns that people are damned for lack of charity—"wrath, and hatred" (x.33). This was the belief of Henry VIII. But then we are again told that only the "chosen" can get to heaven (x.57, echoing ix.53)—the Calvinist or extreme Protestant position. The contradiction between charity and predestination as entrance requirements could perhaps be reconciled if one took the mediating position that the source of good deeds, one's own spontaneous feeling of charity or brotherly love that gets one into heaven, is not self-generated but infused by God at his own pleasure—a position expounded by St. Augustine.

In the House of Holiness (x.21; 27.9), one is surprised to see Redcrosse despair again—another contradiction and one resolvable as a paradox. As Luther says (Thesis 18 for *Heidelberg Disputation*, 1518, in Luther, 502), a Christian needs to experience moral despair in order to learn his or her own moral helplessness and need of grace. This time Redcrosse's suicidal thoughts are thwarted emblematically when he grasps the anchor of Speranza, or hope. Speranza's anchor may symbolize the advice Una dispensed the first time: the assurance of God's mercy for repented sin and even—who knows—a Calvinist assurance that he is among the "chosen" (ix.53).

Having attained an inspiring vision of heaven (x.57), Redcrosse engages in a complex dialogue about his own aspirations with the Hermit Contemplation. Here too, good deeds, at least of the more worldly and spectacular sort, receive endorsement in Cleopolis and from Gloriana, the Faerie Queen who reigns there. To become one of Gloriana's courtiers in Cleopolis, one must achieve something worthy of fame (x.58–59), whereas to gain entrance to the New Jerusalem, one need not do anything, just be divinely "chosen" and forgiven (x.57). Surprisingly for a Christian mentor, the Hermit says Redcrosse must win fame in Cleopolis before he can go to heaven (x.59–60). The Hermit's meritocratic discourse here is not that of Christianity, but that of romance and of classical epic. One possible resolution is that the two cities and their contrasting lifestyles are appropriate, respectively, for youth and for old age. Whatever its meaning, this postponement of heaven and the contemplative life prepares us for another postponement: Redcrosse's announcement that he cannot marry Una now, only become engaged to her, because he has to go back and finish his tour of duty for Gloriana (xii.18; 41). The first postponement also prepares us for the fact that subsequent books of the poem (until the very last stanzas of Book Seven) are not about getting to heaven, but about winning fame (and the hand of one's beloved) on this earth. The ambivalent relationship between the cities is paralleled by that of their inhabitants. Even though everyone, including the poet-speaker, calls him an Elf, Redcrosse learns that he is really a Briton (x.60; 64–67). One of the differences is that Elves never get to see the New Jerusalem (52.2–6), whereas qualified Britons are apparently welcome in Cleopolis and in the two holy places, the Mount of Contemplation and the New Jerusalem. Further differences between the races will emerge in Book Two, Canto Ten.

11. Climax

Spenser's choice of a dragon instead of a human as principal antagonist avoids the guilt attendant upon most chivalric battles—a guilt invoked both by Despaire and by the Hermit Contemplation (ix.43.3–6; x.60.8–9). Humans are redeemable and hence cannot be killed without some guilt. Animals such as dragons also yield more readily than do humans to symbolic interpretation. Symbolism brings one sort of grandeur—the grandeur of generality. The phrase "that old Dragon" (Arg.xi) quotes Rev. 20.2: "the dragon that olde serpent which is the devill and Satan." This means that, on at least one level, Spenser's dragon represents the devil. This symbolism accords with the fact that Spenser's dragon occasioned Adam and Eve's fall, albeit a sinless one, allegorized by their imprisonment in the brazen tower ("Letter"; vii.44).

The dragon is killed conclusively, although Archimago and Duessa return to deceive (xii.24–36). Spenser even makes fun of low-class simpletons who think the dragon is still alive (xii.10). At the crucifixion, Christ

irrevocably bound the devil, according to biblical exegesis and much me-
dieval literature, even though the latter's subordinates continue to work
on earth; at the end of the world, the devil himself, as a dragon, will ul-
timately be cast by an angel into a lake of fire where he will burn for ever
and ever (Rev. 20.10). How can a mere human like Redcrosse kill Satan
once and for all and rescue Adam and Eve? The answer must be, as some
readers have averred with greater or lesser degrees of emphasis, that at
least on the third day Redcrosse somehow transcends mere humanity and
is or typifies the god-man Christ.

If Redcrosse is overachieving on Day Three by doing what Christ
alone could do, perhaps on Day One he is underachieving and showing
how vulnerable mankind was when Christ had not yet come. Redcrosse
is ignominiously defeated (xi.30.9), so much so that both the dragon and
Una believe him to be dead (xi.31–32). The armor that heats up and
paradoxically harms him could be shown to symbolize Mosaic law,
man's sole protection against the devil during the period from Moses to
Christ. When, on the second morning, he arises refreshed from the well
into which the dragon has cast him, the poet-speaker conjectures that
either "his baptized hands now greater grew," or his sword was hardened
in "that holy water" (xi.36); in either case, the well symbolizes baptism,
the initiatory sacrament. As an individual on the literal level, Redcrosse
must have become a Christian long before—certainly when he had
"God to frend" (i.28.7), most likely when, as a lowly rustic, he first
donned the enchanted armor and "seemed the goodliest man in al that
company, and was well liked of the Lady" ("Letter"). It seems as if he
has assumed the role of mankind and it is only now, in that role, that he
gets baptized or enters the Christian era; for on the second day, Red-
crosse achieves more. He finally acts like the good Christian he has be-
come in the House of Holiness; he cannot kill the dragon, but he holds
his own against him; he is defeated not by a blow from the dragon, but
only by his own weakness (xi.45; 48.9), and nobody thinks he is dead.
The balm from the tree that shelters him on the second night is suscep-
tible to several interpretations (e.g., divine grace in general, or the oil
imposed at confirmation), each with its own inadequacies; in context,
the most convincing interpretation is as the second of the two sacra-
ments recognized by Protestants, namely Holy Communion or the
Eucharist. Since the well and the tree both allegorize privileges or
necessities, specifically of the Christian, both of them seem to go with
Day Two as its frame. Holy Communion also represents a transition to
Day Three, in that it effects a union between the Christian and Christ
such as could be allegorized, with pardonable exaggeration, by Red-
crosse's becoming Christ on the third day.

Among the many sources for the dragon fight, especially the victorious third day (e.g., Hawes's *Example of Virtue*), there are three fights with a dragon and/or Satan involving a hero who is a holy being or Christ himself: an angel's imprisonment of "that old Dragon" in Rev. 20.1–3, St. George's killing of a dragon and rescue of a princess in his Legend, and Christ's binding of Satan and rescue of Adam and Eve in the Harrowing of Hell. This last event is hinted at in the Bible, briefly mentioned in the Apostle's Creed, and first narrated in the indubitably apocryphal yet immensely popular Gospel of Nicodemus. Because there are so many retellings of it that Spenser could have known (e.g., *Piers Plowman* B, Passus 18), I cite parallels from the ultimate source, the Gospel of Nicodemus, in a modern scholarly translation. Just as Redcrosse fights for three days, so Christ harrows Hell during the three days while his body is dead. Just as a watchman on the castle tower heralds Redcrosse (xii.2), so prophets—often troped in the Old Testament as watchmen, sometimes "wayting," sometimes on towers (e.g., Isa. 21.5–12; Jer. 31.6; Ezek. 3.17, 33.2–7; Hab. 2.1)—herald Christ's entrance into Hell (James 124–5, Latin A; Greek). Hell's brazen gates are opened on command (James 133, Latin A; James 134, Latin B). Christ wrestles down Satan and leads out of Hell Adam, Eve, and Old Testament patriarchs and prophets—beneficiaries similar to some of those who emerge from the brazen tower after Redcrosse's victory (xii.2–5). Christ leads his flock into Paradise—a Paradise explicitly identified in one version (the Greek, James 141) as "Eden." The Harrowing of Hell gives Christ a chance to battle like a knight. Medieval men retold this apocryphal story endlessly in literature and art—probably because it satisfied their well-known predilection for violence, whereas the Christ portrayed in the gospels must have seemed something of a doormat.

A well-intentioned man under Mosaic and/or natural law, a Christian, and Christ: they differ in how far each is a match for the devil. The first two stages are chronological; but the third stage, Christ's victory, occurred partly at the crucifixion and will occur completely at the end of the world (Rev. 20). Spenser's climactic incident does not use Christianity to correct romance, but fuses the two traditions through an element of combat that he has managed to find in the Christian tradition, thus giving the story an archetypal resonance.

12. Indeterminacy versus Closure

How much of Redcrosse's victory over the dragon depends upon God, and how much on the knight? To judge from the knight's strenuous effort on the second day, framed by the help of two magical objects on the two nights and assisted by Una's prayers, it seems to result from a cooperation of the two. But we cannot be sure because Spenser's report of Una's answer to this question in the last lines of the canto contains a deliberately ambiguous pronoun: "Then God she praysd, and thankt her faithfull knight, / That had atchievde so great a conquest by his might" —whose might, the knight's or God's? (xi.55). It is only in Book Two that Spenser solves this internal debate with a Christian-humanist compromise: in the dragon fight, says the now-perfected Redcrosse, God supplied the power and he the good will (II.i.33). This compromise could represent the solution; but if so, Spenser has deliberately left Book One in indeterminacy because in it, the seemingly normative poet-speaker has said that even one's good will comes from God (x.1.9). Besides this question of divine versus human causes of salvation, Spenser leaves at least two other questions unanswered: 1) Since fame is the only immortality Faeries have (x.59), whereas Britons, and Britons alone, can go to heaven (x.52.3), what is the relation between Britons and Faeries, between Cleopolis and the New Jerusalem or heaven? 2) Since Book One seems to emphasize heaven and to assign God full responsibility for who gets there, whereas Book Two, as II.i.32–33 indicates, affirms some human role in getting to heaven, what is the difference in outlook between Book One and Book Two? Some critics believe that Book Two, and indeed each succeeding book, presupposes Book One and its Christianity as a foundation, if only because Edmund Spenser was a Christian. But others object that this unifying faith ignores the contradictions between Book One and succeeding books, and the latter's general tendencies toward the secular, e.g., *"Cupid's* wanton snare / As hell she hated, chaste in worke and will" (x.30) versus the poet's comparison of an angel to Cupid in II.viii.6, and the admission of Cupid to the Garden of Adonis provided he checks his weapons at the door (III.vi.49.8–9). A.S.P. Woodhouse (1949) controversially claimed that Book One and the later books differ as do the realms, respectively, of grace and of nature. This difference is more usefully conceived as that between the viewpoints of a narrowly exclusive Christianity and of a syncretic Christian humanism (Kaske, 1975). The narrowly exclusive Christianity of Book One, be the discourse Catholic or Protestant, is expressed, for example, by Charissa's hatred of Cupid (x.30), by x.1, and by the Hermit's "blood can nought but sin, and wars but sorrows yield. . . . As for loose loves they'are vaine, and vanish into nought" (x.60.9; 62.9). It is from the syncretic point of view that Book Two attempts a compromise about free will, and therefore Book Two may not answer every question posed by Book One; e.g., it does not agree and cannot deal with the total bankruptcy of natural man described in x.1.

While the conquest of the dragon is complete, the free-will debate remains unresolved. Another frustration, for the characters as well as for the reader, is that after the victory celebration, Duessa and her emissary Archimago attempt to claim Redcrosse for Duessa in the presence of Una's parents. Una exposes their plot and generously exonerates Redcrosse, and her father imprisons Archimago, but the poet warns the reader that Archimago will resurface yet again. Redcrosse is betrothed to Una in a wedding-like ceremony in which the same syncretism of the secular and the sacred that melds romance battles and Christian ones in the dragon fight is exhibited in miniature: in the miraculous infusion of the song of the angels into a love song (xii.39). Another frustration occurs when Redcrosse sojourns with her happily for a time, almost fulfilling the generic romance ending—"And so they got married and lived happily ever after"—but then reveals that they cannot marry for six years, not until Redcrosse shall have finished his suddenly announced tour of duty for the Faerie Queen. Even in this, the most conclusive book of *The Faerie Queene*, a few threads, both of plot and of meaning, are deliberately left hanging.

THE FAERIE
QVEENE.

Difpofed into twelue books,

Fashioning
XII. Morall vertues.

LONDON
Printed for William Ponfonbie.
1590.

Title page to the 1590 edition of *The Faerie Queene* (STC 23081).

TO THE MOST MIGH-
TIE AND MAGNIFI-
CENT EMPRESSE ELI-
ZABETH, BY THE
GRACE OF GOD QVEENE
OF ENGLAND, FRANCE
AND IRELAND DE-
FENDER OF THE FAITH
&c.

Her most humble

Seruant:

Ed. Spenser

The first Booke of
the Faerie Queene.
Contayning
The Legend of the Knight
of the Red Crosse,
OR
Of Holinesse.

1   Lo I the man, whose Muse whylome[1] did maske,
     As time her taught, in lowly Shephards weeds,[2]
     Am now enforst a farre unfitter taske,
     For trumpets sterne to chaunge mine Oaten reeds:[3]
     And sing of Knights and Ladies gentle deeds,
     Whose praises having slept in silence long,
     Me, all too meane, the sacred Muse areeds[4]
     To blazon broade[5] emongst her learned throng:
     Fierce warres and faithfull loves shall moralize my song.[6]

---

[1] **whylome:** a while ago.

[2] **weeds:** clothes. Spenser identifies himself as the man who wrote pastorals, i.e., *The Shepheardes Calender,* 1579. He echoes what were then thought to be the four autobiographical opening lines of Virgil's *Aeneid,* now known to be by a later hand: "Ille ego, qui quondam gracili modulatus avena / carmen, . . . at nunc horrentia martis / arma virumque cano," etc.: "I am he who once tuned my song on a slender reed [*the Eclogues*], . . . but now of Mars' bristling arms I sing and the man who . . . etc." (trans. ACH). Spenser thus aligns his career with the Virgilian career pattern of first writing eclogues or pastorals, then graduating to heroic poetry. For terms, see Introduction, 6. Spenser's Muse "did maske . . . in lowly Shephards weeds" because he wrote under the persona of a shepherd and

under the pseudonym Immerito—"unworthy." "As time her taught" implies that the low persona fits his amateur status and relative youth back then.

[3] I.e., to change from pastoral to heroic poetry. Metonymy.

[4] **areeds:** instructs. Spenser adopts the topos of authorial modesty characteristic of almost all of his personas. The "sacred Muse" is Spenser's usual epithet for the muse (ACH).

[5] **To blazon broade:** to proclaim abroad with a trumpet.

[6] I.e., my song shall moralize fierce wars and faithful loves, imparting to these materials of romance a moral dimension, for example by allegory. Direct object comes before verb and subject comes after verb; Spenser often inverts word order.

3

2 Helpe then, O holy Virgin chiefe of nyne,[1]
    Thy weaker[2] Novice to performe thy will,
    Lay forth out of thine everlasting scryne[3]
    The antique rolles, which there lye hidden still,
    Of Faerie knights and fayrest *Tanaquill*,[4]
    Whom that most noble Briton Prince[5] so long
    Sought through the world, and suffered so much ill,
    That I must rue his undeserved wrong:[6]
   O helpe thou my weake wit, and sharpen my dull tong.

3 And thou most dreaded impe[7] of highest *Jove*,
    Faire *Venus* sonne, that with thy cruell dart
    At that good knight so cunningly didst rove,[8]
    That glorious fire it kindled in his hart,
    Lay now thy deadly Heben[9] bowe apart,
    And with thy mother mylde come to mine ayde:[10]
    Come both, and with you bring triumphant *Mart*,[11]
    In loves and gentle jollities arraid,
   After his murdrous spoyles and bloudie rage allayd.

---

[1] One of the nine muses, either Clio, Muse of history, or Calliope, the muse of heroic poetry. ACH favors Calliope; he quotes Roche quoting Spenser's authorized commentator E.K., to the effect that Calliope is "the first glorye of the Heroicall verse" (on *Shepheardes Calender,* "April," 100); and *The Faerie Queene* is a heroic poem.

[2] **weaker:** too weak.

[3] **scryne:** chest, coffer.

[4] One of the (rarely used) names for Gloriana, queen of Faerie Land, who in turn represents in the political allegory Queen Elizabeth; see "Letter to Raleigh."

[5] I.e., Arthur.

[6] This love quest for Gloriana represents Spenser's creative rewriting of the Arthur story, based on folktales of knights seeking elusive fairy mistresses. For Arthur's account of it, see ix.6–15.

[7] **impe:** offspring.

[8] **rove:** shoot.

[9] **Heben:** ebony.

[10] If Cupid lays down his weapons, Spenser usually portrays him in a positive light, as here; the armed Cupid, however, is either ambivalent, as he was to Arthur (line 3), or downright malicious.

[11] Mars, from the oblique case of his name in Latin: Mars, Martis, etc. Like Cupid, he has here been domesticated. "Mars and Venus represent respectively war and love, the two . . . subjects of the poem" (ACH).

4   And with them eke, O Goddesse heavenly bright,[1]
             Mirrour of grace and Majestie divine,[2]
             Great Ladie of the greatest Isle, whose light
             Like *Phoebus* lampe[3] throughout the world doth shine,
             Shed thy faire beames into mine feeble eyne,
             And raise my thoughtes too humble and too vile,
             To thinke of that true glorious type of thine,[4]
             The argument of mine afflicted stile:[5]
       The which to heare, vouchsafe, O dearest dread[6] a while.

---

[1] **eke:** also; **Goddesse heavenly bright:** Queen Elizabeth, who, like the Muse, can inspire mortals to write poetry. She too is a "Goddesse," a fairly common term for monarchs in the Middle Ages and the Renaissance.

[2] Cf. Wisd. 7.26: "For she is the brightnes of the everlasting light, the undefiled mirroure of the majestie of God" (ACH, quoting the Geneva Bible, as I do throughout this edition). Spenser often links both Elizabeth and Una to the biblical personification Wisdom or Sapience; see Introduction, 9. Elizabeth is first a pagan, then a Judeo-Christian deity.

[3] *Phoebus* **lampe:** the sun.

[4] Type is meant in the biblical sense, figura or prototype; i.e., a person analogous to you, my queen, in the past. Spenser means Gloriana, who is the "argument" of the poem: i.e., the titular heroine, the Faerie Queen. As the poem progresses, however, Gloriana is referred to less and less; and she appears in propria persona only in the "Letter to Raleigh," and in Arthur's problematic dream (ix.2–16).

[5] **mine afflicted stile:** my humble writing style, to which the poet asks the Queen to listen. His style is humble or afflicted because, according to him, it is not very good—the modesty topos again.

[6] **O dearest dread:** O you whom I both love and fear. Oxymoron. Also applied to women who are loved in a sexual way.

Canto One

The Patrone of true Holinesse,
Foule Errour doth defeate:
Hypocrisie him to entrappe,
Doth to his home entreate.

1 A Gentle Knight was pricking on the plaine,
   Ycladd[1] in mightie armes and silver shielde,
   Wherein old dints of deepe woundes did remaine,
   The cruell markes of many a bloody fielde;
   Yet armes till that time did he never wield:
   His angry steede did chide his foming bitt,
   As much disdayning to the curbe to yield:
   Full jolly knight he seemd, and faire did sitt,
As one for knightly giusts[2] and fierce encounters fitt.

2 And on his brest a bloodie Crosse he bore,
   The deare remembrance of his dying Lord,
   For whose sweete sake that glorious badge he wore,
   And dead as living ever him ador'd:
   Upon his shield the like was also scor'd,
   For soveraine hope, which in his helpe he had:
   Right faithfull true he was in deede and word,
   But of his cheere[3] did seeme too solemne sad;
Yet nothing did he dread, but ever was ydrad.[4]

3 Upon a great adventure he was bond,
   That greatest *Gloriana* to him gave,
   That greatest Glorious Queene of *Faery* lond,
   To winne him worshippe, and her grace to have,
   Which of all earthly thinges he most did crave;

---

[1] **Ycladd:** clad; "y–" is the sign of the perfect passive participle. "The Letter to Raleigh" identifies Redcrosse's armor as the armor of the Christian man described by Paul in Eph. 6.11–17.

[2] **giusts:** jousts.

[3] **cheere:** behavior, here chiefly facial expression.

[4] **ydrad:** dreaded.

And ever as he rode his hart did earne,[1]
  To prove his puissance in battell brave
  Upon his foe, and his new force to learne;
Upon his foe, a Dragon horrible and stearne.

4   A lovely Ladie rode him faire beside,
       Upon a lowly Asse more white then snow,
       Yet she much whiter, but the same did hide
       Under a vele, that wimpled[2] was full low,
       And over all a blacke stole shee did throw,
       As one that inly mournd: so was she sad,
       And heavie sate upon her palfrey slow:
       Seemed in heart some hidden care she had,
And by her in a line[3] a milkewhite lambe she lad.

5   So pure and innocent, as that same lambe,
       She was in life and every vertuous lore,[4]
       And by descent from Royall lynage came
       Of ancient Kinges and Queenes, that had of yore
       Their scepters stretcht from East to Westerne shore,
       And all the world in their subjection held,
       Till that infernall feend with foule uprore
       Forwasted all their land, and them expeld:
Whom to avenge, she had this knight from far compeld.

6   Behind her farre away a Dwarfe[5] did lag,
       That lasie seemd in being ever last,
       Or wearied with bearing of her bag
       Of needments at his backe. Thus as they past,
       The day with cloudes was suddeine overcast,
       And angry *Jove* an hideous storme of raine

---

[1] **earne:** yearn.

[2] **wimpled:** falling in folds around her face and neck.

[3] **in a line:** on a lead. The lamb is never mentioned again; therefore it must be purely emblematic. Literally it derives from the lamb that the princess leads with her for their mutual sacrifice to the dragon in the St. George legend; see Jacobus de Voragine,

3:125–34. It could symbolize Christ the Lamb of God (Rev. 21.2–3, 9–11), whom Redcrosse resembles at his and Una's betrothal (xii.36–4).

[4] **lore:** doctrines and edifying literature.

[5] The Dwarfe perhaps symbolizes reason, prudence, or common sense; cf. the Palmer in Book Two.

Did poure into his Lemans[1] lap so fast,
      That everie wight[2] to shrowd it did constrain,
And this faire couple eke to shroud themselves were fain.[3]

7   Enforst to seeke some covert nigh at hand,
          A shadie grove not farr away they spide,
          That promist ayde the tempest to withstand:
          Whose loftie trees yclad[4] with sommers pride,
          Did spred so broad, that heavens light did hide,
          Not perceable with power of any starr:
          And all within were pathes and alleies wide,
          With footing worne, and leading inward farr:
      Fair harbour that them seemes,[5] so in they entred ar.

8   And foorth they passe, with pleasure forward led,
          Joying to heare the birdes sweete harmony,
          Which therein shrouded from the tempest dred,
          Seemd in their song to scorne the cruell sky.
          Much can they praise the trees so straight and hy,[6]
          The sayling Pine, the Cedar proud and tall,
          The vine-propp Elme, the Poplar never dry,
          The builder Oake, sole king of forrests all,
      The Aspine good for staves, the Cypress funerall.

9   The Laurell, meed[7] of mightie Conquerours
          And Poets sage, the Firre that weepeth still,
          The Willow worne of forlorne Paramours,
          The Eugh obedient to the benders will
          The Birch for shaftes, the Sallow for the mill,
          The Mirrhe sweete bleeding in the bitter wound,
          The warlike Beech, the Ash for nothing ill,
          The fruitfull Olive, and the Platane round,
      The carver Holme, the Maple seeldom inward sound.

---

[1] **Lemans:** mistress's.

[2] **wight:** human being.

[3] **eke:** also; **fain:** eager, happy to do something.

[4] **ycladd:** clad.

[5] **them seemes:** it seems to them; the verb here is impersonal and takes the dative. Forms of the word "seems" occur frequently in the first part of Book One.

[6] The catalogue of trees is traditional, conveying a sense of plenitude. See ACH for preceding catalogues of trees and the reason for each of Spenser's epithets; all annotators cite Chaucer's *Parliament of Fowles,* 176–82.

[7] **meed:** reward, in the form of the laurel crown.

10 Led with delight, they thus beguile the way,
   Untill the blustring storme is overblowne;
   When weening to returne,[1] whence they did stray,
   They cannot finde that path, which first was showne,
   But wander too and fro in waies unknowne,
   Furthest from end then, when they neerest weene,
   That makes them doubt, their wits be not their owne:
   So many pathes, so many turnings seene,
  That which of them to take, in diverse doubt they been.[2]

11 At last resolving forward still to fare,
   Till that some end they finde or in or out,
   That path they take, that beaten seemd most bare,
   And like to lead the labyrinth about;
   Which when by tract[3] they hunted had throughout,
   At length it brought them to a hollowe cave,
   Amid the thickest woods. The Champion stout
   Eftsoones[4] dismounted from his courser brave,
  And to the Dwarfe a while his needlesse spere he gave.

12 "Be well aware," quoth then that Ladie milde,
   "Least suddaine mischiefe ye too rash provoke:
   The danger hid, the place unknowne and wilde,
   Breedes dreadfull doubts: Oft fire is without smoke,
   And perill without show: therefore your hardy stroke
   Sir knight with-hold, till further tryall made."
   "Ah Ladie" (sayd he) "shame were to revoke,
   The forward footing for an hidden shade:[5]
  Vertue gives her selfe light, through darkenesse for to wade."[6]

13 "Yea but" (quoth she) "the perill of this place
   I better wot[7] then you, though nowe too late,
   To wish you backe returne with foule disgrace,

---

[1] **weening to return:** supposing they can return.

[2] Some commentators relate this wood to the *selva oscura,* or "dark wood," in which Dante's Pilgrim finds himself lost in the beginning of *The Divine Comedy.*

[3] **tract:** traces.

[4] **Eftsoones:** immediately.

[5] I.e., it would be shameful to turn back because of obscuring shadows.

[6] Cf. 14.4–5 and x.1, which passages undercut this heroic-sounding speech, showing it to be a revelation of Redcrosse's spiritual overconfidence.

[7] **wot:** know.

Yet wisedome warnes, whilest foot is in the gate,
To stay the steppe, ere forced to retrate.
This is the wandring wood, this *Errours den,*
A monster vile, whom God and man does hate:
Therefore I read[1] beware." "Fly fly" (quoth then
The fearefull Dwarfe:) "this is no place for living men."

14   But full of fire and greedy hardiment,
The youthfull knight could not for ought be staide,
But forth unto the darksom hole he went,
And looked in: his glistring armor made
A litle glooming light, much like a shade,
By which he saw the ugly monster plaine,
Halfe like a serpent horribly displaide,
But th'other halfe did womans shape retaine,
Most lothsom, filthie, foule, and full of vile disdaine.

15   And as she lay upon the durtie ground,
Her huge long taile her den all overspred,
Yet was in knots and many boughtes[2] upwound,
Pointed with mortall sting. Of her there bred,
A thousand yong ones, which she dayly fed,
Sucking upon her poisnous dugs, eachone
Of sundrie shapes, yet all ill favored:
Soone as that uncouth light upon them shone,
Into her mouth they crept, and suddain all were gone.

16   Their dam upstart, out of her den effraide,
And rushed forth, hurling her hideous taile
About her cursed head, whose folds displaid
Were stretcht now forth at length without entraile.[3]
She lookt about, and seeing one in mayle
Armed to point,[4] sought backe to turne againe;
For light she hated as the deadly bale,[5]
Ay wont[6] in desert darknes to remaine,
Where plain none might her see, nor she see any plaine.

---

[1] **read:** counsel.

[2] **boughtes:** coils.

[3] **without entraile:** without coiling.

[4] **Armed to point:** fully armed.

[5] **bale:** death or grave damage.

[6] **wont:** accustomed.

17 Which when the valiant Elfe[1] perceiv'd, he lept
   As Lyon fierce upon the flying pray,
   And with his trenchand[2] blade her boldly kept
   From turning backe, and forced her to stay:
   Therewith enrag'd, she loudly gan to bray,
   And turning fierce, her speckled taile advaunst,
   Threatning her angrie sting, him to dismay:
   Who nought aghast, his mightie hand enhaunst:[3]
The stroke down from her head unto her shoulder glaunst.

18 Much daunted with that dint, her sence was dazd,
   Yet kindling rage her selfe she gathered round,
   And all attonce her beastly bodie raizd
   With doubled forces high above the ground:
   Tho[4] wrapping up her wrethed sterne arownd,
   Lept fierce upon his shield, and her huge traine[5]
   All suddenly about his body wound,
   That hand or foot to stirr he strove in vaine:
God helpe the man so wrapt in *Errours* endlesse traine.

19 His Lady sad to see his sore constraint,
   Cride out, "Now now Sir knight, shew what ye bee
   Add faith unto your force,[6] and be not faint:
   Strangle her, els she sure will strangle thee."
   That when he heard, in great perplexitie,
   His gall did grate for griefe and high disdaine,
   And knitting all his force[7] got one hand free,
   Wherewith he grypt her gorge with so great paine,
That soone to loose her wicked bands did her constraine.

20 Therewith she spewd out of her filthie maw
   A floud of poyson horrible and blacke,
   Full of great lumps of flesh and gobbets raw,
   Which stunck so vildly, that it forst him slacke,
   His grasping hold, and from her turne him backe:

---

[1] **Elfe:** literally a male fairy, but apparently here used generally for any inhabitant of Faerie Land; cf. x.60.1–2; x.64–5.

[2] **trenchand:** sharp.

[3] **enhaunst:** raised.

[4] **Tho:** Then.

[5] **traine:** tail.

[6] Cf. 2 Pet. 1.5.

[7] Cf. i.24.6.

Her vomit full of bookes and papers was,[1]
With loathly frogs[2] and toades, which eyes did lacke,
And creeping sought way in the weedy gras:
Her filthie parbreake[3] all the place defiled has.

21   As when old father *Nilus*[4] gins to swell
With timely pride above the *Aegyptian* vale,
His fattie waves doe fertile slime outwell,
And overflow each plaine and lowly dale:
But when his later ebbe gins t'avale,[5]
Huge heapes of mudd he leaves, wherein there breed
Ten thousand kindes of creatures partly male
And partly femall of his fruitful seed;
Such ugly monstrous shapes elswher may no man reed.[6]

22   The same so sore annoyed has the knight,
That welnigh choked with the deadly stinke,
His forces faile, ne can no longer fight.
Whose corage when the feend perceivd to shrinke,
She poured forth out of her hellish sinke
Her fruitfull cursed spawne of serpents small,
Deformed monsters, fowle, and blacke as inke,
Which swarming all about his legs did crall,
And him encombred sore, but could not hurt at all.

23   As gentle Shepheard in sweete eventide,
When ruddy *Phebus* gins to welke[7] in west,
High on an hill, his flocke to vewen wide,
Markes which doe byte their hasty supper best,
A cloud of cumbrous gnattes doe him molest,
All striving to infixe their feeble stinges,

---

[1] Symbolizing, among other things, theological writings, in which error is difficult to avoid.

[2] Cf. Rev. 16.13.

[3] **parbreake:** vomit.

[4] The river Nile. "Spenser often uses the Latin forms of proper names as here"

(TPR). Spenser employs this same comparison in III.vi.8–9.

[5] **gins t'avale:** begins to abate.

[6] **reed:** see. This usage occurs only in Spenser, and frequently there. See also III.ix.2.3; V.xii.39 (OED, "read," 4).

[7] **welke:** fade, sink. An epic simile in the manner of Homer.

That from their noyance he no where can rest,
But with his clownish[1] hands their tender wings,
He brusheth oft, and oft doth mar their murmurings.[2]

24   Thus ill bestedd,[3] and fearefull more of shame,
      Then of the certeine perill he stood in,
      Halfe furious unto his foe he came,
      Resolvd in minde all suddenly to win,
      Or soone to lose, before he once would lin;[4]
      And stroke at her with more then manly force,[5]
      That from her body full of filthie sin
      He raft her hatefull heade without remorse;
A streame of cole black blood forth gushed from her corse.

25   Her scattred brood, soone as their Parent deare
      They saw so rudely falling to the ground,
      Groning full deadly, all with troublous feare,
      Gathred themselves about her body round,
      Weening their wonted[6] entrance to have found
      At her wide mouth: but being there withstood
      They flocked all about her bleeding wound,
      And sucked up their dying mothers bloud,
Making her death their life, and eke her hurt their good.

26   That detestable sight him much amazde,
      To see th'unkindly Impes[7] of heaven accurst,
      Devoure their dam; on whom while so he gazd,
      Having all satisfide their bloudy thurst,
      Their bellies swolne he saw with fulnesse burst,
      And bowels gushing forth: well worthy end
      Of such as drunke her life, the which them nurst;
      Now needeth him no lenger labour spend,
His foes have slaine themselves, with whom he should contend.

---

[1] **clownish:** rustic.

[2] Onomatopoeia.

[3] **bestedd:** situated.

[4] **lin:** leave off.

[5] **more then manly force:** more than what a man could do—evidently the effect of adding faith unto his force, recommended in 19.3. Cf. vii.6.4; ix.48.7.

[6] **wonted:** accustomed.

[7] **unkindly Impes:** unnatural children.

27   His Lady seeing all, that chaunst, from farre
        Approcht in hast to greet his victorie,
        And saide, "Faire knight, borne under happie starre,
        Who see your vanquisht foes before you lye:
        Well worthie be you of that Armory,[1]
        Wherein ye have great glory wonne this day,
        And proov'd your strength on a strong enimie,
        Your first adventure: many such I pray,
And henceforth ever wish, that like succeed it may."

28   Then mounted he upon his Steede againe,
        And with the Lady backward sought to wend;
        That path he kept, which beaten was most plaine,
        Ne ever would to any byway bend,
        But still did follow one unto the end,
        The which at last out of the wood them brought.
        So forward on his way (with God to frend)[2]
        He passed forth, and new adventure sought,
Long way he traveiled, before he heard of ought.

29   At length they chaunst to meet upon the way
        An aged Sire, in long blacke weedes[3] yclad,
        His feete all bare, his beard all hoarie gray,
        And by his belt his booke he hanging had;
        Sober he seemde, and very sagely sad,
        And to the ground his eyes were lowly bent,
        Simple in shew, and voide of malice bad,
        And all the way he prayed as he went,
And often knockt his brest, as one that did repent.

30   He faire the knight saluted, louting low,[4]
        Who faire him quited,[5] as that courteous was:
        And after asked him, if he did know
        Of straunge adventures, which abroad did pas.
        "Ah my deare Sonne" (quoth he) "how should, alas,

---

[1] **Armory:** armor.

[2] **to frend:** as friend. Whatever his missteps, he is now in a good relationship with God.

[3] **weedes:** garments. The long black garment, the book hanging by the belt, and knocking the breast are Roman Catholic attributes. Cf. *OF,* 2.12–3, in which Angelica meets the hypocritical old hermit.

[4] **louting low:** bowing low.

[5] **faire him quited:** returned the salutation politely.

Silly[1] old man, that lives in hidden cell,
Bidding his beades all day for his trespas,[2]
Tydings of warre and worldly trouble tell?
With holy father sits not with such thinges to mell.[3]

31   But if of daunger which hereby doth dwell,
      And homebredd evil ye desire to heare,
      Of a straunge man I can you tidings tell,
      That wasteth all this countrie farre and neare."
      "Of such" (saide he) "I chiefly doe inquere,
      And shall thee well rewarde to shew the place,
      In which that wicked wight[4] his dayes doth weare:
      For to all knighthood it is foule disgrace,
That such a cursed creature lives so long a space."

32   "Far hence" (quoth he) "in wastfull[5] wildernesse
      His dwelling is, by which no living wight[6]
      May ever passe, but thorough great distresse."[7]
      "Now" (saide the Ladie) "draweth toward night,
      And well I wote, that of your later[8] fight
      Ye all forwearied[9] be: for what so strong,
      But wanting rest will also want of might?
      The Sunne that measures heaven all day long,
At night doth baite[10] his steedes the *Ocean* waves emong.

33   "Then with the Sunne take Sir, your timely rest,
      And with new day new worke at once begin:
      Untroubled night they say gives counsell best."
      "Right well Sir knight ye have advised bin,"

---

[1] **silly:** innocent.

[2] If "beades" bears its modern meaning, as it seems to do in iii.13.6–9, then praying with the aid of beads is saying the rosary, which is a Romanist activity. Contrast with Caelia, in x.3.8, who bids her beads only at night, whereas she is occupied with good deeds during the day.

[3] **mell:** meddle. I.e., it is not fitting for a holy father to concern himself with such things.

[4] **wight:** person.

[5] **wastfull:** desolate.

[6] **wight:** person.

[7] Since we never again hear of this villain (except in a patent lie by Archimago in iii.29.1–6), Archimago must have just made him up to engage Redcrosse's interest.

[8] **wote:** know; **later:** recent. Spenser often appends "-er" to an adjective just to gain a needed short syllable.

[9] **forwearied:** very wearied.

[10] **baite:** give rest and food to.

Quoth then that aged man; "the way to win
Is wisely to advise: now day is spent;
Therefore with me ye may take up your In[1]
For this same night." The knight was well content:
So with that godly father to his home they went.

34   A litle lowly Hermitage it was,
          Downe in a dale, hard by a forests side,
          Far from resort of people, that did pas
          In traveill to and froe: a litle wyde[2]
          There was an holy chappell edifyde,[3]
          Wherein the Hermite dewly wont[4] to say
          His holy thinges[5] each morne and eventyde:
          Thereby a christall streame did gently play,
Which from a sacred fountaine welled forth alway.

35   Arrived there the litle house they fill,
          Ne looke for entertainement, where none was:
          Rest is their feast, and all thinges at their will;[6]
          The noblest mind the best contentment has.
          With faire discourse the evening so they pas:
          For that olde man of pleasing wordes had store,
          And well could file his tongue as smooth as glas,[7]
          He told of Saintes and Popes, and evermore
He strowd[8] an *Ave-Mary* after and before.

36   The drouping Night thus creepeth on them fast,
          And the sad humor[9] loading their eye liddes,
          As messenger of *Morpheus*[10] on them cast
          Sweet slombring deaw, the which to sleep them biddes:
          Unto their lodgings then his guestes he riddes:[11]

---

[1] **take up your In:** take up residence as at an inn.

[2] **wyde:** off to one side.

[3] **edifyde:** built.

[4] **wont:** was accustomed.

[5] **holy thinges:** the monastic offices for morning and evening.

[6] I.e., rest is entertainment to them; and because they desire nothing, they have "all things at their will" (TPR).

[7] He was a "smooth talker."

[8] **strowd:** interspersed. The "Hail Mary" is "the principal prayer of the rosary" (TPR), moreover, he apparently says it in Latin; Protestants associated this prayer with Catholic Mariolatry.

[9] **humor:** moisture.

[10] God of sleep.

[11] **riddes:** dispatches.

Where when all drownd in deadly sleepe he findes,
He to his studie goes, and there amiddes
His magick bookes and artes of sundrie kindes,
He seekes out mighty charmes, to trouble sleepy minds.

37 Then choosing out few words most horrible,
(Let none them read) thereof did verses frame,
With which and other spelles like terrible,
He bad awake blacke *Plutoes* griesly Dame,[1]
And cursed heven, and spake reprochful shame
Of highest God, the Lord of life and light,
A bold bad man, that dar'd to call by name
Great *Gorgon*,[2] prince of darknes and dead night,
At which *Cocytus* quakes and *Styx* is put to flight.

38 And forth he cald out of deepe darknes dredd
Legions of Sprights,[3] the which like litle flyes
Fluttring about his everdamned hedd,
A waite whereto their service he applyes,
To aide his friendes, or fray[4] his enemies:
Of those he chose out two, the falsest twoo,
And fittest for to forge true-seeming lyes;
The one of them he gave a message too,
The other by him self staide other worke to doo.

39 He making speedy way through spersed ayre,[5]
And through the world of waters wide and deepe,
To *Morpheus*[6] house doth hastily repaire.
Amid the bowels of the earth full steepe,
And low, where dawning day doth never peepe,
His dwelling is; there *Tethys*[7] his wet bed

---

[1] Pluto's wife, Proserpina, queen of hell.

[2] Demogorgon, the progenitor of all the gods. Mentioned again at v.22.5ff. Like "Cocytus," chosen largely for its sound. "Even mention of his name makes the rivers of hell (Cocytus and Styx) tremble" (TPR).

[3] **Sprights:** spirits.

[4] **fray:** frighten.

[5] **He:** the sprite with the message; **spersed ayre:** the air that parted to let him through.

[6] See *Metamorphoses,* 11:592–632; Chaucer, *The Book of the Duchess,* 155ff, which also contains a farcical awakening.

[7] Wife of Ocean, hence goddess of the sea; here the sea itself.

> Doth ever wash,[1] and *Cynthia* still doth steepe
> In silver deaw his ever-drouping hed,[2]
> Whiles sad Night over him her mantle black doth spred.

40   Whose double gates he findeth locked fast,
        The one faire fram'd of burnisht Yvory,
        The other all with silver overcast;[3]
        And wakeful dogges before them farre doe lye,
        Watching to banish Care their enimy,
        Who oft is wont to trouble gentle Sleepe.
        By them the Sprite doth passe in quietly,
        And unto *Morpheus* comes, whom drowned deepe
In drowsie fit he findes: of nothing he takes keepe.[4]

41   And more, to lulle him in his slumber soft,
        A trickling streame from high rock tumbling downe
        And ever drizling raine upon the loft,[5]
        Mixt with a murmuring winde, much like the sowne[6]
        Of swarming Bees, did cast him in a swowne:
        No other noyse, nor peoples troublous cryes,
        As still are wont t'annoy the walled towne,
        Might there be heard: but carelesse Quiet lyes,
Wrapt in eternall silence farre from enimyes.[7]

42   The Messenger approching to him spake,
        But his waste wordes retournd to him in vaine:
        So sound he slept, that nought mought him awake.
        Then rudely he him thrust, and pusht with paine,
        Whereat he gan to stretch: but he againe
        Shooke him so hard, that forced him to speake.

---

[1] **wash:** as waves wash a gently sloping shore. Why a wet bed is soporific remains unexplained; it would make more sense if the "bed" were the Ocean's bed; one would have to conjecture either that Spenser said "his" when he meant "her," or that he forgot that Tethys is female.

[2] Cynthia is the moon. Dew materializes at night, when the moon is visible; astrology associates her with moisture.

[3] The Gates of Sleep are from Homer, *Odyssey*, 19.562–67, and *Aeneid*, 6.893–96. They are pictured as side-by-side alterna-tives; the gate of horn channels true dreams and is not mentioned, being replaced by a gate of silver; the gate of ivory channels false dreams, and the sprite exits through it at 44.6.

[4] **fit:** mood; **keepe:** notice.

[5] **loft:** ceiling (OED, 5c).

[6] **sowne:** sound.

[7] Spenser flaunts his skill at creating a mood by means of rhetoric and versification. Here and elsewhere, he slips easily into per-sonification.

As one then in a dreame, whose dryer braine[1]
Is tost with troubled sights and fancies weake,
He mumbled soft, but would not all his silence breake.

43   The Sprite[2] then gan more boldly him to wake,
      And threatned unto him the dreaded name
      Of *Hecate:*[3] whereat he gan to quake,
      And lifting up his lompish head, with blame
      Halfe angrie asked him, for what he came.
      "Hether" (quoth he) "me *Archimago*[4] sent,
      He that the stubborne Sprites can wisely tame,
      He bids thee to him send for his intent
A fit false dreame, that can delude the sleepers sent."[5]

44   The God obayde, and calling forth straight way
      A diverse dreame out of his prison darke,
      Delivered it to him, and downe did lay
      His heavie head, devoide of careful carke,[6]
      Whose sences all were straight benumbd and starke.
      He backe returning by the Yvorie dore,
      Remounted up as light as chearefull Larke,
      And on his litle winges the dreame he bore,
In hast unto his Lord, where he him left afore.

45   Who all this while with charmes and hidden artes,
      Had made a Lady of that other Spright,
      And fram'd of liquid ayre her tender partes
      So lively and so like in all mens sight,
      That weaker sence it could have ravisht quight:
      The maker selfe for all his wondrous witt,

---

[1] **dryer braine:** too-dry brain. See *SE,* "dreams."

[2] **Sprite:** spirit.

[3] The queen of Hades, another name for Proserpina; in Natalis Comes (Natale Conti, Spenser's and the Elizabethans' favorite mythographer, for whose comments on each god mentioned by Spenser, translated into English, see Lotspeich) the patroness of black magic and goddess of dreams.

[4] Here Archimago is named for the first time. He is both "master of images" and "master-magician." Protestants charged that Catholic ritual was supposed to operate like magic, without considering the spiritual state of the performer. He symbolizes the devil as tempter and owes something to the False Prophet in Rev., as well as to "the disguised hermit in Ariosto's *OF* 2.12–3 and the enchanter Malagigi in Tasso's *Rinaldo* I.31" (M&P).

[5] **sent:** senses.

[6] **careful carke:** worry.

Was nigh beguiled with so goodly sight:
Her all in white he clad, and over it
Cast a black stole, most like to seeme for *Una* fit.[1]

46   Now when that ydle[2] dreame was to him brought,
        Unto that Elfin knight he bad him fly,
        Where he slept soundly void of evil thought,
        And with false shewes abuse his fantasy,
        In sort as he him schooled privily:
        And that new creature borne without her dew,[3]
        Full of the makers guyle with usage sly
        He taught to imitate that Lady trew,
Whose semblance she did carrie under feigned hew.[4]

47   Thus well instructed, to their worke they haste,
        And comming where the knight in slomber lay,
        The one upon his hardie head him plaste,
        And made him dreame of loves and lustfull play,
        That nigh his manly hart did melt away,
        Bathed in wanton blis and wicked joy:
        Then seemed him[5] his Lady by him lay,
        And to him playnd, how that false winged boy,[6]
Her chaste hart had subdewd, to learn Dame pleasures toy.[7]

48   And she her selfe of beautie soveraigne Queene,
        Fayre *Venus* seemde unto his bed to bring
        Her, whom he waking evermore did weene,
        To bee the chastest flowre, that aye did spring
        On earthly braunch, the daughter of a king,
        Now a loose Leman[8] to vile service bound:
        And eke the *Graces* seemed all to sing,
        Hymen iō Hymen,[9] dauncing all around,
Whylst freshest *Flora*[10] her with Yvie girlond crownd.

---

[1] Una means "one," i.e., consistent, in Latin. In this she contrasts with Duessa, the first syllable of whose name means "two," i.e., duplicitous. See *SE*, "Una." "Una is not named until the duplicate, false image has been created" (TPR); Spenser customarily defers naming his characters.

[2] **ydle:** baseless.

[3] **without her dew:** unnaturally.

[4] **hew:** physical appearance.

[5] **seemed him:** it seemed to him.

[6] **playnd:** complained; **false winged boy:** Cupid. So also "blind God" below.

[7] **Dame pleasures toy:** lovemaking.

[8] **Leman:** mistress.

[9] **Hymen iō Hymen:** a chant at Roman weddings; here ironical.

[10] Goddess of spring and flowers, but also the name of a famous harlot in classical

49   In this great passion of unwonted[1] lust,
          Or wonted feare of doing ought amis,
          He starteth up, as seeming to mistrust,
          Some secret ill, or hidden foe of his:
          Lo there before his face his Ladie is,
          Under blacke stole hyding her bayted hooke,
          And as halfe blushing offred him to kis,
          With gentle blandishment and lovely looke,
      Most like that virgin true, which for her knight him took.

50   All cleane dismayd to see so uncouth sight,
          And halfe enraged at her shamelesse guise,[2]
          He thought have slaine her in his fierce despight,[3]
          But hastie heat tempring with sufferance wise,
          He stayde his hand, and gan himselfe advise
          To prove his sense, and tempt her faigned truth.
          Wringing her hands in wemens piteous wise,
          Tho can she weepe, to stirre up gentle ruth,[4]
      Both for her noble blood, and for her tender youth.

51   And sayd, "Ah Sir, my liege Lord and my love,
          Shall I accuse the hidden cruell fate,
          And mightie causes wrought in heaven above,
          Or the blind God, that doth me thus amate,[5]
          For hoped love to winne me certaine hate?
          Yet thus perforce he bids me do, or die.
          Die is my dew: yet rew my wretched state
          You, whom my hard avenging destinie
      Hath made judge of my life or death indifferently.

52   "Your owne dear sake forst me at first to leave
          My Fathers kingdom," There she stopt with teares;
          Her swollen hart her speech seemd to bereave,
          And then againe begonne, "My weaker yeares
          Captiv'd to fortune and frayle worldly feares
          Fly to your fayth for succour and sure ayde:

Rome; here used disparagingly, as classical gods usually are in Book One; cf. II.ii.6.5.

[1] **unwonted:** unaccustomed.

[2] **guise:** behavior.

[3] **despight:** wrath.

[4] **Tho can:** then did; **ruth:** pity.

[5] **amate:** dismay; here by forcing her to offer herself to Redcrosse and perhaps thus disgust him, as she indeed does, though he cleverly pretends not to understand what she is suggesting.

Let me not die in languor and long teares."
"Why Dame" (quoth he) "what hath ye thus dismayd?
What frayes[1] ye, that were wont to comfort me affrayd?"

53   "Love of your selfe," she saide, "and deare[2] constraint
      Lets me not sleepe, but waste the wearie night
      In secret anguish and unpittied plaint,
      Whiles you in carelesse sleepe are drowned quight."
      Her doubtfull words made that redoubted knight
      Suspect her truth: yet since no'untruth he knew,
      Her fawning love with foule disdainefull spight
      He would not shend,[3] but said, "Dear dame I rew,
That for my sake unknowne such griefe unto you grew.

54   "Assure your selfe, it fell not all to ground;
      For all so deare as life is to my hart,
      I deeme your love, and hold me[4] to you bound;
      Ne let vaine feares procure your needlesse smart,
      Where cause is none, but to your rest depart."
      Not all content, yet seemd she to appease
      Her mournefull plaintes, beguiled of her art,[5]
      And fed with words, that could not chose but please,
So sliding softly forth, she turnd as to her ease.

55   Long after lay he musing at her mood,
      Much griev'd to thinke that gentle Dame so light,[6]
      For whose defence he was to shed his blood.
      At last dull wearines of former fight
      Having yrockt a sleepe his irkesome spright,
      That troublous dreame gan freshly tosse his braine,
      With bowres, and beds, and ladies deare delight:
      But when he[7] saw his labour all was vaine,
With that misformed spright he backe returnd againe.

---

[1] **frayes:** frightens.

[2] **deare:** here, dire, an unusual use; for the normal use, see line 8 of this stanza.

[3] **shend:** rebuke.

[4] **hold me:** consider myself.

[5] **plaintes:** complaints; **beguiled of her art:** being disappointed that her women's wiles did not succeed in seducing him.

[6] **light:** wanton, forth-putting.

[7] I.e., the sprite who was administering the dream, as in stanza 47. The "misformed sprite" is the one who is impersonating Una (ii.2). Their failure shows that Redcrosse has so far resisted temptation and remained sinless, though his priggish desire to slay the false Una is worrisome.

Canto Two

The guilefull great Enchaunter[1] parts
The Redcrosse Knight from Truth:
Into whose stead faire falshood steps,
And workes him woefull ruth.[2]

1   By this the Northerne wagoner had set
       His sevenfold teme behind the stedfast starre,
       That was in Ocean waves yet never wet,
       But firme is fixt, and sendeth light from farre
       To al, that in the wide deepe wandring arre:[3]
       And chearefull Chaunticlere[4] with his note shrill
       Had warned once, that *Phoebus* fiery carre,[5]
       In hast was climbing up the Easterne hill,
   Full envious that night so long his roome did fill.

2   When those accursed messengers of hell,
       That feigning dreame, and that faire-forged Spright
       Came to their wicked maister, and gan tel
       Their bootelesse paines, and ill succeeding night:
       Who all in rage to see his skilfull might
       Deluded so, gan threaten hellish paine
       And sad *Proserpines*[6] wrath, them to affright.
       But when he saw his threatning was but vaine,
   He cast about, and searcht his baleful bokes againe.

---

[1] **great Enchaunter:** one indubitable etymology of "Archimago."

[2] **ruth:** damage.

[3] These five lines constitute a conspicuously abstruse astronomical way of telling time. The "Northerne wagoner" is the constellation Boötes, the ox-driver. His "sevenfold teme" are the seven bright stars of Ursa Major, identified with the Plough or Charles' Wain in England and the Big Dipper in the U.S.; the "stedfast starre" is the Pole Star or North Star, which was thought never to move, and so never to set into the ocean (TPR).

[4] **Chaunticlere:** the rooster.

[5] *Phoebus* **fiery carre:** the chariot of the sun, pictured as climbing up the bulging surface of his underground orbit toward the eastern horizon.

[6] Proserpina is the wife of Pluto and therefore the queen of Hell.

3   Eftsoones he tooke that miscreated faire,[1]
         And that false other Spright,[2] on whom he spred
         A seeming body of the subtile aire,
         Like a young Squire, in loves and lusty hed
         His wanton daies that ever loosely led,[3]
         Without regard of armes and dreaded fight:
         Those twoo he tooke, and in a secrete bed,
         Covered with darkenes and misdeeming night,
    Them both together laid, to joy in vaine delight.

4   Forthwith he runnes with feigned faithfull hast
         Unto his guest, who after troublous sights
         And dreames gan now to take more sound repast,[4]
         Whom suddenly he wakes with fearfull frights,
         As one aghast with feends or damned sprights,
         And to him cals, "Rise rise unhappy Swaine,
         That here wex[5] old in sleepe, whiles wicked wights
         Have knit themselves in *Venus* shamefull chaine;[6]
    Come see, where your false Lady doth her honor staine."

5   All in amaze he suddenly up start
         With sword in hand, and with the old man went;
         Who soone him brought into a secret part,
         Where that false couple were full closely ment[7]
         In wanton lust and leud enbracement:
         Which when he saw, he burnt with gealous fire,
         The eie of reason was with rage yblent,[8]
         And would have slaine them in his furious ire,
    But hardly[9] was restreined of that aged sire.

[1] **Eftsoones:** immediately; **that miscre-ated faire:** that unnaturally created beauty.

[2] I.e., the one who formerly manipulated the sexual dream.

[3] I.e., that ever loosely led his wanton days. Word order is inverted for sake of rhyme.

[4] **repast:** repose.

[5] **wex:** wax, i.e., become.

[6] I.e., linked themselves in intercourse.

[7] **closely ment:** tightly or secretly united.

[8] I.e., the passion of rage blinded the eye of reason. See also ii.12.4: "Will was his guide, and grief led him astray." These diagnoses are in terms of the faculty-psychology common in older literature. Reason is not doing its job—to control the will and, through it, the passions such as rage and grief.

[9] **hardly:** with difficulty.

6 Retourning to his bed in torment great,
  And bitter anguish of his guilty sight,
  He could not rest, but did his stout heart eat,
  And wast his inward gall with deepe despight,[1]
  Yrkesome of life,[2] and too long lingring night.
  At last faire *Hesperus*[3] in highest skie
  Had spent his lampe, and brought forth dawning light,
  Then up he rose, and clad him hastily;
The dwarfe him brought his steed: so both away do fly.

7 Now when the rosy fingred Morning faire,
  Weary of aged *Tithones*[4] saffron bed,
  Had spred her purple robe through deawy aire,
  And the high hils *Titan* discovered,[5]
  The royall virgin shooke of drousy hed,
  And rising forth out of her baser bowre,
  Lookt for her knight, who far away was fled,
  And for her dwarfe, that wont to wait each howre;
Then gan she wail and weepe, to see that woeful stowre.[6]

8 And after him she rode with so much speede,
  As her slowe beast could make; but all in vaine:
  For him so far had borne[7] his light-foot steede,
  Pricked with wrath and fiery fierce disdaine,
  That him to follow was but fruitlesse paine;
  Yet she her weary limbes would never rest,
  But every hil and dale, each wood and plaine
  Did search, sore grieved in her gentle brest,
He so ungently left her, whome she loved best.

9 But subtill *Archimago* when his guests
  He saw divided into double parts,
  And *Una* wandring in woods and forrests,
  Th'end of his drift,[8] he praisd his divelish arts,

---

[1] **despight:** wrath.

[2] **Yrksome of life:** finding life irksome.

[3] Venus positioned as the morning star.

[4] Aurora, goddess of the dawn, loved Tithonus and persuaded the gods to grant him immortality; but she forgot to obtain for him eternal youth, so that he lived but just went on getting older.

[5] *Titan:* the sun; **discovered:** uncovered them for mortal watchers.

[6] **stowre:** time of distress.

[7] **borne:** carried off.

[8] **Th'end of his drift:** the goal of his plan.

That had such might over true meaning harts:
Yet rests not so, but other meanes doth make,
How he may worke unto her further smarts:
For her he hated as the hissing snake,
And in her many troubles did most pleasure take.

10   He then devisde himselfe how to disguise;
For by his mighty science he could take
As many formes and shapes in seeming wise,
As ever *Proteus*[1] to himselfe could make:
Sometime a fowle, sometime a fish in lake,
Now like a foxe, now like a dragon fell,[2]
That of himselfe he ofte for feare would quake,
And oft would flie away. O who can tell
The hidden powre of herbes, and might of Magick spel?

11   But now seemde best, the person to put on
Of that good knight, his late beguiled guest:
In mighty armes he was yclad anon:
And silver shield, upon his coward brest
A bloody crosse, and on his craven crest
A bounch of heares discolourd diversly:[3]
Full jolly knight he seemde, and wel addrest,[4]
And when he sate uppon his courser free,
Saint George[5] himselfe ye would have deemed him to be.

12   But he the knight, whose semblaunt he did beare,
The true *Saint George* was wandred far away,
Still flying from his thoughts and gealous feare;
Will was his guide, and griefe led him astray.
At last him chaunst to meete upon the way
A faithlesse Sarazin[6] all armde to point,

---

[1] A god of the sea, also a shapeshifter. He will appear in person in Book Four.

[2] **fell:** ruthless.

[3] **heares discolourd diversly:** hairs of various colors; i.e., a plume. Arthur's plume is similar (vii.32).

[4] **addrest:** readied.

[5] Redcrosse is here named for the first time. He has been called St. George in ii.11.9, but in x.61 we learn he earns this name only when he kills the dragon, and he may not even know his name is George; hence critics, and indeed, most of the time, the poet-speaker, call him Redcrosse. This description echoes the description of Redcrosse in i.1.

[6] **Sarazin:** Saracen, a pagan or infidel—epithets ignorantly applied to Muslims such as the feared and hated Turks.

In whose great shield was writ with letters gay
    Sans foy:[1] full large of limbe and every joint
He was, and cared not for God or man a point.

13   Hee had a faire companion of his way,
        A goodly Lady[2] clad in scarlot red,
        Purfled[3] with gold and pearle of rich assay,
        And like a *Persian* mitre[4] on her hed
        Shee wore, with crowns and owches[5] garnished,
        The which her lavish lovers to her gave;
        Her wanton palfrey all was overspred
        With tinsell trappings, woven like a wave,
Whose bridle rung with golden bels and bosses[6] brave.

14   With faire disport[7] and courting dalliaunce
        She intertainde her lover all the way:
        But when she saw the knight his speare advaunce,
        Shee soone left off her mirth and wanton play,
        And bad her knight addresse him to the fray:
        His foe was nigh at hand. He prickte with pride[8]
        And hope to winne his Ladies hearte that day,
        Forth spurred fast: adowne his coursers side
The red bloud trickling staind the way, as he did ride.

---

[1] Means "without faith" in French. His brothers are Sansloy (without law) and Sansjoy (without joy). The Sans brothers are the villains threatening Redcrosse and Una in the middle cantos. The faith Sansfoy lacks is not only religious but also, on the allegorical level, sexual, in that he reflects Redcrosse, who has recently broken his "faith" to Una by deserting her; whereas Redcrosse will praise Una for her "wondrous faith" to him.

[2] Duessa here appears for the first time. She will appear in every book up through Book Five, in which she is finally executed. In Book One, she represents the Scarlet Whore of Babylon (Rev. 17–18.3), whom Protestant commentators on Rev. took to be a prophecy of the corrupt state of the Catholic Church in the last days of the world. She appears with all her apocalyptic attributes in vii.16ff.

[3] **Purfled:** embroidered.

[4] **mitre:** a bishop's hat. Persia is associated with opulence, decadence, and tyranny, and so was the Roman Church.

[5] **owches:** brooches.

[6] **bosses:** ornamental knobs, here, on the ends of the bridle bit.

[7] **disport:** wanton gestures.

[8] **prickte with pride:** spurred by pride as he spurs his horse, but also with sexual overtones.

15   The knight of the *Redcrosse*[1] when him he spide,
          Spurring so hote with rage dispiteous,
          Gan fairely couch his speare,[2] and towards ride:
          Soone meete they both, both fell[3] and furious,
          That daunted with theyr forces hideous,
          Their steeds doe stagger and amazed stand,
          And eke themselves too rudely rigorous,
          Astonied[4] with the stroke of their owne hand,
     Doe backe rebutte,[5] and ech to other yealdeth land.

16   As when two rams stird with ambitious pride,
          Fight for the rule of the rich fleeced flocke,
          Their horned fronts so fierce on either side,
          Doe meete, that with the terror of the shocke
          Astonied both, stand sencelesse as a blocke,
          Forgetfull of the hanging victory:
          So stood these twaine, unmoved as a rocke,
          Both staring fierce, and holding idely,
     The broken reliques of their former cruelty.[6]

17   The *Sarazin*[7] sore daunted with the buffe
          Snatcheth his sword, and fiercely to him flies;
          Who well it wards, and quyteth cuff with cuff:[8]
          Each others equall puissaunce envies,
          And through their iron sides with cruell spies[9]
          Does seeke to perce: repining[10] courage yields
          No foote to foe. The flashing fier flies
          As from a forge out of their burning shields,
     And streams of purple bloud new dies the verdant fields.

---

[1] This is the first time he is called Redcrosse.

[2] **couch his speare:** bring it down from its normally vertical traveling position to the horizontal fighting position, and lay it in its rest.

[3] **fell:** ruthless.

[4] **Astonied:** stunned.

[5] **rebutte:** recoil.

[6] I.e., their now-broken spears. The spear was the first weapon of the first phase, the horseback, of knightly combat.

[7] *Sarazin:* Saracen, Muslim.

[8] **quyteth cuff with cuff:** returns blow for blow.

[9] **cruell spies:** corrected from *F.E.* in defiance of 1590 and 1596 editions, which had the tautological word "cruelties." In a bold metaphor, the corrector (who, if not Spenser, must have had at least some input from him) probably envisioned each combatant discovering and aiming for the chinks in his opponent's armor.

[10] **repining:** weakening, fading.

18   "Curse on that Crosse" (quoth then the *Sarazin)*
          "That keepes thy body from the bitter fitt;[1]
          Dead long ygoe I wote thou haddest bin,
          Had not that charme from thee forwarned itt:[2]
          But yet I warne thee now assured sitt,[3]
          And hide thy head." Therewith upon his crest
          With rigor so outrageous he smitt,
          That a large share it hewd out of the rest,
And glauncing downe his shield, from blame him fairely blest.[4]

19   Who thereat wondrous wroth, the sleeping spark
          Of native vertue[5] gan eftsoones revive,
          And at his haughty helmet making mark,
          So hugely stroke, that it the steele did rive,[6]
          And cleft his head. He tumbling downe alive,
          With bloudy mouth his mother earth did kis,
          Greeting his grave: his grudging ghost did strive
          With the fraile flesh; at last it flitted is,
Whether[7] the soules doe fly of men, that live amis.

20   The Lady when she saw her champion fall,
          Like the old ruines of a broken towre,
          Staid not to waile his woefull funerall,
          But from him fled away with all her powre;
          Who after her as hastily gan scowre,[8]
          Bidding the dwarfe with him to bring away

---

[1] **bitter fitt:** death, possibly referring to the phase of trembling and stretching that occurs during a violent death.

[2] Spenser contrives to make Sansfoy curse the cross to emphasize his enmity to Christianity. Sansfoy believes there is something efficacious about the cross. Because many Catholics did so, too, some commentators say Spenser could not have believed it. But there are other instances in the poem at which a material cross does seem efficacious. As we shall see in Canto Ten, Spenser retained some Catholic beliefs. See Kaske, 1999, 88–9.

[3] **assured sitt:** hold onto your saddle.

[4] **from blame him fairely blest:** from harm it preserved him; "it" (line 8) refers by squinting syntax to the shield, which does, to an extent, operate as Sansfoy complained that it does.

[5] **native vertue:** his own natural strength (from Latin *virtus*); cf. the "more than manly force" by which he kills Errour in i.24.6 (ACH).

[6] **rive:** split.

[7] **whether:** whither, to which.

[8] **scowre:** run, pursue.

The *Sarazins* shield, signe of the conqueroure,[1]
　　Her soone he overtooke, and bad to stay,
For present cause was none of dread her to dismay.

21　　Shee turning backe with ruefull countenaunce,
　　　　Cride, "Mercy mercy Sir vouchsafe to show
　　　　On silly[2] Dame, subject to hard mischaunce,
　　　　And to your mighty wil." Her humblesse low
　　　　In so ritch weedes and seeming glorious show,
　　　　Did much emmove his stout heroicke heart,
　　　　And said, "Deare dame, your suddein overthrow
　　　　Much rueth me;[3] but now put feare apart,
And tel, both who ye be, and who that tooke your part."

22　　Melting in teares, then gan shee thus lament;
　　　　"The wreched woman, whom unhappy howre
　　　　Hath now made thrall[4] to your commandement,
　　　　Before that angry heavens list to lowre,[5]
　　　　And fortune false betraide me to thy powre,
　　　　Was, (O what now availeth that I was?)
　　　　Borne the sole daughter of an Emperour,[6]
　　　　He that the wide West under his rule has,
And high hath set his throne, where *Tiberis* doth pas.

23　　"He in the first flowre of my freshest age,
　　　　Betrothed me unto the onely haire
　　　　Of a most mightly king, most rich and sage;
　　　　Was never Prince so faithfull and so faire,
　　　　Was never Prince so meeke and debonaire;[7]
　　　　But ere my hoped day of spousall shone,

---

[1] **signe of the conqueroure:** sign that he had conquered Sansfoy. Taking some souvenir from a conquered enemy is a chivalric convention; it can symbolize the acquisition of some trait of the enemy.

[2] **silly:** innocent

[3] **rueth me:** causes me to pity you.

[4] **thrall:** prisoner.

[5] **lowre:** frown, scowl.

[6] Duessa's father, as Emperor of the West, stands for the Pope, the head of Western or Roman Catholicism, as evidenced by the fact that he dwells on the banks of the Tiber. Protestants called the Pope "The Bishop of Rome." Contrast Una and her father, who, although their seat is Eden, rule "from East to Western shore"—i.e., the entire world, thus representing the church that is truly "Catholic," i.e., universal, including, for example, the Eastern or Greek Orthodox Church.

[7] **debonaire:** gentle, gracious; a virtue proper for the late-medieval knight.

My dearest Lord fell from high honors staire,
Into the hands of hys accursed fone,
And cruelly was slaine, that shall I ever mone.

24   "His blessed body spoild of lively breath,
Was afterward, I know not how, convaid
And fro me hid: of whose most innocent death
When tidings came to mee unhappy maid,
O how great sorrow my sad soule assaid.[1]
Then forth I went his woefull corse to find,
And many yeares throughout the world I straid,
A virgin widow, whose deepe wounded mind
With love, long time did languish as the striken hind.

25   "At last it chaunced this proud *Sarazin,*
To meete me wandring, who perforce me led
With him away, but yet could never win
The Fort, that Ladies hold in soveraigne dread.[2]
There lies he now with foule dishonor dead,
Who whiles he livde, was called proud *Sansfoy,*
The eldest of three brethren, all three bred
Of one bad sire, whose youngest is *Sansjoy,*
And twixt them both was born the bloudy bold *Sansloy.*

26   "In this sad plight, friendlesse, unfortunate,
Now miserable I *Fidessa*[3] dwell,
Craving of you in pitty of my state,
To doe none ill, if please ye not doe well."
He in great passion al this while did dwell,
More busying his quicke eies, her face to view,

---

[1] **assaid:** tested.

[2] I.e., virginity. Cf. "For that I would not yeeld, that to Sansfoy I gave" (iv.47.9). This lie as to Fidessa's sexual status is one of several distortions in her autobiography. There is no reason, however, to doubt her characterization of her "captor" and his family. What is revealing, whether true or false, conscious or unconscious, is her hints at her role as the Roman Church, e.g., her mitre and her fixation on the dead body of her "Lord," paralleling the Catholic tendency to place the body of Christ on their crosses, making them into crucifixes.

[3] Duessa's pseudonym replaces the first syllable of her name with "Fid-" from Latin *fides,* or faith—the same meaning that the syllable bears later (x.12–13, 18–21) in the name of Fidelia, or faith, who, like Duessa, wields a golden cup, magic, and a reptilian beast. The contrast hints to the reader that Fidessa means faith in the wrong object. It is ironic that she is paired with Sansfoy, or "without faith."

Then his dull eares, to heare what shee did tell,
  And said, "faire Lady hart of flint would rew
The undeserved woes and sorrowes, which ye shew.

27   "Henceforth in safe assuraunce may ye rest,
      Having both found a new friend you to aid,
      And lost an old foe, that did you molest:
      Better new friend then an old foe is said."
      With chaunge of chear[1] the seeming simple maid
      Let fal her eien, as shamefast to the earth,
      And yeelding soft, in that she nought gain-said,
      So forth they rode, he feining seemely merth,[2]
And shee coy lookes: so dainty they say maketh derth.[3]

28   Long time they thus together traveiled,
      Til weary of their way, they came at last,
      Where grew two goodly trees, that faire did spred
      Their armes abroad, with gray mosse overcast,
      And their greene leaves trembling with every blast,[4]
      Made a calme shadowe far in compasse round:
      The fearefull Shepheard often there aghast
      Under them never sat, ne wont there sound
His mery oaten pipe, but shund th'unlucky ground.

29   But this good knight soone as he them can[5] spie,
      For the coole shade him thither hastly got:
      For golden *Phoebus* now that mounted hie,
      From fiery wheeles of his faire chariot
      Hurled his beame so scorching cruell hot,
      That living creature mote[6] it not abide;
      And his new Lady it endured not.
      There they alight, in hope themselves to hide
From the fierce heat, and rest their weary limbs a tide.[7]

---

[1] **chear:** external demeanor.

[2] **feining seemely merth:** forcing himself
to utter appropriate pleasantries.

[3] The meaning and relevance of this
proverb is not clear. A.C. Hamilton sug-
gests, "Fastidiousness makes one precious
(**derth:** costliness) to another, implying

here that her coyness makes her seem more
worthy to be wooed."

[4] **blast:** puff, breath; OED sense 2, obso-
lete.

[5] **can:** did.

[6] **mote:** might, past tense.

[7] **a tide:** a while.

30   Faire seemely pleasaunce each to other makes,
        With goodly purposes[1] there as they sit:
        And in his falsed[2] fancy he her takes
        To be the fairest wight, that lived yit;
        Which to expresse, he bends his gentle wit,
        And thinkng of those braunches greene to frame
        A girlond[3] for her dainty forehead fit,
        He pluckt a bough; out of whose rifte there came
Smal drops of gory bloud, that trickled down the same.[4]

31   Therewith a piteous yelling voice was heard,
        Crying, "O spare with guilty hands to teare
        My tender sides in this rough rynd embard,[5]
        But fly, ah fly far hence away, for feare
        Least to you hap, that happened to me heare,
        And to this wretched Lady, my deare love,
        O too deare love, love bought with death too deare."
        Astond he stood, and up his heare did hove,[6]
And with that suddein horror could no member[7] move.

32   At last when as the dreadfull passion
        Was overpast, and manhood well awake,[8]
        Yet musing at the straunge occasion,
        And doubting much his sence, he thus bespake;
        "What voice of damned Ghost from *Limbo*[9] lake,
        Or guilefull spright wandring in empty aire,
        Both which fraile men doe oftentimes mistake,[10]
        Sends to my doubtful eares these speaches rare,
And ruefull plaints, me bidding guiltlesse blood to spare?"

---

[1] **purposes:** topics of conversation.

[2] **falsed:** false, deluded.

[3] **girlond:** garland, leafy crown.

[4] This begins the episode of Fradubio. The motif of a man transformed into a tree that bleeds and speaks when wounded can be found in *Aeneid,* 3.22–48; Dante, *Inferno,* 13; and *OF,* 6.26–53; see Kennedy. Somewhat as Fradubio predicts, Redcrosse, in abandoning Una and taking up with Duessa, is making the same mistake as Fradubio did; hence he is his "brother" (TPR).

[5] **embard:** imprisoned.

[6] **Astond:** stunned, astonished; **heare did hove:** hair did stand on end.

[7] **member:** part of his body.

[8] **manhood well awake:** reason was in control of his passions (TPR).

[9] The uppermost and least-threatening part of hell, but perhaps by metonymy for all of hell; for tradition does not record any particular lake in Limbo.

[10] **mistake:** mislead; not in OED.

33   Then groning deep, "Nor damned Ghost," (quoth he,)
            "Nor guileful sprite to thee these words doth speake,
            But once a man *Fradubio*,[1] now a tree,
            Wretched man, wretched tree; whose nature weake
            A cruell witch her cursed will to wreake,
            Hath thus transformd, and plast in open plaines,
            Where *Boreas*[2] doth blow full bitter bleake,
            And scorching Sunne does dry my secret vaines:
      For though a tree I seme, yet cold and heat me paines."

34   "Say on *Fradubio* then, or[3] man, or tree,"
            Quoth then the knight, "by whose mischievous arts
            Art thou misshaped thus, as now I see?
            He oft finds med'cine, who his griefe imparts;
            But double griefs afflict concealing harts,
            As raging flames who striveth to suppresse."[4]
            "The author[5] then" (said he) "of all my smarts,
            Is one *Duessa* a false sorceresse,
      That many errant[6] knights hath broght to wretchednesse.

35   "In prime of youthly yeares, when corage hott
            The fire of love and joy of chevalree
            First kindled in my brest, it was my lott
            To love this gentle Lady, whome ye see,
            Now not a Lady, but a seeming tree;
            With whome as once I rode accompanyde,
            Me chaunced of a knight encountred bee,
            That had a like faire Lady by his syde,
      Lyke a faire Lady, but did fowle *Duessa* hyde.

36   "Whose forged beauty he did take in hand,
            All other Dames to have exceded farre;
            I in defence of mine did likewise stand,
            Mine, that did then shine as the Morning starre:
            So both to batteill fierce arraunged arre,
            In which his harder fortune was to fall

---

[1] Means "Brother Doubt."
[2] *Boreas:* the north wind.
[3] **or:** whether.

[4] I.e., hearts that conceal grief suffer doubly, as he who strives to suppress raging flames often increases them.
[5] **author:** originator.
[6] **errant:** on a quest, wandering.

Under my speare: such is the dye[1] of warre:
  His Lady left as a prise martiall,[2]
Did yield her comely person, to be at my call.

37   "So doubly lov'd of ladies unlike faire,
  Th' one seeming such, the other such indeede,
  One day in doubt I cast for to compare,
  Whether in beauties glorie did exceede;
  A Rosy girlond was the victors meede:[3]
  Both seemde to win, and both seemde won to bee,
  So hard the discord was to be agreede.
  Fralissa was as faire, as faire mote[4] bee,
And ever false *Duessa* seemde as faire as shee.

38   "The wicked witch now seeing all this while
  The doubtfull ballaunce equally to sway,
  What not by right, she cast to win by guile,
  And by her hellish science raisd streight way
  A foggy mist, that overcast the day,
  And a dull blast, that breathing on her[5] face,
  Dimmed her former beauties shining ray,
  And with foule ugly forme did her disgrace:
Then was she fayre alone, when none was faire in place.[6]

39   "Then cride she out, 'fye, fye, deformed wight,
  Whose borrowed beautie now appeareth plaine
  To have before bewitched all mens sight;
  O leave her soone, or let her soone be slaine.'
  Her loathly visage viewing with disdaine,
  Eftsoones I thought her such, as she me told,
  And would have kild her; but with faigned paine,
  The false witch did my wrathfull hand with-hold:
So left her, where she now is turnd to treen mould.[7]

---

[1] **dye:** singular of "dice." Fradubio courteously attributes his victory to chance.

[2] **prise martiall:** spoil or booty left from an armed conflict.

[3] **meede:** reward.

[4] *Fralissa:* "frail," from Italian "fralezza" (ACH); **mote:** might, past tense.

[5] I.e., Fralissa's.

[6] **in place:** in the present place.

[7] **treen mould:** form of a tree.

40   "Thensforth I tooke *Duessa* for my Dame,
            And in the witch unweeting[1] joyd long time,
            Ne ever wist, but that she was the same,
            Till on a day (that day is everie Prime,[2]
            When Witches wont do penance for their crime)
            I chaunst to see her in her proper hew,[3]
            Bathing herselfe in origane and thyme:[4]
            A filthy foule old woman I did vew,
        That ever to have toucht her, I did deadly rew.

41   "Her neather partes misshapen, monstruous,
            Were hidd in water, that I could not see,
            But they did seeme more foule and hideous,
            Then womans shape man would beleeve to bee.
            Thens forth from her most beastly companie
            I gan refraine, in minde to slipp away,
            Soone as appeard safe opportunitie:
            For danger great, if not assurd decay[5]
        I saw before mine eyes, if I were knowne to stray.

42   "The divelish hag by chaunges of my cheare[6]
            Perceiv'd my thoughts, and drownd in sleepie night,
            With wicked herbes and oyntments did besmeare
            My body all, through charmes and magicke might,
            That all my senses were bereaved quight:
            Then brought she me into this desert waste,
            And by my wretched lovers side me pight,[7]
            Where now enclosd in wooden wals full faste,
        Banisht from living wights, our wearie daies we waste."

43   "But how long time," said then the Elfin knight,
            "Are you in this misformed hous to dwell?"
            "We may not chaunge" (quoth he) "this evill plight,

---

[1] **unweeting:** unawares.

[2] **Prime:** probably spring.

[3] **proper hew:** her own natural form.

[4] **origane and thyme:** to heal scabs, with which Duessa is afflicted, as we learn at viii.47.8–9; as recommended in Gerarde, *Herball;* noted Todd, 1805. Thyme is the first herb recommended in Fracastoro, *Syphilis* (2.174–75), as a cure for syphilis (ACH).

[5] **decay:** destruction.

[6] **cheare:** expression and/or mood (OED, "cheer," 2 and 3).

[7] **pight:** planted.

Till we be bathed in a living well;[1]
This is the terme prescribed by the spell."
"O how," sayd he, "mote I that well out find,
That may restore you to your wonted well?"[2]
"Time and suffised[3] fates to former kynd
Shall us restore, none else from hence may us unbynd."[4]

44   The false *Duessa*, now *Fidessa* hight,[5]
Heard how in vaine *Fradubio* did lament,
And knew well all was true. But the good knight
Full of sad feare and ghastly dreriment,[6]
When all this speech the living tree had spent,
The bleeding bough did thrust into the ground,
That from the blood he might be innocent,
And with fresh clay did close the wooden wound:
Then turning to his Lady, dead with feare her fownd.

45   Her seeming dead he fownd with feigned feare,
As all unweeting of that well she knew,[7]
And paynd himselfe with busie care to reare
Her out of carelesse swowne.[8] Her eylids blew
And dimmed sight with pale and deadly hew
At last she up gan lift: with trembling cheare[9]
Her up he tooke, too simple and too trew,
And oft her kist. At length all passed feare,
He set her on her steede, and forward forth did beare.

---

[1] Redcrosse will be bathed in the life-giving Well of Life in xi.29–30, an act that is identified as baptism. This hints that Fradubio and Fralissa are in need of baptism, but the meaning is not entirely clear. The present "living well" may be simply divine grace in general, as in John 4.13–4 and Rev. 22.1.

[2] **wonted well:** usual state of well-being.

[3] **suffised:** satisfied.

[4] The literal meaning of this mythic prophecy is not entirely clear. The fates (read God?) are angry. They will eventually relent; then, and only then, they will restore the pair to former kynd—i.e., to their former species. Allegorically, the prophecy seems to constitute a skewed myth of Adam's fall and redemption, in which females are innocent but have to suffer with their mates. "Fates all satisfied" occurs in Merlin's prophecy at III.iii.44.7.

[5] **hight:** called.

[6] **dreriment:** gloom.

[7] I.e., as if ignorant of what she knew only too well.

[8] **carelesse swowne:** unconscious, or, supposedly unconscious, swoon.

[9] **cheare:** disposition as manifested by external demeanor (OED, "cheer," 3).

Canto Three

Forsaken Truth long seekes her love,
And makes the Lyon mylde,
Marres blind Devotions mart,[1] *and fals*
In hand of leachour vylde.

1   Nought is there under heav'ns wide hollownesse,
         That moves more deare compassion of mind,
         Then beautie brought t'unworthie wretchednesse
         Through envies snares or fortunes freakes unkind:
         I, whether lately through her[2] brightnes blynd,
         Or through alleageance and fast fealty,
         Which I do owe unto all womankynd,
         Feele my hart perst with so great agony,
When such I see, that all for pitty I could dy.

2   And now it is empassioned so deepe,
         For fairest *Unaes* sake, of whom I sing,
         That my frayle eies these lines with teares do steepe,
         To thinke how she through guylefull handeling
         Though true as touch,[3] though daughter of a king,
         Though faire as ever living wight was fayre,
         Though nor in word nor deede ill meriting,
         Is from her knight divorced in despayre
And her dew loves deryv'd[4] to that vile witches shayre.

3   Yet she most faithfull Ladie all this while
         Forsaken, wofull, solitarie mayd
         Far from all peoples preace,[5] as in exile,
         In wildernesse and wastfull deserts strayd,

---

[1] **mart:** traffic, business, projects. "To mar someone's market" was a slang term for frustrating or disgracing them.

[2] I.e., beauty's.

[3] **true as touch:** true as a touchstone: "A very smooth, fine-grained, black or dark-colored variety of quartz or jasper . . . used for testing the quality of gold and silver alloys by the colour of the streak produced by rubbing them upon it" (OED, "touch," 6, and "touchstone").

[4] **deryv'd:** diverted.

[5] **preace:** gathering, congregating.

To seeke her knight; who subtily betrayd
Through that late vision, which th'Enchaunter wrought
Had her abandond. She of nought affrayd,
Through woods and wastnes wide him daily sought;
Yet wished tydinges none of him unto her brought.

4   One day nigh wearie of the yrkesome way,
      From her unhastie beast she did alight,
      And on the grasse her dainty limbs did lay
      In secrete shadow, far from all mens sight:
      From her fayre head her fillet she undight,[1]
      And layd her stole aside. Her angels face
      As the great eye of heaven shyned bright,
      And made a sunshine in the shady place;
Did never mortall eye behold such heavenly grace.

5   It fortuned out of the thickest wood
      A ramping[2] Lyon rushed suddeinly,
      Hunting full greedy after salvage blood;[3]
      Soone as the royall virgin he did spy,
      With gaping mouth at her ran greedily,
      To have attonce devourd her tender corse:
      But to the pray when as he drew more ny,
      His bloody rage aswaged with remorse,
And with the sight amazd, forgat his furious forse.

---

[1] I.e., she took off her headband.

[2] **ramping:** rearing up to attack, as a "lion rampant" does in heraldry. The lion's alliance with Una, whatever its meaning, partakes of folkore and myth. "Common lore maintains that 'the lion will not touch the true prince' (Shakespeare, *1 Henry IV,* 2.4.271–72); that it protects virgins; and . . . aids the faithful. . ." (ACH). The lion is common in medieval romance, e.g., Guy of Warwick in the romance of that name; Percival in Malory's *Le Morte D'Arthur;* the virgin heroine of *Bevis of Hampton* (M&P); and Yvain in Chrétien's romance of that name. Since he is good yet destructive, the meaning of Una's lion is problematic. He breaks the "wicket" of Abessa and Corceca and kills Abessa's "sugar daddy." According to another interpretation, "as primate of the beasts, Una's lion represents the force of nature's law, supporting neglected or despised truth" (M&P). See Richard Hooker's "Sermon on Faith in the Elect" (delivered 1585–1586) in *Works,* 3:481: "Lions, beasts ravenous by nature, . . . have as it were religiously adored the very flesh of the faithful man." For use of the lion in an erotic context, see *Amoretti,* 20.5–8: "the Lyon that is Lord of power . . . disdeigneth to devoure / The silly lambe that to his might doth yield" (ACH).

[3] **salvage blood:** the blood of wild beasts.

6   In stead thereof he kist her wearie feet,
       And lickt her lilly hands with fawning tong,
       As he her wronged innocence did weet.[1]
       O how can beautie maister the most strong,
       And simple truth subdue avenging wrong?
       Whose yielded pryde and proud submission,
       Still dreading death, when she had marked long,
       Her hart gan melt in great compassion,
And drizling teares did shed for pure affection.

7   "The Lyon Lord of everie beast in field"
       Quoth she, "his princely puissance doth abate,
       And mightie proud to humble weake does yield,
       Forgetfull of the hungry rage, which late
       Him prickt, in pittie of my sad estate:[2]
       But he my Lyon, and my noble Lord
       How does he find in cruell hart to hate
       Her that him lov'd, and ever most adord,
As the God of my life? why hath he me abhord?"

8   Redounding teares did choke th'end of her plaint,
       Which softly ecchoed from the neighbour wood;
       And sad to see her sorrowfull constraint
       The kingly beast upon her gazing stood;
       With pittie calmd, downe fell his angry mood.
       At last in close hart shutting up her payne,
       Arose the virgin borne of heavenly brood,[3]
       And to her snowy Palfrey got agayne,
To seeke her strayed Champion, if she might attayne.[4]

9   The Lyon would not leave her desolate,
       But with her went along, as a strong gard
       Of her chast person, and a faythfull mate
       Of her sad troubles and misfortunes hard:
       Still when she slept, he kept both watch and ward,
       And when she wakt, he wayted diligent,

---

[1] **weet:** know.

[2] **estate:** state.

[3] **heavenly brood:** divine ancestry. See also iii.28.9 and x.9.3. Since Una's parents are Adam and Eve, as we learn in vii.44 and II.i.1.5, perhaps Spenser refers to the fact that God, while not precisely begetting them, created them with his own hands, without any mediating element; see Gen. 1.20–7.

[4] **attayne:** attain him; i.e., overtake him.

With humble service to her will prepard:
From her fayre eyes he tooke commandement,
And ever by her lookes conceived her intent.

10   Long she thus traveiled through deserts wyde,
        By which she thought her wandring knight shold pas,
        Yet never shew of living wight espyde;
        Till that at length she found the troden gras,
        In which the tract[1] of peoples footing was,
        Under the steepe foot of a mountaine hore;
        The same she followes, till at last she has
        A damzell spyde slow footing[2] her before,
        That on her shoulders sad[3] a pot of water bore.

11   To whom approching she to her gan call,
        To weet,[4] if dwelling place were nigh at hand;
        But the rude wench her answerd nought at all,
        She could not heare, nor speake, nor understand;[5]
        Till seeing by her side the Lyon stand,
        With suddeine feare her pitcher downe she threw,
        And fled away: for never in that land
        Face of fayre Lady she before did vew,
        And that dredd Lyons looke her cast in deadly hew.[6]

12   Full fast she fled, ne ever lookt behynd,
        As if her life upon the wager lay,
        And home she came, whereas her mother blynd[7]
        Sate in eternall night: nought could she say,

---

[1] **tract:** trace.

[2] **slow footing:** walking slowly.

[3] **sad:** bent down, as if with sadness.

[4] **weet:** learn.

[5] Abessa's inability to hear and understand alludes to the several passages in the gospels in which Christ laments that his hearers do not understand and employs metaphors of ears and hearing, e.g., Mark 4.9–12. That she cannot speak seems an addition to Scripture and perhaps refers to the reputed meekness and passivity of the Catholic rank and file, and of Catholic women generally. With her water pot, Abessa is also analogous to the Samaritan woman at the well (John 4.13) who, though she eventually under-stands Christ, exhibits sexual immorality and spiritual obtuseness. The mountain may suggest Mount Sinai, where Moses received the Law (alluded to in x.53), because Corceca is legalistic in her devotions. See King, 54–6; "Abessa, Corceca, Kirkrapine" in *SE*. Compare Una's selfish indifference to Abessa, Corceca, and Kirkrapine with her concern for the souls of the Satyrs in Canto Six.

[6] I.e., made her turn as pale as a corpse.

[7] Christ frequently calls his opponents blind; see note to 18.4 below. Ignorance was another fault that Protestants saw in the Catholic rank and file; see Ignaro (viii.30–37).

But suddeine catching hold did her dismay
With quaking hands, and other signes of feare:
. Who full of ghastly fright and cold affray,[1]
Gan shut the dore. By this arrived there
Dame *Una,* weary Dame, and entrance did requere.[2]

13   Which when none yielded, her unruly Page
With his rude clawes the wicket[3] open rent,
And let her in; where of his cruell rage
Nigh dead with feare, and faint astonishment,
Shee found them both in darkesome corner pent;
Where that old woman day and night did pray
Upon her beads devoutly penitent;
Nine hundred *Pater nosters* every day,
And thrise nine hundred *Aves* she was wont to say.[4]

14   And to augment her painefull penaunce more,
Thrise every weeke in ashes shee did sitt,
And next her wrinkled skin rough sackecloth wore,
And thrise three times did fast from any bitt:
But now for feare her beads she did forgett.
Whose needelesse dread for to remove away,
Faire *Una* framed words and count'naunce fitt:
Which hardly[5] doen, at length she gan them pray,
That in their cotage small that night she rest her may.[6]

15   The day is spent, and commeth drowsie night,
When every creature shrowded is in sleepe;
Sad *Una* downe her laies in weary plight,

---

[1] **affray:** fear.

[2] **requere:** request.

[3] **wicket:** a small door. I.e., he rent the wicket open. Evidently he did not completely destroy it, because it later presents an obstacle to Kirkrapine.

[4] Spenser describes Corceca in terms of the defects of Catholic laity, ignorant and too legalistically ritualistic and quantitative in their approach to their devotions. She "thrice three times did fast from any bitt" (14.4). That she counts her prayers shows that she thinks they are meritorious and hence that God will be pleased by mere repetition. "Beads" can mean prayers, but here they seem to be physical rosary beads on which prayers were counted. Ashes, sackcloth, and fasting are characteristic of Catholic devotion, though Protestants too believed in fasting—see the Hermit's advice to Redcrosse in x.52—and Spenser apparently even endorsed sackcloth and ashes (x.26). The difference seems to be not in the practices themselves, but in the underlying attitude: Protestants focus on the heart and do not keep score. Corceca, however, seems at least to have been sincerely misled.

[5] **hardly:** with difficulty.

[6] I.e., that she may rest herself in their small cottage that night.

And at her feete the Lyon watch doth keepe:
In stead of rest, she does lament, and weepe
For the late losse of her deare loved knight,
And sighes, and grones, and evermore does steepe
Her tender brest in bitter teares all night,
All night she thinks too long, and often lookes for light.

16   Now when *Aldeboran* was mounted hye
Above the shinie *Cassiopeias* chaire,[1]
And all in deadly sleepe did drowned lye,
One knocked at the dore, and in would fare;[2]
He knocked fast, and often curst, and sware,
That ready entraunce was not at his call:
For on his backe a heavy load he bare
Of nightly stelths and pillage severall,[3]
Which he had got abroad by purchas criminall.[4]

17   He was to weete a stout and sturdy thiefe,
Wont to robbe Churches of their ornaments,
And poore mens boxes of their due reliefe,
Which given was to them for good intents;[5]
The holy Saints of their rich vestiments
He did disrobe, when all men carelesse slept,
And spoild the Priests of their habiliments,[6]
Whiles none the holy things in safety kept;[7]
Then he by conning sleights in at the window crept.[8]

---

[1] Aldeboran is a star in the constellation Taurus. Cassiopeia is a chair-shaped constellation. Aldeboran would be above Cassiopeia in the sky after midnight in late August or in the autumn. This is another instance of the astronomical way of telling time common in older literature.

[2] **fare:** come.

[3] **severall:** of various kinds.

[4] **purchas criminall:** robbery.

[5] Kirkrapine steals the money from the "poor box" or "alms-box" in the church—money that virtuous people had given for relief of the poor. Either a Catholic or a Protestant could have committed this crime.

[6] **habiliments:** attire—here, vestments.

[7] Despoiling religious statues of those beautiful clothes in which pious Catholics customarily arrayed them, and stealing the rich vestments of the clergy from their closets were crimes committed chiefly by opportunistic Protestant iconoclasts against Catholic churches. In confirmation of the sympathy with the statues here implied, Spenser later condemns the Protestant vandalism of Catholic statues in the person of the Blatant Beast (VI.xii.25).

[8] See John 10.1–2: "Verely, verely I say unto you, He that entreth not in by the doore into the sheepfold, but climeth up another way, he is a thiefe and a robber."

18   And all that he by right or wrong could find,
           Unto this house he brought, and did bestow
           Upon the daughter of this woman blind,
           Abessa daughter of *Corceca* slow,[1]
           With whom he whoredome usd, that few did know,
           And fed her fatt with feast of offerings,
           And plenty, which in all the land did grow;
           Ne spared he to give her gold and rings:
       And now he to her brought part of his stolen things.

19   Thus long the dore with rage and threats he bett,[2]
           Yet of those fearfull women none durst rize,
           The Lyon frayed them, him in to lett:[3]
           He would no lenger stay him to advize,[4]
           But open breakes the dore in furious wize,
           And entring is; when that disdainfull beast
           Encountring fierce, him suddein doth surprize,
           And seizing cruell clawes on trembling brest,
       Under his Lordly foot him proudly hath supprest.

20   Him booteth not resist, nor succour call,
           His bleeding hart is in the vengers hand,
           Who streight him rent in thousand peeces small,
           And quite dismembred hath: the thirsty land
           Dronke up his life; his corse left on the strand.[5]
           His fearefull freends weare out the wofull night,
           Ne dare to weepe, nor seeme to understand
           The heavie hap,[6] which on them is alight,
       Affraid, least to themselves the like mishappen might.

[1] Abessa's name could come from the Latin *Ab-esse,* to be absent. It also suggests "Abbess," the female head of a religious house; and her dwelling somewhat resembles a nunnery. Corceca means blind heart, or, as the Argument says, "blind devotion," a skewed echo of St. Paul's criticism of the classical pagans in their degenerate state: "their foolish heart was ful of darkenesse" (Rom. 1.21; see also Eph. 4.17–8). Both women are foolish.

[2] **bett:** past tense of "beat."

[3] I.e., the presence of the Lion made them afraid to get up and let him in.

[4] I.e., he would not wait any longer to advise himself—i.e., to consider what to do.

[5] **strand:** ground.

[6] **heavie hap:** grievous accident. Some have suggested that in his rough treatment of Abessa, Corceca, and Kirkrapine, the lion represents Henry VIII—instigator of the English Reformation, yet also of the dissolution of the monasteries, an act which Spenser criticizes (see *Ruins of Time,* 418; *Var.* 207, on iii.5ff; King, 54–6; and *SE,* "Abessa, Corceca, Kirkrapine").

21   Now when broad day the world discovered has,
        Up *Una* rose, up rose the lyon eke,[1]
      And on their former journey forward pas,
      In waies unknowne, her wandring knight to seeke,
      With paines far passing that long wandring *Greeke,*
      That for his love refused deitye;[2]
      Such were the labours of this Lady meeke,
      Still seeking him, that from her still did flye,
Then furthest from her hope, when most she weened nye.

22   Soone as she parted thence, the fearfull twayne,
        That blind old woman and her daughter dear
      Came forth, and finding *Kirkrapine*[3] there slayne,
      For anguish great they gan to rend their heare,
      And beat their brests, and naked flesh to teare.
      And when they both had wept and wayld their fill,
      Then forth they ran like two amazed deare,
      Halfe mad through malice, and revenging will,
To follow her, that was the causer of their ill.

23   Whome overtaking, they gan loudly bray,
        With hollow houling, and lamenting cry,
      Shamefully at her rayling all the way,
      And her accusing of dishonesty,
      That was the flowre of faith and chastity;
      And still amidst her rayling she[4] did pray,
      That plagues, and mischiefes, and long misery
      Might fall on her, and follow all the way,
And that in endlesse error she might ever stray.

24   But when she saw her prayers nought prevaile,
        Shee backe retourned with some labour lost;
      And in the way, as shee did weepe and waile,
      A knight her mett in mighty armes embost,[5]
      Yet knight was not for all his bragging bost,[6]

---

[1] **eke:** also.

[2] I.e., Odysseus (Ulysses). Calypso promised him immortality, provided he stay with her forever, but he wanted to get home to his wife Penelope (and his family and estate); Homer, *Odyssey,* 5.203–4—one of the few classical references in this book that are favorable.

[3] *Kirkrapine:* church robbery.

[4] I.e., Corceca.

[5] **embost:** encased.

[6] **bost:** boast.

But subtill *Archimag,* that *Una* sought
By traynes[1] into new troubles to have toste:
Of that old woman tidings he besought,
If that of such a Lady shee could tellen ought.

25   Therewith she gan her passion to renew,
    And cry, and curse, and raile, and rend her heare,
    Saying, that harlott she too lately knew,
    That causd her shed so many a bitter teare,
    And so forth told the story of her feare:
    Much seemed he to mone her haplesse[2] chaunce,
    And after for that Lady did inquere;
    Which being taught, he forward gan advaunce
His fair enchaunted steed, and eke his charmed launce.

26   Ere long he came, where *Una* traveild slow,
    And that wilde Champion wayting her besyde:
    Whome seeing such, for dread hee durst not show
    Him selfe too nigh at hand, but turned wyde
    Unto an hil; from whence when she him spyde,
    By his like seeming shield her knight by name
    Shee weend it was,[3] and towards him gan ride:
    Approching nigh she wist,[4] it was the same,
And with faire fearefull humblesse towards him shee came.

27   And weeping said, "Ah my long lacked Lord,
    Where have ye bene thus long out of my sight?
    Much feared I to have bene quite abhord,
    Or ought have done,[5] that ye displeasen might,
    That should as death unto my deare heart light:
    For since mine eie your joyous sight did mis,
    My chearefull day is turnd to chearelesse night,
    And eke my night of death the shadow is;
But welcome now my light, and shining lampe of blis."

---

[1] **traynes:** deceptions.

[2] **haplesse:** unlucky.

[3] "I.e., by his shield, which seemed to be that of Redcrosse, she supposed him to be her own particular knight" (M&P). Archimago quickly assumes the role. Although she symbolizes truth, Una can be deceived, which seems to characterize her as the human institution of the church, rather than truth in the abstract.

[4] **wist:** knew. Supposition ("weend," line 7) strengthens into knowledge (ACH).

[5] **ought have done:** have done anything.

28 He thereto meeting said, "My dearest Dame,
  Far be it from your thought, and fro my wil,
  To thinke that knighthood I so much should shame,
  As you to leave, that have me loved stil,
  And chose in Faery court of meere goodwil,
  Where noblest knights were to be found on earth:
  The earth shall sooner leave her kindly skil
  To bring forth fruit, and make eternall derth,
 Then I leave you, my liefe, yborn of hevenly berth.[1]

29 "And sooth to say, why I lefte you so long,
  Was for to seeke adventure in straunge place,
  Where *Archimago* said a felon strong
  To many knights did daily worke disgrace;
  But knight he now shall never more deface,
  Good cause of mine excuse, that mote ye please[2]
  Well to accept, and ever more embrace
  My faithfull service, that by land and seas
 Have vowd you to defend. Now then your plaint appease."

30 His lovely words her seemd due recompence
  Of all her passed paines: one loving howre
  For many yeares of sorrow can dispence:[3]
  A dram of sweete is worth a pound of sowre:
  Shee has forgott, how many a woeful stowre[4]
  For him she late endurd; she speakes no more
  Of past: true is, that true love hath no powre
  To looken backe; his eies be fixt before.
 Before her stands her knight, for whom she toyld so sore.

31 Much like, as when the beaten marinere,
  That long hath wandred in the *Ocean* wide,
  Ofte soust in swelling *Tethys* saltish teare,[5]
  And long time having tand his tawney hide,

---

[1] **my liefe:** my beloved; **yborn of hevenly berth:** see note on 8.7.

[2] **mote ye please:** may it please you.

[3] Spenser frequently muses about whether love's pleasures outweigh its pains, and he frequently concludes that certainty is unattainable because intense emotion either lengthens or shortens clock time.

[4] **stowre:** time of turmoil and stress.

[5] "I.e., soaked by the ocean's waves; as in I.i.3.9, Tethys, properly the consort of Oceanus, is identified with the ocean" itself (M&P).

With blustring breath of Heaven, that none can bide,
And scorching flames of fierce *Orions* hound,[1]
Soone as the port from far he has espide,
His chearfull whistle merily doth sound,
And *Nereus* crownes with cups; his mates him pledg around.[2]

32   Such joy made *Una,* when her knight she found;
And eke th'enchaunter joyous seemde no lesse,
Then the glad marchant, that does vew from ground
His ship far come from watrie wildernesse,
He hurles out vowes, and *Neptune*[3] oft doth blesse:
So forth they past, and all the way they spent
Discoursing of her dreadful late distresse,
In which he askt her, what the Lyon ment:
Who told her all that fell[4] in journey, as she went.

33   They had not ridden far, when they might see
One pricking towards them with hastie heat,
Full strongly armd, and on a courser free,
That through his fiersnesse fomed all with sweat,
And the sharpe yron[5] did for anger eat,
When his hot ryder spurd his chauffed[6] side;
His looke was sterne, and seemed still to threat
Cruell revenge, which he in hart did hyde,
And on his shield *Sansloy*[7] in bloody lines was dyde.

34   When nigh he drew unto this gentle payre
And saw the Red-crosse, which the knight did beare,
He burnt in fire, and gan eftsoones prepare
Himselfe to batteill with his couched speare.[8]

---

[1] The Dog Star Sirius, so called because it is ascendant in July and August, the dog days, the hottest months and therefore the months when dogs are most likely to go mad.

[2] The captain pours out a libation to Nereus, god of the Aegean sea, and his sub-ordinates drink a toast to him.

[3] God of the sea.

[4] **fell:** befell.

[5] **yron:** the bit.

[6] **chauffed:** hot through irritation, physical and emotional.

[7] *Sansloy:* without law, lawless, esp. in his sexual appetite; see *SE*, "Sansfoy, Sansjoy, and Sansloy." The three Sans brothers are the villains threatening Redcrosse and Una in the middle cantos. Only Sansloy lives on, seemingly invincible; he reappears at II.ii.18.1.

[8] **couched speare:** a spear put horizontally in its rest for attack.

Loth was that other, and did faint through feare,
To taste th'untryed dint of deadly steele;
But yet his Lady did so well him cheare,
That hope of new good hap he gan to feele;
So bent[1] his speare, and spurd his horse with yron heele.

35   But that proud Paynim[2] forward came so ferce,
        And full of wrath, that with his sharphead speare
        Through vainly crossed shield he quite did perce,[3]
        And had his staggering steed not shronke for feare,
        Through shield and body eke he should him beare:
        Yet so great was the puissance of his push,
        That from his sadle quite he did him beare:[4]
        He tombling rudely downe to ground did rush,
And from his gored wound a well of bloud did gush.

36   Dismounting lightly from his loftie steed,
        He to him lept, in minde to reave[5] his life,
        And proudly said, "Lo there the worthie meed
        Of him, that slew *Sansfoy* with bloody knife;
        Henceforth his ghost freed from repining strife,[6]
        In peace may passen over *Lethe* lake,[7]
        When mourning altars purgd with enimies life,
        The black infernall *Furies* doen aslake:[8]
Life from *Sansfoy* thou tookst, *Sansloy* shall from thee take."

[1] **bent:** aimed, as Sansloy had done, by putting it in the rest.

[2] **Paynim:** pagan, but in Spenser a synonym for Sarazin, as his brother Sansfoy is called in ii.12.6ff.

[3] In the final analysis, the cross is not efficacious, perhaps because the wearer is unworthy of it.

[4] I.e., Sansloy would have thrust the spear through his shield and his body as well.

[5] **reave:** to wrest away.

[6] **repining strife:** mournful restlessness, alluding to the classical belief that the ghost of a murdered man cannot cross the Styx, but must wander until his murder is avenged.

[7] *Lethe* **lake:** Spenser seems to be picturing it as a barrier to souls bound for Hades in place of the River Styx. "At v.10.5–6 this same soul is still 'wayling by blacke Stygian lake,' delayed through desire for revenge" (ACH).

[8] I.e., when his murderer Redcrosse is killed, it will cleanse the altars that have been set afire in his memory and will appease the black infernal Furies (who see that murders are avenged)—a classical idea, as in *Oedipus the King* (lines 25–30, 95–107) by Sophocles and the *Eumenides* (passim) by Aeschylus.

37   Therewith in haste his helmet gan unlace,
         Till *Una* cride, "O hold that heavie hand,
         Deare Sir, what ever that thou be in place:[1]
         Enough is, that thy foe doth vanquisht stand
         Now at thy mercy: Mercy not withstand:[2]
         For he is one the truest knight alive,
         Though conquered now he lye on lowly land,
         And whilest him fortune favourd, fayre did thrive
    In bloudy field: therefore of life him not deprive."

38   Her piteous wordes might not abate his rage,
         But rudely rending up his helmet, would
         Have slayne him streight: but when he sees his age,
         And hoarie head of *Archimago* old,
         His hasty hand he doth amased hold,
         And halfe ashamed, wondred at the sight:
         For the old man well knew he, though untold,[3]
         In charmes and magick to have wondrous might,
    Ne ever wont in field, ne in round lists to fight.[4]

39   And said, "Why *Archimago,* lucklesse syre,
         What doe I see? what hard mishap is this,
         That hath thee hether brought to taste mine yre?
         Or thine the fault, or mine the error is,
         In stead of foe to wound my friend amis?"
         He answered nought, but in a traunce still lay,
         And on those guilefull dazed eyes of his
         The cloude of death did sit. Which doen away,[5]
    He left him lying so, ne would no lenger stay.

40   But to the virgin comes, who all this while
         Amased stands, her selfe so mockt[6] to see
         By him, who has the guerdon[7] of his guile,

---

[1] I.e., whoever you are.

[2] I.e., do not refuse mercy.

[3] I.e., without having to be told, demonstrating "the instinctive kinship among evil characters" (ACH); but it was not instinctive enough; see below.

[4] I.e., he was not used to jousting, either in open country or within a tournament's enclosure. This scene is comic—two villains working against each other. Evil's self-defeating character amuses Spenser.

[5] **which doen away:** when it went away and he showed signs of life.

[6] **mockt:** exposed as naïve.

[7] **guerdon:** reward; in this case, the just punishment.

For so misfeigning[1] her true knight to bee:
Yet is she now in more perplexitie,
Left in the hand of that same Paynim[2] bold,
From whom her booteth not at all to flie;[3]
Who by her cleanly garment catching hold,
Her from her Palfrey pluckt, her visage to behold.

41   But her fiers servant full of kingly aw
And high disdaine, whenas his soveraine Dame
So rudely handled by her foe he saw,
With gaping jawes full greedy at him came,
And ramping on his shield, did weene the same
Have reft[4] away with his sharp rending clawes:
But he was stout, and lust did now inflame
His corage more, that from his griping pawes
He hath his shield redeemd,[5] and forth his swerd he drawes.

42   O then too weake and feeble was the forse
Of salvage[6] beast, his puissance to withstand:
For he was strong, and of so mightie corse,[7]
As ever wielded speare in warlike hand,
And feates of armes did wisely understand.
Eftsoones he perced through his chaufed[8] chest
With thrilling point of deadly yron brand,[9]
And launcht[10] his Lordly hart: with death opprest
He ror'd aloud, whiles life forsooke his stubborne brest.

43   Who now is left to keepe the forlorne maid
From raging spoile of lawlesse victors will?
Her faithfull gard remov'd, her hope dismaid,
Her selfe a yielded pray to save or spill.[11]
He now Lord of the field, his pride to fill,
With foule reproches, and disdaineful spight

---

[1] **misfeigning:** falsely pretending.

[2] **Paynim:** pagan, Saracen.

[3] I.e., to flee from him does not do her any good.

[4] **reft:** snatched.

[5] **redeemd:** regained by effort.

[6] **salvage:** wild.

[7] **corse:** body.

[8] **chaufed:** heated with anger.

[9] I.e., with searching point of deadly iron sword.

[10] **launcht:** pierced.

[11] **spill:** destroy.

Her vildly entertaines,[1] and will or nill,
Beares her away upon his courser light:
Her prayers nought prevaile, his rage is more of might.

44   And all the way, with great lamenting paine,
        And piteous plaintes she filleth his dull eares,
        That stony hart could riven[2] have in twaine,
        And all the way she wetts with flowing teares:
        But he enrag'd with rancor, nothing heares.
        Her servile beast[3] yet would not leave her so,
        But followes her far off, ne ought he feares,
        To be partaker of her wandring woe,
More mild in beastly kind,[4] then that her beastly foe.

---

[1] **vildly entertaines:** treats vilely, badly.

[2] **riven:** split.

[3] **servile beast:** the ass on which she normally rides.

[4] **kind:** in the old sense of nature or species.

Canto Four

To sinfull hous of Pryde, Duessa
guydes the faithfull knight,
Where brothers death to wreak[1] Sansjoy
doth chaleng him to fight.

1   Young knight, what ever that dost armes professe,
     And through long labours huntest after fame,
     Beware of fraud, beware of ficklenesse,
     In choice, and chaunge of thy deare loved Dame,
     Least thou of her believe too lightly[2] blame,
     And rash misweening[3] doe thy hart remove:
     For unto knight there is no greater shame,
     Then lightnesse and inconstancie in love;
That doth this *Redcrosse* knights ensample plainly prove.

2   Who after that he had faire *Una* lorne,[4]
     Through light misdeeming of her loialtie,
     And false *Duessa* in her sted had borne,[5]
     Called *Fidess,* and so supposd to be;
     Long with her traveild, till at last they see
     A goodly building, bravely garnished,[6]
     The house of mightie Prince it seemd to be:
     And towards it a broad high way that led,
All bare through peoples feet, which thether traveiled.[7]

3   Great troupes of people traveild thetherward
     Both day and night, of each degree and place,[8]
     But few returned, having scaped hard,

---

[1] **wreak:** avenge; i.e., to avenge his brother's death.

[2] **too lightly:** too hastily, so also "light misdeeming" in next stanza.

[3] **misweening:** mistaken mistrust.

[4] **lorne:** abandoned.

[5] **borne:** carried off. Not literally, since Duessa has her own horse.

[6] **bravely garnished:** nicely decorated.

[7] See Matt. 7.13: "Enter ye in at the strait gate, for it is the wide gate, and broad way that leadeth to destruction, and many there be which go in thereat."

[8] **degree and place:** social level.

With balefull[1] beggery, or foule disgrace,
Which ever after in most wretched case,
Like loathsome lazars,[2] by the hedges lay.
Thether *Duessa* badd him bend his pace:
For she is wearie of the toilsom way,
And also nigh consumed is the lingring day.

4   A stately Pallace built of squared bricke,[3]
        Which cunningly was without morter laid,
        Whose wals were high, but nothing strong, nor thick
        And golden foile all over them displaid,
        That purest skye with brightnesse they dismaid:
        High lifted up were many loftie towres,
        And goodly galleries far over laid,
        Full of faire windowes, and delightful bowres;
And on the top a Diall told the timely howres.[4]

5   It was a goodly heape[5] for to behould,
        And spake the praises of the workmans witt;
        But full great pittie, that so faire a mould[6]
        Did on so weake foundation ever sitt:
        For on a sandie hill, that still did flitt,
        And fall away, it mounted was full hie,
        That every breath of heaven shaked itt:[7]
        And all the hinder partes, that few could spie,
Were ruinous and old, but painted cunningly.

---

[1] **balefull:** wretched.

[2] **lazars:** lepers.

[3] See the House of Fortune in Guillaume de Lorris and Jean de Meun, *Romance of the Rose,* 127–8. It has an unstable site, beautiful golden parts in front and ugly decaying parts in back, and an unstable mistress, the Goddess Fortune, who is said to have ruined many characters in history.

[4] I.e., it identified each hour as it occurred. The dial is possibly a metonymy for a clock; but a literal sundial sometimes accompanied or replaced a clock on towers. "The clock indicates Time's power over the edifice and its inhabitants, i.e., over the fallen world. An evil parody of Gloriana's Cleopolis and God's New Jerusalem, Lucifera's court opposes the House of Holiness (I.x)" (M&P).

[5] **heape:** building; not in OED, but see the synonymous "pile," sense 4.

[6] **mould:** structure.

[7] See Matt. 7.26–7: "every one that heareth these sayings of mine, and doeth them not, shall be likened unto a foolish man, which built his house upon the sand: And the rain descended, and the floods came, and the winds blew, and beat upon that house: and it fell: and great was the fall of it."

6   Arrived there they passed in forth right;
       For still to all the gates stood open wide,
       Yet charge of them was to a Porter hight[1]
       Cald *Malvenù*,[2] who entrance none denide:
       Thence to the hall, which was on every side
       With rich array and costly arras dight:[3]
       Infinite sortes of people did abide
       There waiting long, to win the wished sight
    Of her, that was the Lady of that Pallace bright.

7   By them they passe, all gazing on them round,
       And to the Presence[4] mount; whose glorious vew
       Their frayle amazed senses did confound:
       In living Princes court none ever knew
       Such endlesse richesse, and so sumpteous shew;
       Ne *Persia* selfe, the nourse of pompous pride
       Like ever saw. And there a noble crew
       Of Lords and Ladies stood on every side,
    Which with their presence fayre, the place much beautifide.

8   High above all a cloth of State[5] was spred,
       And a rich throne, as bright as sunny day,
       On which there sate most brave embellished
       With royall robes and gorgeous array,
       A mayden Queene, that shone as *Titans*[6] ray,
       In glistring gold, and perelesse pretious stone;
       Yet her bright blazing beautie did assay[7]
       To dim the brightnesse of her glorious throne,
    As envying her selfe, that too exceeding shone.

9   Exceeding shone, like *Phoebus* fayrest childe,[8]
       That did presume his fathers fyrie wayne,
       And flaming mouthes of steedes unwonted wilde

---

[1] **hight:** designated.

[2] Cf. *Bienvenu,* the French word for "welcome." *Malvenù* represents a parody of it.

[3] **arras:** tapestry hangings on walls to stop drafts; **dight:** decked.

[4] **the Presence:** an exaggeratedly reverent term for Lucifera on her throne.

[5] **cloth of State:** canopy.

[6] *Titans:* the sun's.

[7] **assay:** seemed to try.

[8] *Phoebus* **fayrest childe:** Phaeton, or Phaethon, who took the "wayne" or chariot of the sun belonging to his father Apollo for an unauthorized spin. When its unmanageable course threatened to set the world on fire, Jupiter killed him with lightning *(Metamorphoses,* 2.1–328).

Through highest heaven with weaker hand to rayne;
Proud of such glory and advancement vayne,
While flashing beames do daze his feeble eyen,
He leaves the welkin way[1] most beaten playne,
And rapt[2] with whirling wheeles, inflames the skyen,
With fire not made to burne, but fayrely for to shyne.

10   So proud she shyned in her princely state,
Looking to heaven; for earth she did disdayne,
And sitting high; for lowly[3] she did hate:
Lo under neath her scornefull feete, was layne
A dreadfull Dragon with an hideous trayne,[4]
And in her hand she held a mirrhour bright,
Wherein her face she often vewed fayne.[5]
And in her selfe-lov'd semblance tooke delight;
For she was wondrous faire, as any living wight.

11   Of griesly *Pluto* she the daughter was,
And sad *Proserpina* the Queene of hell;
Yet did she thinke her pearelesse worth to pas
That parentage, with pride so did she swell,
And thundring *Jove,* that high in heaven doth dwell,
And wield[6] the world, she claymed for her syre,
Or if that any else did *Jove* excell:
For to the highest she did still aspyre,
Or if ought higher were then that, did it desyre.

12   And proud *Lucifera*[7] men did her call,
That made her selfe a Queene, and crownd to be,
Yet rightfull kingdome she had none at all,
Ne heritage of native soveraintie,

---

[1] **welkin way:** an imaginary path that the sun follows in the sky.

[2] **rapt:** carried away.

[3] **lowly:** lowliness.

[4] **trayne:** here, tail.

[5] **fayne:** happily.

[6] **wield:** control.

[7] Lucifera's name and parentage link her with Satan, who is her chauffeur (see stanza 36 below). Yet the manifestations of her pride here seem not to be against God, like Lucifer's (Isa. 14.12–4), but against other people. She therefore seems to be pride in general, which could encompass both these different kinds of pride and could appropriately participate in the parade of the Seven Deadly Sins, beginning Stanza 18. "She is presumably the opposite of that other 'may-den Queene,' Elizabeth, but some suspect that Spenser's satire does not quite exempt his monarch and her court" (M&P).

But did usurpe with wrong and tyrannie
Upon the scepter, which she now did hold:
Ne ruld her Realme with lawes, but pollicie,[1]
And strong advizement of six wisards old,
That with their counsels bad her kingdome did uphold.

13   Soone as the Elfin knight in presence came,
And false *Duessa* seeming Lady fayre,
A gentle Husher,[2] *Vanitie* by name
Made rowme, and passage for them did prepaire:
So goodly brought them to the lowest stayre
Of her high throne, where they on humble knee
Making obeysaunce, did the cause declare,
Why they were come, her roiall state to see,
To prove the wide report of her great Majestee.

14   With loftie eyes, halfe loth to looke so lowe,
She thancked them in her disdainefull wise,
Ne other grace vouchsafed them to showe
Of Princesse worthy, scarse them bad arise.
Her Lordes and Ladies all this while devise
Themselves to setten forth to straungers sight:
Some frounce their curled heare in courtly guise,[3]
Some prancke their ruffes, and others trimly dight[4]
Their gay attyre: each others greater pride does spight.[5]

15   Goodly they all that knight doe entertayne,
Right glad with him to have increast their crew;
But to *Duess'* each one himselfe did payne
All kindnesse and faire courtesie to shew;
For in that court whylome[6] her well they knew:
Yet the stout Faery mongst the middest crowd[7]
Thought all their glorie vaine in knightly vew,
And that great Princesse too exceeding prowd,
That to strange knight no better countenance allowd.

---

[1] **pollicie:** politics, political cunning.

[2] **Husher:** usher.

[3] **frounce:** frizz; **guise:** manner, behavior.

[4] **prancke their ruffes:** arrange in folds the stiff, disk-shaped collars worn by Elizabethan ladies and gentlemen on state occasions; **dight:** arrange.

[5] I.e., each considers the other too proud and criticizes him or her for it.

[6] **whylome:** formerly.

[7] **the middest crowd:** the very middle of the crowd.

16   Suddein upriseth from her stately place
          The roiall Dame, and for her coche doth call;
          All hurtlen[1] forth, and she with princely pace,
          As faire *Aurora* in her purple pall,
          Out of the East the dawning day doth call:
          So forth she comes: her brightnes brode doth blaze;
          The heapes of people thronging in the hall,
          Doe ride each other,[2] upon her to gaze:
      Her glorious glitterand[3] light doth all mens eies amaze.

17   So forth she comes, and to her coche does clyme,
          Adorned all with gold, and girlonds[4] gay,
          That seemd as fresh as *Flora* in her prime,
          And strove to match, in roiall rich array,
          Great *Junoes* golden chayre,[5] the which they say
          The Gods stand gazing on, when she does ride
          To *Joves* high hous through heavens bras-paved way[6]
          Drawne of fayre Pecocks, that excell in pride,
      And full of *Argus* eyes their tayles dispredden wide.[7]

18   But this was drawne of six unequall[8] beasts,
          On which her six sage Counsellours did ryde,
          Taught to obay their bestiall beheasts,

---

[1] **hurtlen:** rush in response to Lucifera's whim.

[2] **ride each other:** they literally climb on each other's backs in order to get their heads high enough to see her, illustrating how ambition objectifies and uses other people.

[3] **glitterand:** glittering. The "-nd" ending is an allowable, if somewhat medieval, variant. In this poem it is used only once more, to describe Arthur's armor at vii.29.4. The hard *d* is less mellifluous than "-ng" and conjures up a radiance that is more glaring.

[4] **girlonds:** garlands.

[5] **chayre:** chariot.

[6] **heavens bras-paved way:** the Milky Way, which, according to Ovid, is the road on which the gods travel in their chariots to the house of Jove (*Metamorphoses*, 1.168–71). Ovid says it is shining white, which would

more aptly be described as silver or pearl than brass.

[7] Homer (*Iliad,* 5.720ff.) describes Juno's chariot in this way, but Spenser also allegorizes the peacocks within another tradition as symbolizing pride. "Ovid (*Metamorphoses,* 1.590–726) tells how Juno set the hundred eyes of Argus, killed by Mercury at Jove's command, in her peacock's tail" (M&P)—an etiological myth. The smoothly lengthening Alexandrine mimes the gradual widening of the tails.

[8] **unequall:** highly diverse in species and hence not an effective team. I.e., six of the deadly sins or capital vices (sinful tendencies), with Lucifera or pride representing the seventh, the originary sin. All six counselors and their emblematic mounts are hitched to Lucifera's wagon or coach, which is driven by Satan. For primary sources and critics, see *SE,* "sins, deadly";

With like conditions to their kindes[1] applyde:
Of which the first, that all the rest did guyde,
Was sluggish *Idlenesse* the nourse of sin;
Upon a slouthfull Asse he chose to ryde,
Arayd in habit blacke, and amis[2] thin,
Like to an holy Monck, the service to begin.

19   And in his hand his Portesse[3] still he bare,
That much was worne, but therein little redd,
For of devotion he had little care,
Still drownd in sleepe, and most of his dais dedd;
Scarse could he once uphold his heavie hedd,
To looken, whether it were night or day:
May seeme the wayne[4] was very evill ledd,
When such an one had guiding of the way,
That knew not, whether right he went, or else astray.[5]

20   From worldly cares himselfe he did esloyne,[6]
And greatly shunned manly exercise,
From everie worke he chalenged essoyne,[7]
For contemplation sake: yet otherwise,
His life he led in lawlesse riotise;
By which he grew to grievous malady;
For in his lustlesse limbs through evill guise[8]
A shaking fever raignd continually:
Such one was *Idlenesse,* first of this company.

21   And by his side rode loathsome *Gluttony,*
Deformed creature, on a filthie swyne,
His belly was upblowne with luxury;
And eke with fatnesse swollen were his eyne,

---

for these and also individual symbols, see ACH notes on 18–35, both general and local; also Cullen, 14–5, 40–1. The attributes of the vices, with the exception of Sloth, are mostly traditional and difficult to trace to any one source.

[1] **kindes:** species; i.e., the counselors resembled their respective mounts.

[2] **amis:** priestly vestment or monk's hood.

[3] **Portesse:** breviary or prayer book.

[4] **wayne:** wain, wagon, chariot.

[5] Sloth has some nontraditional attributes here that associate him with monks. This constitutes anti–Catholic satire and seems to come from Stephen Bateman's *Cristall Glasse of Reformation* (1590), a Protestant work; see illustration of Sloth from it in *SE*.

[6] **esloyne:** withdrew himself from legal jurisdiction.

[7] **chalenged essoyne:** claimed exemption. Like "esloyne" above, it is a legal term.

[8] **evill guise:** debauched behavior.

And like a Crane his necke was long and fyne,[1]
With which he swallowd up excessive feast,
For want whereof poore people oft did pyne,[2]
And all the way, most like a brutish beast,
He spued up his gorge, that all did him deteast.

22   In greene vine leaves he was right fitly clad;
        For other clothes he could not weare for heat,
        And on his head an yvie girland had,
        From under which fast trickled downe the sweat:
        Still as he rode, he somewhat[3] still did eat,
        And in his hand did beare a bouzing can,
        Of which he supt so oft, that on his seat
        His dronken corse[4] he scarse upholden can,
    In shape and life more like a monster, then a man.

23   Unfit he was for any worldly thing,
        And eke unhable once to stirre or go,
        Not meet to be of counsell to a king,
        Whose mind in meat and drinke was drowned so,
        That from his frend he seeldome knew his fo:
        Full of diseases was his carcas blew,[5]
        And a dry dropsie[6] through his flesh did flow,
        Which by misdiet daily greater grew:
    Such one was *Gluttony*, the second of that crew.

24   And next to him rode lustfull *Lechery*,
        Upon a bearded Gote, whose rugged heare,
        And whally[7] eies (the signe of gelosy,)
        Was like the person selfe, whom he did beare:
        Who rough, and blacke, and filthy did appeare,
        Unseemely man to please faire Ladies eye;
        Yet he of Ladies oft was loved deare,
        When fairer faces were bid standen by:
    O who does know the bent of womens fantasy?

---

[1] **fyne:** thin. There is a traditional story that a glutton wished his neck were as long as a crane's so that he could savor his food longer.

[2] **pyne:** starve.

[3] **somewhat:** something.

[4] **corse:** body.

[5] **blew:** livid.

[6] **dry dropsie:** a disease that causes excessive thirst.

[7] **whally:** showing much white, glaring.

25   In a greene gowne he clothed was full faire,
        Which underneath did hide his filthinesse,
        And in his hand a burning hart he bare,
        Full of vaine follies, and new fanglenesse;[1]
        For he was false, and fraught with ficklenesse,
        And learned had to love with secret lookes,
        And well could daunce, and sing with ruefulnesse,
        And fortunes tell, and read in loving bookes,[2]
    And thousand other waies, to bait his fleshly hookes.

26   Inconstant man, that loved all he saw,
        And lusted after all, that he did love,
        Ne would his looser life be tide to law,
        But joyd weake wemens hearts to tempt, and prove
        If from their loyall loves he might them move;
        Which lewdnes fild him with reprochfull pain
        Of that foule evill,[3] which all men reprove,
        That rotts the marrow, and consumes the braine:
    Such one was *Lechery*, the third of all this traine.

27   And greedy *Avarice* by him did ride,
        Uppon a Camell[4] loaden all with gold;
        Two iron coffers hong on either side,
        With precious metall full, as they might hold,
        And in his lap an heap of coine he told;[5]
        For of his wicked pelfe[6] his God he made,
        And unto hell him selfe for money sold;
        Accursed usury was all his trade,
    And right and wrong ylike in equall ballaunce waide.[7]

28   His life was nigh unto deaths dore yplaste,
        And thred-bare cote, and cobled shoes hee ware,
        Ne scarse good morsell all his life did taste,
        But both from backe and belly still did spare,

---

[1] **new fanglenesse:** here, sexual infidelity.

[2] **loving bookes:** handbooks on the art of love.

[3] **foule evill:** venereal disease.

[4] Spenser gives him this mount in order to call to mind Christ's statement that "it is easier for a camell to go through the eye of a needle than for a rich man to enter into the kingdome of God." See Matt. 19.24; Mark 10.25; Luke 18.25.

[5] **told:** counted.

[6] **pelfe:** a contemptuous term for wealth.

[7] I.e., he didn't care whether he did right or wrong, so long as it made money.

To fill his bags, and richesse to compare;[1]
Yet childe ne kinsman living had he none
To leave them to; but thorough daily care
To get, and nightly feare to lose his owne,
He led a wretched life unto him selfe unknowne.[2]

29   Most wretched wight, whom nothing might suffise,
          Whose greedy lust did lacke in greatest store,
          Whose need had end, but no end covetise,
          Whose welth was want, whose plenty made him pore,
          Who had enough, yett wished ever more,
          A vile disease, and eke in foote and hand
          A grievous gout tormented him full sore,
          That well he could not touch, nor goe, nor stand:
     Such one was *Avarice*, the forth of this faire band.

30   And next to him malicious *Envy* rode,
          Upon a ravenous wolfe, and still did chaw
          Betweene his cankred[3] teeth a venemous tode,
          That all the poison ran about his chaw;[4]
          But inwardly he chawed his owne maw[5]
          At neibors welth, that made him ever sad;
          For death it was, when any good he saw,
          And wept, that cause of weeping none he had,
     But when he heard of harme, he wexed[6] wondrous glad.

31   All in a kirtle of discolourd say[7]
          He clothed was, ypaynted full of eies;
          And in his bosome secretly there lay
          An hatefull Snake, the which his taile uptyes
          In many folds, and mortall sting implyes.[8]
          Still as he rode, he gnasht his teeth, to see
          Those heapes of gold with griple[9] Covetyse,
          And grudged at the great felicitee
     Of proud *Lucifera*, and his owne companee.

---

[1] **compare:** to obtain, from Latin *comparare*.

[2] **unto him selfe unknowne:** he lacks the self-knowledge to perceive what a wretched life his avarice has created.

[3] **cankred:** infected.

[4] **chaw:** jaw.

[5] **maw:** stomach.

[6] **wexed:** became—past tense of the verb "wax."

[7] **a kirtle of discolourd say:** a multi-colored outer garment of a close-woven material like serge.

[8] **implyes:** enfolds, from Latin *implicare*.

[9] **griple:** greedy, tenacious.

32 He hated all good workes and vertuous deeds,
  And him no lesse, that any like did use,[1]
  And who with gratious bread the hungry feeds,
  His almes for want of faith he doth accuse;
  So every good to bad he doth abuse:[2]
  And eke the verse of famous Poets witt
  He does backebite, and spightfull poison spues
  From leprous mouth on all, that ever writt:
Such one vile *Envy* was, that fifte in row did sitt.

33 And him beside rides fierce revenging *Wrath,*
  Upon a Lion, loth for to be led;
  And in his hand a burning brond[3] he hath,
  The which he brandisheth about his hed;
  His eies did hurle forth sparcles fiery red,
  And stared sterne on all, that him beheld,
  As ashes pale of hew and seeming ded;
  And on his dagger still his hand he held,
Trembling through hasty rage, when choler[4] in him sweld.

34 His ruffin raiment all was staind with blood,
  Which he had spilt, and all to rags yrent,[5]
  Through unadvized rashnes woxen wood;[6]
  For of his hands he had no governement,
  Ne car'd for blood in his avengement:
  But when the furious fitt was overpast,
  His cruell facts[7] he often would repent;
  Yet wilfull man he never would forecast,
How many mischieves should ensue his heedlesse hast.

35 Full many mischiefes follow cruell *Wrath;*
  Abhorred bloodshed, and tumultuous strife,
  Unmanly murder, and unthrifty scath,[8]
  Bitter despight, with rancours rusty knife,

---

[1] **that any like did use:** anyone that did perform them.

[2] **abuse:** make it appear bad. The personification of envy recurs frequently in the poem, perhaps because this vice, by making people reluctant to acknowledge achievement, subverts the entire honor system.

[3] **brond:** sometimes sword, but here probably brand.

[4] **choler:** the inward disposition, or "humor," that expresses itself in wrath.

[5] **yrent:** torn.

[6] **wood:** crazy.

[7] **facts:** deeds.

[8] **unmanly:** inhuman; **unthrifty scath:** self-destructive harm.

And fretting griefe the enemy of life;
All these, and many evils moe haunt ire,
The swelling Splene,[1] and Frenzy raging rife,
The shaking Palsey, and Saint *Fraunces* fire:[2]
Such one was *Wrath,* the last of this ungodly tire.[3]

36   And after all upon the wagon beame[4]
       Rode *Sathan,* with a smarting whip in hand,
       With which he forward lasht the laesy[5] teme,
       So oft as *Slowth* still in the mire did stand.
       Huge routs[6] of people did about them band,
       Showting for joy, and still before their way
       A foggy mist had covered all the land;
       And underneath their feet, all scattered lay
Dead sculls and bones of men, whose life had gone astray.

37   So forth they marchen in this goodly sort,
       To take the solace of the open aire,
       And in fresh flowring fields themselves to sport;
       Emongst the rest rode that false Lady faire,
       The foule *Duessa,* next unto the chaire
       Of proud *Lucifer',* as one of the traine:
       But that good knight would not so nigh repaire,[7]
       Him selfe estraunging from their joyaunce vaine,
Whose fellowship seemd far unfitt for warlike swaine.

38   So having solaced themselves a space,
       With pleasaunce of the breathing[8] fields yfed,
       They backe retourned to the princely Place;
       Whereas an errant[9] knight in armes ycled,

---

[1] **Splene:** in Renaissance physiology, the organ responsible for wrath.

[2] **Saint *Fraunces* fire:** an unknown disease; Spenser presumably meant St. Anthony's fire (ACH). It is called *erysipelas,* which Thomas Cooper defines as, "An inflammation or sore with redness rounde about, which procedeth of choler and causeth a fever in the bodie."

[3] **tire:** not in OED, but presumably means "procession."

[4] **beame:** the beam or tongue of Lucifera's coach or wagon, to which the six counselors and their mounts are hitched. Since we have already been treated to a portrait of Lucifera, or pride, none is given here.

[5] **laesy:** lazy.

[6] **routs:** crowds.

[7] **repaire:** betake himself; as yet, Redcrosse still disapproves and holds himself aloof.

[8] **breathing:** exhaling fragrance.

[9] **errant:** on a quest, wandering.

And heathnish shield, wherein with letters red
Was writt *Sansjoy,* they new arrived find:
Enflam'd with fury and fiers hardy hed,[1]
He seemd in hart to harbour thoughts unkind,
And nourish bloody vengeaunce in his bitter mind.

39   Who when the shamed shield of slaine *Sansfoy*
He spide with that same Fary champions page,
Bewraying[2] him, that did of late destroy
His eldest brother, burning all with rage
He to him lept, and that same envious gage[3]
Of victors glory from him snacht away:
But th'Elfin knight, which ought that warlike wage,[4]
Disdaind to loose the meed he wonne in fray,
And him rencountring fierce, reskewd the noble pray.

40   Therewith they gan to hurtlen[5] greedily,
Redoubted battaile ready to darrayne,[6]
And clash their shields, and shake their swerds on hy,
That with their sturre they troubled all the traine;
Till that great Queene upon eternall paine
Of high displeasure, that ensewen might,
Commaunded them their fury to refraine,
And if that either to that shield had right,
In equall lists[7] they should the morrow next it fight.

41   "Ah dearest Dame," quoth then the Paynim bold,
"Pardon the error of enraged wight,
Whome great griefe made forgett the raines to hold
Of reasons rule, to see this recreaunt knight,
No knight, but treachour full of false despight
And shameful treason, who through guile hath slayn

---

[1] **hardy hed:** boldness.

[2] **bewraying:** unconsciously revealing.

[3] **envious gage:** envied pledge.

[4] **ought that warlike wage:** owned that spoil of war.

[5] **to hurtlen:** here, to rush together; see "All hurtlen" in iv.16.3; "-en" is the sign of both the infinitive and the present plural in Middle English.

[6] **darrayne:** "engage in order to vindicate a claim (a legal term)" (ACH).

[7] **in equall lists:** in impartial formal combat.

      The prowest[1] knight, that ever field did fight,
      Even stout *Sansfoy* (O who can then refrayn?)
   Whose shield he beares renverst,[2] the more to heap disdayn.

42   "And to augment the glorie of his guile,
      His dearest love the faire *Fidessa* loe
      Is there possessed of the traytour vile,
      Who reapes the harvest sowen by his foe,
      Sowen in bloodie field, and bought with woe:
      That brothers hand shall dearely well requight
      So be,[3] O Queene, you equall favour showe."
      Him litle answerd th'angry Elfin knight;
   He never meant with words, but swords to plead his right.

43   But threw his gauntlet as a sacred pledg,
      His cause in combat the next day to try:
      So been they parted both, with harts on edg,
      To be aveng'd each on his enimy.
      That night they pas in joy and jollity,
      Feasting and courting both in bowre and hall;
      For Steward was excessive *Gluttony,*
      That of his plenty poured forth to all;
   Which doen, the Chamberlain *Slowth* did to rest them call.

44   Now whenas darkesome night had all displayd
      Her coleblacke curtein over brightest skye,
      The warlike youthes on dayntie couches layd,
      Did chace away sweet sleepe from sluggish eye,
      To muse on meanes of hoped victory.
      But whenas *Morpheus* had with leaden mace,
      Arrested all that courtly company,
      Uprose *Duessa* from her resting place,
   And to the Paynims lodging comes with silent pace.

45   Whom broad awake she findes, in troublous fitt,[4]
      Forecasting, how his foe he might annoy,
      And him amoves with speaches seeming fitt:

---

[1] **prowest:** the knight with the most prowess or fighting ability.

[2] **renverst:** upside down or inside out in token of defeat.

[3] **So be:** if.

[4] **fitt:** mood.

"Ah deare *Sansjoy,* next dearest to *Sansfoy,*
Cause of my new griefe, cause of my new joy,
Joyous, to see his ymage in mine eye,
And greevd, to thinke how foe did him destroy,
That was the flowre of grace and chevalrye;
Lo his *Fidessa* to thy secret faith I flye."

46   With gentle wordes he can[1] her fayrely greet,
      And bad say on the secrete of her hart.
      Then sighing soft, "I learne that litle sweet
      Oft tempted is," (quoth she) "with muchell smart:
      For since my brest was launcht[2] with lovely dart
      Of deare *Sansfoy,* I never joyed howre,
      But in eternall woes my weaker[3] hart
      Have wasted, loving him with all my powre,
And for his sake have felt full many an heavie stowre.

47   "At last when perils all I weened past,
      And hop'd to reape the crop of all my care,
      Into new woes unweeting I was cast,
      By this false faytor, who unworthie ware[4]
      His worthie shield, whom he with guilefull snare
      Entrapped slew, and brought to shamefull grave.
      Me silly[5] maid away with him he bare,
      And ever since hath kept in darksom cave,
For that I would not yeeld, that to *Sansfoy* I gave.[6]

48   "But since faire Sunne hath sperst[7] that lowring clowd,
      And to my loathed life now shewes some light,
      Under your beames I will me safely shrowd,
      From dreaded storme of his disdainfull spight:
      To you th'inheritance belonges by right
      Of brothers prayse, to you eke longes[8] his love.

---

[1] **can:** did.

[2] **launcht:** pierced.

[3] **weaker:** too weak.

[4] **faytor:** imposter; **ware:** wore.

[5] **silly:** innocent.

[6] I.e., because I would not yield to Red-crosse that which I gave to Sansfoy. This proves Duessa was lying when she told Redcrosse that she never yielded her "fort" to Sansfoy (ii.25).

[7] **sperst:** dispersed.

[8] **longes:** belongs.

Let not his love, let not his restlesse spright,
  Be unreveng'd, that calles to you above
From wandring *Stygian*[1] shores, where it doth endlesse move."

49   Thereto said he, "faire Dame be nought dismaid
         For sorrowes past; their griefe is with them gone:
         Ne yet of present perill be affraid:
         For needlesse feare did never vantage none,[2]
         And helplesse hap it booteth not to mone.
         Dead is *Sansfoy,* his vitall paines[3] are past,
         Though greeved ghost for vengeance deep do grone
         He lives, that shall him pay his dewties last,[4]
And guiltie Elfin blood shall sacrifice in hast."

50   "O But I feare the fickle freakes"[5] (quoth shee)
         "Of fortune false, and oddes of armes in field."
         "Why dame" (quoth he) "what oddes can ever bee,
         Where both doe fight alike, to win or yield?"
         "Yea but" (quoth she) "he beares a charmed shield,
         And eke enchaunted armes, that none can perce,
         Ne none can wound the man, that does them wield."
         "Charmed or enchaunted" (answerd he then ferce)[6]
"I no whitt reck, ne you the like need to reherce.[7]

51   "But faire *Fidessa,* sithens[8] fortunes guile,
         Or enimies powre hath now captived you,
         Returne from whence ye came, and rest a while
         Till morrow next, that I the Elfe subdew,
         And with *Sansfoyes* dead dowry you endew."[9]
         "Ay me, that is a double death" (she said)
         "With proud foes sight my sorrow to renew:
         Where ever yet I be, my secrete aide
Shall follow you." So passing forth she him obaid.

---

[1] *Stygian:* of the river Styx, which surrounded classical Hades, and to the land side of which were consigned the spirits of those who either lacked proper burial or were murdered but unavenged. See also notes on *Lethe* Lake and the Furies, above at iii.36.

[2] **did never vantage none:** never did any good to anyone.

[3] **vitall paines:** the pains he suffered in life.

[4] **pay his dewties last:** that shall do for him the last duty; i.e., avenging his murder.

[5] **freakes:** whims.

[6] **ferce:** fiercely.

[7] I.e., I do not care at all and you do not need to tell me about it.

[8] **sithens:** since.

[9] I.e., "endow you with the dowry of the dead Sansfoy" (M&P).

Canto Five

The faithfull knight in equall field
subdewes his faithlesse foe,
Whom false Duessa saves, and for
his cure to hell does goe.

1   The noble hart, that harbours vertuous thought,
        And is with childe of[1] glorious great intent,
        Can never rest, untill it forth have brought
        Th'eternall brood of glorie excellent:
        Such restlesse passion did all night torment
        The flaming corage of that Faery knight,
        Devizing, how that doughtie turnament
        With greatest honour he atcheiven might;
    Still did he wake, and still did watch for dawning light.

2   At last the golden Orientall gate
        Of greatest heaven gan to open fayre,
        And *Phoebus* fresh, as brydegrome to his mate,
        Came dauncing forth, shaking his deawie hayre:
        And hurld his glistring beams through gloomy ayre.
        Which when the wakeful Elfe perceivd, streight way
        He started up, and did him selfe prepayre,
        In sunbright armes, and battailous array:[2]
    For with that Pagan proud he combatt will that day.

3   And forth he comes into the commune hall,
        Where earely waite him many a gazing eye,
        To weet what end to straunger knights may fall.
        There many Minstrales maken melody,
        To drive away the dull melancholy,
        And many Bardes, that to the trembling chord

---

[1] **with childe of:** travailing in birth with. Elizabethan writers generally and Spenser in particular employ metaphors of feminine experience, such as insemination, pregnancy, childbearing, and lactation.

[2] **battailous array:** warlike equipment.

Can tune their timely[1] voices cunningly,
And many Chroniclers, that can record
Old loves, and warres for Ladies doen by many a Lord.

4   Soone after comes the cruell Sarazin,
In woven maile all armed warily,
And sternly lookes at him, who not a pin
Does care for looke of living creatures eye.
They bring them wines of *Greece* and *Araby*,
And daintie spices fetcht from furthest *Ynd*,[2]
To kindle heat of corage privily:[3]
And in the wine a solemne oth they bynd
T'observe the sacred lawes of armes, that are assynd.

5   At last forth comes that far renowmed Queene,
With royall pomp and princely majestie;
She is ybrought unto a paled[4] greene,
And placed under stately canapee,
The warlike feates of both those knights to see.
On th'other side in all mens open vew
Duessa placed is, and on a tree
Sansfoy his shield is hangd with bloody hew:
Both those the lawrell girlonds to the victor dew.[5]

6   A shrilling trompett sownded from on hye,
And unto battaill bad them selves addresse:[6]
Their shining shieldes about their wrestes[7] they tye,
And burning blades about their heades doe blesse,[8]
The instruments of wrath and heavinesse:
With greedy force each other doth assayle,
And strike so fiercely, that they doe impresse
Deepe dinted furrowes in the battred mayle:
The yron walles to ward their blowes are weak and fraile.

---

[1] **timely:** measured.

[2] **Ynd:** East Indies.

[3] **privily:** inwardly.

[4] **paled:** fenced.

[5] Duessa and the shield of Sansfoy take the place of the laurel garlands usually given to victors. Metaphor.

[6] I.e., bade or told them to address themselves.

[7] **wrestes:** wrists.

[8] **blesse:** brandish, flourish.

7   The Sarazin was stout, and wondrous strong,
      And heaped blowes like yron hammers great:
      For after blood and vengeance he did long.
      The knight was fiers, and full of youthly heat,
      And doubled strokes, like dreaded thunders threat:
      For all for praise and honour he did fight,
      Both stricken stryke, and beaten both doe beat,
      That from their shields forth flyeth firie light,
And hewen helmets deepe shew marks of eithers might.

8   So th'one for wrong, the other strives for right:
      As when a Gryfon[1] seized of his pray,
      A Dragon fiers encountreth in his flight,
      Through widest ayre making his ydle way,
      That would his rightfull ravine[2] rend away:
      With hideous horror both together smight,
      And souce so sore, that they the heavens affray:[3]
      The wise Southsayer seeing so sad sight,
Th'amazed vulgar telles of warres and mortall fight.[4]

9   So th'one for wrong, the other strives for right,
      And each to deadly shame would drive his foe:
      The cruell steele so greedily doth bight
      In tender flesh, that streames of blood down flow,
      With which the armes, that earst[5] so bright did show
      Into a pure vermillion now are dyde:
      Great ruth in all the gazers harts did grow,
      Seeing the gored woundes to gape so wyde,
That victory they dare not wish to either side.

10   At last the Paynim chaunst to cast his eye,
      His suddein eye,[6] flaming with wrathfull fyre,
      Upon his brothers shield, which hong thereby:

---

[1] A huge and mythical monster combining the body of a lion with the head and wings of an eagle.

[2] **ravine:** captured prey.

[3] **souce:** strike; **affray:** affect, e.g., as with an eclipse. For comparable celestial hyperboles, see "And molten starres doe droppe like weeping eyes," etc., vi.6.5–8.

[4] I.e., the wise prophet or soothsayer, seeing a sight so sad, tells the amazed common people that war and mortal battle are impending.

[5] **earst:** formerly.

[6] **suddein eye:** quick-glancing eye.

Therewith redoubled was his raging yre,
And said, "Ah wretched sonne of wofull syre,
Doest thou sit wayling by blacke *Stygian* lake,
Whylest here thy shield is hangd for victors hyre,
And sluggish german doest thy forces slake,[1]
To after-send his foe, that him may overtake?

11   "Goe caytive[2] Elfe, him quickly overtake,
And soone redeeme from his long wandring woe,
Goe guiltie ghost, to him my message make,
That I his shield have quit[3] from dying foe."
Therewith upon his crest he stroke him so,
That twise he reeled, readie twise to fall;
End of the doubtfull battaile deemed tho[4]
The lookers on, and lowd to him gan call
The false *Duessa,* "Thine the shield, and I, and all."[5]

12   Soone as the Faerie heard his Ladie speake,
Out of his swowning dreame he gan awake,
And quickning faith, that earst was woxen[6] weake,
The creeping deadly cold away did shake:
Tho mov'd with wrath, and shame, and Ladies sake,
Of all attonce he cast[7] avengd to be,
And with so'exceeding furie at him strake,
That forced him to stoupe upon his knee;
Had he not stouped so, he should have cloven bee.

---

[1] **german:** brother; **doest thy forces slake:** slackens the force he ought to be exercising on your behalf. "Sansjoy's reaction recalls that of Aeneas, who, momentarily inclined to spare the defeated Turnus, is once again roused to fury by the sight of the dead Pallas's sword belt on the shoulder of Turnus" (M&P; *Aeneid,* 12.938–52).

[2] **caytive:** base.

[3] **quit:** recovered. Alludes to the tradition that a spirit of a dead person cannot cross the Styx and enter Hades, but must wander until certain duties are performed—here, avenging the dead person's murder.

[4] **tho:** then.

[5] In "lowd to him" and "Thine the shield," the antecedents of "him" and "Thine" hover ambiguously between Redcrosse and Sansloy; neither Spenser nor Duessa will say whom she is encouraging. Although Sansjoy currently has the upper hand and is therefore the most likely candidate, in the next stanza the unsuspecting Redcrosse applies it to himself and is inspired to win thereby. The satire is on him and, perhaps, on chivalry itself.

[6] **earst was woxen:** formerly had become.

[7] **cast:** planned.

13   And to him said, "Goe now proud Miscreant,
        Thy selfe thy message do to german deare,[1]
        Alone he wandring thee too long doth want:
        Goe say, his foe thy shield with his doth beare."
        Therewith his heavie hand he high gan reare,
        Him to have slaine; when lo a darkesome clowd
        Upon him fell: he no where doth appeare,
        But vanisht is. The Elfe him calls alowd,
    But answer none receives: the darkness him does shrowd.[2]

14   In haste *Duessa* from her place arose,
        And to him running sayd, "O prowest[3] knight,
        That ever Ladie to her love did chose,
        Let now abate the terrour of your might,
        And quench the flame of furious despight,
        And bloodie vengeance; lo th'infernall powres
        Covering your foe with cloud of deadly night,
        Have borne him hence to *Plutoes* balefull bowres.[4]
    The conquest yours, I yours, the shield, and glory yours."

15   Not all so satisfide, with greedy eye
        He sought all round about, his thirsty blade
        To bathe in blood of faithlesse enimy;
        Who all that while lay hid in secret shade:
        He standes amazed, how he thence should fade.
        At last the trumpets Triumph sound on hie,
        And running Heralds humble homage made,
        Greeting him goodly with new victorie,
    And to him brought the shield, the cause of enmitie.

16   Wherewith he goeth to that soveraine Queene,
        And falling her before on lowly knee,
        To her makes present of his service seene:
        Which she accepts, with thankes, and goodly gree,[5]

---

[1] **do:** deliver; **german deare:** your dear relative.

[2] The motif of a god (or in this case, a sorceress) sending a cloud to rescue a favorite warrior in danger has parallels in Homer,

Iliad, 3.380; *Aeneid* 5.808–11; and *GL,* 7.44–45.

[3] **prowest:** superlative of prow; having the most prowess.

[4] **balefull bowres:** deathly chambers.

[5] **gree:** favor.

Greatly advauncing[1] his gay chevalree.
So marcheth home, and by her takes the knight,[2]
Whom all the people followe with great glee,
Shouting, and clapping all their hands on hight,
That all the ayre it fils, and flyes to heaven bright.

17   Home is he brought, and layd in sumptuous bed:
    Where many skilfull leaches him abide,[3]
    To salve his hurts, that yet still freshly bled.
    In wine and oyle they wash his woundes wide,
    And softly can embalme[4] on everie side.
    And all the while, most heavenly melody
    About the bed sweet musicke did divide,[5]
    Him to beguile of griefe and agony:
And all the while *Duessa* wept full bitterly.

18   As when a wearie traveiler that strayes
    By muddy shore of broad seven-mouthed *Nile,*
    Unweeting of the perillous wandring wayes,
    Doth meete a cruell craftie Crocodile,
    Which in false griefe hyding his harmefull guile,
    Doth weepe full sore, and sheddeth tender teares:
    The foolish man, that pitties all this while
    His mournefull plight, is swallowd up unwares,
Forgetfull of his owne, that mindes anothers cares.

19   So wept *Duessa* untill eventyde,
    That[6] shyning lampes in *Joves* high house were light:
    Then forth she rose, ne lenger would abide,
    But comes unto the place, where th'Hethen knight
    In slombring swownd nigh voyd of vitall spright,[7]
    Lay cover'd with inchaunted cloud all day:

---

[1] **advauncing:** praising.

[2] I.e., takes Redcrosse by her in her coach, which symbolizes pride in the sin parade. He has been sucked into Lucifera's superficial society (cf. his earlier aloofness) and has, in particular, felt pride.

[3] **leaches him abide:** doctors wait for him.

[4] **can embalme:** did anoint.

[5] **musicke did divide:** did run a division, did sing or play a descant—a melody harmonizing with the main melody.

[6] **that:** when.

[7] I.e., in a slumbering swoon with his vital spirit almost gone. Vital spirit probably means "the breath of life," "the animating or vital principle in men (and animals)" (OED).

Whom when she found, as she him left in plight,[1]
To wayle his wofull case she would not stay,
But to the Easterne coast of heaven makes speedy way.

20   Where griesly *Night*,[2] with visage deadly sad,
       That *Phoebus* chearefull face durst never vew,
       And in a foule blacke pitchy mantle clad,
       She findes forth comming from her darksome mew,[3]
       Where she all day did hide her hated hew.
       Before the dore her yron charot[4] stood,
       Already harnessed for journey new;
       And coleblacke steedes yborne of hellish brood,
That on their rusty bits did champ, as they were wood.[5]

21   Who when she saw *Duessa* sunny bright,
       Adornd with gold and jewels shining cleare,
       She greatly grew amazed at the sight,
       And th'unacquainted light began to feare:
       For never did such brightnes there appeare,
       And would have backe retyred to her cave,
       Untill the witches speach she gan to heare,
       Saying, "yet O thou dreaded Dame, I crave
Abyde, till I have told the message, which I have."

22   She stayd, and foorth *Duessa* gan proceede,
       "O thou most auncient Grandmother of all,
       More old then *Jove*, whom thou at first didst breede,
       Or that great house of Gods caelestiall,
       Which wast begot in *Daemogorgons* hall,
       And sawst the secrets of the world unmade,

---

[1] I.e., when she found him in the same plight as that in which she had left him. His condition, while serious, was stable.

[2] Spenser derives Night's origin, age, and appearance from data in Comes, *Mythologia*, 3.12, but he adds subjective depth to her speeches. "She numbers among her descendants Duessa and Aveugle, father of the three Sans brothers. . . . She is the eldest of the gods because she existed before the world was formed and before the Olympian gods were begotten in Demogorgon's hall (chaos). . . . See I.i.37–38 and iv.2.47" (TPR). She is not just the complement of day as in VII.vii.44, but primeval chaos or even nothingness—hence an appropriate ancestor for three brothers named "Sans-," or "without." Night accedes to Duessa's request and the two women go back and fetch Sansjoy, who has been lying on the field in the cloud.

[3] **mew:** den, narrow place.

[4] **charot:** chariot.

[5] **wood:** mad, crazy.

Why suffredst thou thy Nephewes deare to fall[1]
With Elfin sword, most shamefully betrade?
Lo where the stout *Sansjoy* doth sleepe in deadly shade.

23   "And him before, I saw with bitter eyes
      The bold *Sansfoy* shrinck underneath his speare;
      And now the pray of fowles in field he lyes,
      Nor wayld of friends, nor layd on groning beare,[2]
      That whylome was to me too dearely deare.
      O what of Gods then boots it to be borne,
      If old *Aveugles* sonnes so evill heare?[3]
      Or who shall not great *Nightes* children scorne,
  When two of three her Nephews are so fowle forlorne?

24   "Up then, up dreary Dame, of darknes Queene,
      Go gather up the reliques of thy race,
      Or else goe them avenge, and let be seene,
      That dreaded *Night* in brightest day hath place,
      And can the children of fayre light deface."
      Her feeling speaches some compassion mov'd
      In hart, and chaunge in that great mothers face:
      Yet pitty in her hart was never prov'd
  Till then: for evermore she hated, never lov'd.

25   And said, "Deare daughter rightly may I rew
      The fall of famous children borne of mee,
      And good successes, which their foes ensew:[4]
      But who can turne the streame of destinee,
      Or breake the chayne of strong necessitee,
      Which fast is tyde to *Joves* eternall seat.
      The sonnes of Day he favoureth, I see,
      And by my ruines thinkes to make them great:
  To make one great by others losse, is bad excheat.[5]

---

[1] **Nephewes:** grandsons, here and *passim*.

[2] **beare:** bier.

[3] **so evill heare:** are not esteemed (Latin: *audire male*) (TPR). "Aveugle" means blind. He is the father of the three Sans- brothers—one of whom is dead, while this one is on point of death.

[4] **which their foes ensew:** which attend their foes.

[5] **excheat:** a variant spelling of "escheat," a legal term; forfeiture, esp. of goods to the king when there is no legal heir.

26   "Yet shall they not escape so freely all;
      For some shall pay the price of others guilt:
      And he the man that made *Sansfoy* to fall,
      Shall with his owne blood price, that he hath spilt.[1]
      But what art thou, that telst of Nephews kilt?"
      "I that do seeme not I, *Duessa* ame,"
      Quoth she, "how ever now in garments gilt,
      And gorgeous gold arrayd I to thee came;
    Duessa I, the daughter of Deceipt and Shame."

27   Then bowing downe her aged backe, she kist
      The wicked witch, saying, "In that fayre face
      The false resemblaunce of Deceipt, I wist
      Did closely lurke; yet so true-seeming grace
      It carried, that I scarse in darksome place
      Could it discerne, though I the mother bee
      Of falshood, and roote of *Duessaes* race.
      O welcome child, whom I have longd to see,
    And now have seene unwares. Lo now I goe with thee."

28   Then to her yron wagon she betakes,
      And with her beares the fowle welfavourd[2] witch:
      Through mirkesome[3] aire her ready way she makes.
      Her twyfold Teme, of which two blacke as pitch,
      And two were browne, yet each to each unlich,[4]
      Did softly swim away, ne ever stamp,
      Unlesse she chaunst their stubborne mouths to twitch;
      Then foming tarre,[5] their bridles they would champ,
    And trampling the fine element,[6] would fiercely ramp.

29   So well they sped, that they be come at length
      Unto the place, whereas the Paynim lay,
      Devoid of outward sence, and native strength,
      Coverd with charmed cloud from vew of day,
      And sight of men, since his late luckelesse fray.

---

[1] **price, that he hath spilt:** pay the price for blood that he has spilled.

[2] **fowle welfavourd:** ugly-beautiful, an oxymoron; she is beautiful on the outside and ugly on the inside.

[3] **mirkesome:** murky.

[4] **unlich:** unlike.

[5] **foming tarre:** these horses were so sinister that even their saliva was black.

[6] **fine element:** air.

His cruell wounds with cruddy[1] bloud congeald,
   They binden up so wisely, as they may,
   And handle softly, till they can be heald:
So lay him in her charett,[2] close in night conceald.

30   And all the while she stood upon the ground,
   The wakefull dogs did never cease to bay,
   As giving warning of th'unwonted sound,
   With which her yron wheeles did them affray,
   And her darke griesly looke them much dismay;
   The messenger of death, the ghastly owle
   With drery shrickes did also her bewray;[3]
   And hungry wolves continually did howle,
At her abhorred face, so filthy and so fowle.

31   Thence turning backe in silence softe they stole,
   And brought the heavy corse with easy pace
   To yawning gulfe of deepe *Avernus* hole.[4]
   By that same hole an entraunce darke and bace
   With smoake and sulphur hiding all the place,
   Descends to hell: there creature never past,
   That backe retourned without heavenly grace;
   But dreadfull *Furies,* which their chaines have brast,[5]
And damned sprights sent forth to make ill[6] men aghast.

32   By that same way the direfull dames doe drive
   Their mournefull charett, fild with rusty blood,[7]
   And downe to *Plutoes* house are come bilive:[8]
   Which passing through, on every side them stood
   The trembling ghosts with sad amazed mood,
   Chattring their iron teeth, and staring wide

---

[1] **cruddy:** clotted.

[2] **charett:** chariot, cart.

[3] **bewray:** manifest the presence of.

[4] Avernus is a lake near Naples, but is traditionally pictured as a cavelike entrance to Hades, used by Aeneas (*Aeneid,* 6.237–63). There are many echoes of *Aeneid,* Book Six, in this episode. It seems as if challenging Virgil may have been Spenser's motive for creating it, for it has no effect on the plot.

[5] *Furies:* spirits who inspire vengeance, see note to iii.36; **brast:** burst.

[6] **ill:** a common Elizabethan contraction of evil.

[7] **rusty blood:** old, dried blood. On the phrase in iv.35.4, ACH notes, "usually the word suggests 'filthy' or 'defiled' from use, not disuse."

[8] **bilive:** quickly.

With stony eies; and all the hellish brood
Of feends infernall flockt on every side,
To gaze on erthly wight, that with the Night durst ride.

33   They pas the bitter waves of *Acheron,*
      Where many soules sit wailing woefully,
      And come to fiery flood of *Phlegeton,*[1]
      Whereas the damned ghosts in torments fry,
      And with sharp shrilling shriekes doe bootlesse cry,
      Cursing high *Jove,* the which them thither sent.
      The house of endlesse paine is built thereby,
      In which ten thousand sorts of punishment
      The cursed creatures doe eternally torment.

34   Before the threshold dreadfull *Cerberus*[2]
      His three deformed heads did lay along,[3]
      Curled with thousand adders venemous,
      And lilled[4] forth his bloody flaming tong:
      At them he gan to reare his bristles strong,
      And felly gnarre,[5] untill Dayes enemy
      Did him appease; then downe his taile he hong
      And suffered them to passen quietly:
      For she in hell and heaven had power equally.

35   There was *Ixion* turned on a wheele,[6]
      For daring tempt the Queene of heaven to sin;
      And *Sisyphus* an huge round stone did reele[7]
      Against an hill, ne might from labour lin;[8]
      There thristy *Tantalus* hong by the chin;[9]

[1] Acheron and Phlegeton are rivers of Hell. Phlegeton is a river of fire.

[2] The three-headed dog that guards the gate to Hell.

[3] **did lay along:** stretched out on the ground.

[4] **lilled:** lolled, two syllables.

[5] **felly gnarre:** snarl viciously.

[6] This catalogue of sufferers in hell, of which Virgil and the literature of the Middle Ages and Renaissance offer many examples, follows the list in Comes' *Mythologia* (6.16) in order and wording, as Lotspeich has noted (74). These men and deities all sought what cannot be obtained from the gods (6.16–22). Spenser adds to this list Theseus from Comes' list of illustrious men (7.9), and the fifty sisters (9.17). "Three are guilty of sexual assault against goddesses, three of scorning or rebelling against the gods, and the fifty sisters of slaying their husbands" (ACH); for further details, see TPR and ACH.

[7] **reele:** roll.

[8] **lin:** cease.

[9] **hong by the chin:** suspended up to the chin in water (ACH); a daring visualization of Tantalus' standard punishment of being always about to drink but unable to do so.

And *Tityus* fed a vultur on his maw;
Typhoeus joynts were stretched on a gin,[1]
Theseus condemned to endlesse slouth[2] by law
And fifty sisters water in leke[3] vessels draw.

36   They all beholding worldly wights in place,[4]
          Leave off their worke, unmindfull of their smart,
          To gaze on them; who forth by them do pace,
          Till they be come unto the furthest part:
          Where was a Cave ywrought by wondrous art,
          Deepe, darke, uneasy, dolefull, comfortlesse,
          In which sad *Aesculapius* far apart
          Emprisond was in chaines remedilesse,
     For that *Hippolytus* rent corse he did redresse.[5]

37   *Hippolytus* a jolly huntsman was,
          That wont in charett chace the foming bore;
          He all his Peeres in beauty did surpas,
          But Ladies love as losse of time forbore:
          His wanton stepdame[6] loved him the more,
          But when she saw her offred sweets refusd
          Her love she turnd to hate, and him before
          His father fierce of treason false accusd,
     And with her gealous termes his open eares abusd.[7]

38   Who all in rage his Sea-god syre besought,[8]
          Some cursed vengeaunce on his sonne to cast:
          From surging gulf two Monsters streight were brought,

---

[1] **gin:** engine; in this case, a rack. Lotspeich finds no source for this punishment, but TPR points out that this is traditionally the punishment of Tityus, above, which Spenser has transferred to Typhoeus.

[2] **endlesse slouth:** endless sloth, sitting in a chair for eternity.

[3] **leke:** leaky.

[4] **in place:** in that place.

[5] Hippolytus was dragged to death as a result of the passion and deceit of his stepmother Phaedra (*Aeneid*, 7.761ff). Virgil says Apollo and Diana reassembled him into a new man called Virbius. Spenser got the notion that Aesculapius, a god of medicine, restored Hippolytus from *Metamorphoses* (15.497ff) and Boccacio, *De Genealogia Deorum* (10.50). See M&P.

[6] I.e., Phaedra.

[7] I.e., she convinced the gullible father Theseus that Hippolytus had tried to seduce her, thus arousing his jealousy.

[8] Theseus, in a rage, prayed to his father, the sea god Neptune, who sent two sea monsters to frighten the horses that drew Hippolytus' chariot and so cause an accident, dragging their master to death.

With dread whereof his chacing steedes aghast,
Both charett swifte and huntsman overcast.
His goodly corps on ragged cliffs yrent,[1]
Was quite dismembred, and his members chast
Scattered on every mountaine, as he went,
That of *Hippolytus* was lefte no moniment.[2]

39   His cruell stepdame seeing what was donne,
Her wicked daies with wretched knife did end,
In death avowing th'innocence of her sonne.
Which hearing his rash Syre, began to rend
His heare,[3] and hasty tong, that did offend:
Tho gathering up the relicks of his smart[4]
By *Dianes* meanes, who was *Hippolyts* frend,
Them brought to *Aesculape,* that by his art
Did heale them all againe, and joyned every part.

40   Such wondrous science in mans witt to rain[5]
When *Jove* avizd, that could the dead revive,
And fates expired could renew again,[6]
Of endlesse life he might him not deprive,
But unto hell did thrust him downe alive,
With flashing thunderbolt ywounded sore:
Where long remaining, he did alwaies strive
Him selfe with salves to health for to restore,
And slake the heavenly fire, that raged evermore.

41   There auncient Night arriving, did alight
From her nigh weary wayne,[7] and in her armes
To *Æsculapius* brought the wounded knight:
Whome having softly disaraid of armes,
Tho gan to him discover all his harmes,
Beseeching him with prayer, and with praise,

---

[1] **yrent:** torn.

[2] **moniment:** monument or identifiable remains. But there must have been something left because the remains are gathered in the next lines.

[3] **heare:** hair.

[4] I.e., the remains of Hippolytus.

[5] **rain:** reign.

[6] I.e., could literally give a person a new lease on life, after his destined time on earth had expired.

[7] **wayne:** cart; variant spelling of "wain," as in iv.9.2 and iv.19.7.

If either salves, or oyles, or herbes, or charmes
A fordonne[1] wight from dore of death mote raise,
He would at her request prolong her nephews daies.

42   "Ah Dame" (quoth he) "thou temptest me in vaine,
      To dare the thing, which daily yet I rew,
      And the old cause of my continued paine
      With like attempt to like end to renew.
      Is not enough, that thrust from heaven dew
      Here endlesse penaunce for one fault I pay,
      But that redoubled crime with vengeance new
      Thou biddest me to eeke? Can Night defray[2]
The wrath of thundring *Jove,* that rules both night and day?"

43   "Not so" (quoth she) "but sith that heavens king
      From hope of heaven hath thee excluded quight,
      Why fearest thou, that canst not hope for thing,
      And fearest not, that more thee hurten might,
      Now in the powre of everlasting Night?
      Goe to then, O thou far renouned sonne
      Of great *Apollo,* shew thy famous might
      In medicine, that els[3] hath to thee wonne
Great pains, and greater praise, both never to be donne."[4]

44   Her words prevaild: And then the learned leach[5]
      His cunning hand gan to his wounds to lay,
      And all things els, the which his art did teach:
      Which having seene, from thence arose away
      The mother of dredd darkenesse, and let stay
      Aveugles sonne there in the leaches cure,[6]
      And backe retourning tooke her wonted way,
      To ronne her timely race, whilst *Phoebus* pure
In westerne waves his weary wagon did recure.[7]

---

[1] **fordonne:** ruined, exhausted, "done in."

[2] **eeke:** augment; **defray:** discharge a debt by paying; "buy off."

[3] **els:** already.

[4] **donne:** finished.

[5] **leach:** doctor.

[6] We never hear any more about Sansjoy in the poem as we have it. But at the beginning of Canto Six, we learn that Redcrosse is "yet half sad," just as in i.2 his "cheer," his outward behavior, was "too solemne sad." It is as if a piece of Sansjoy is embedded in Redcrosse; perhaps that is what makes it impossible for Redcrosse to kill him.

[7] **recure:** refresh.

45   The false *Duessa* leaving noyous[1] Night,
        Returnd to stately pallace of Dame *Pryde;*
        Where when she came, she found the Faery knight
        Departed thence, albee[2] his woundes wyde
        Not throughly heald, unready were to ryde.
        Good cause he had to hasten thence away;
        For on a day his wary Dwarfe had spyde,
        Where in a dungeon deepe huge nombers lay
    Of caytive[3] wretched thralls, that wayled night and day.

46   A ruefull sight, as could be seene with eie;
        Of whom he learned had in secret wise
        The hidden cause of their captivitie,
        How mortgaging their lives to *Covetise,*
        Through wastfull Pride, and wanton Riotise,[4]
        They were by law of that proud Tyrannesse
        Provokt with *Wrath,* and *Envyes* false surmise,
        Condemned to that Dongeon mercilesse,
    Where they should live in wo, and dye in wretchednesse.

47   There was that great proud king of *Babylon,*[5]
        That would compell all nations to adore,
        And him as onely God to call upon,
        Till through celestiall doome[6] thrown out of dore,
        Into an Oxe he was transformd of yore:
        There also was king *Croesus,* that enhaunst

---

[1] **noyous:** harmful.

[2] **albee:** albeit, although.

[3] **caytive:** here, captive.

[4] **Riotise:** riotous behavior, like that of Lechery in iv.20.5.

[5] Nebuchadnezzar (Dan. 3–6). In the Bible, he only becomes like a beast; he does not actually become an ox; see esp. Dan. 4.30. Spenser may have found this further indignity in Gower's *Confessio amantis,* I.2972–3. The following list of victims, like the hell-dwellers they resemble, is also traditional: those listed come mostly either from Plutarch, *Lives of the Noble Grecians and Romans;* or from Chaucer's "Monk's Tale" and its source, Boccaccio's *De Casibus Virorum Illustrium,* which last two contributed Nebuchadnezzar, Croesus, and Antiochus (stanza 47), Alexander (48), Julius Caesar and his opponent Pompey (49), and Sthenobia or Cenobia (50). Spenser, unlike other authors, sees all their bad ends as punishments for their sins, esp. pride (ACH; M&P); though it is hard to see how Scipio, usually much admired, deserves this charge, T. Cooper accuses Scipio not of pride, but only of trusting fortune and the voice of the people.

[6] **celestiall doome:** God's judgment.

His hart too high through his great richesse store;[1]
And proud *Antiochus,* the which advaunst
His cursed hand gainst God, and on his altares daunst.[2]

48   And them long time before, great *Nimrod* was,
        That first the world with sword and fire warrayd;[3]
        And after him old *Ninus* far did pas
        In princely pomp, of all the world obayd;[4]
        There also was that mightie Monarch[5] layd
        Low under all, yet above all in pride,
        That name of native syre did fowle upbrayd,
        And would as *Ammons* sonne be magnifide,
    Till scornd of God and man a shamefull death he dide.

49   All these together in one heape were throwne,
        Like carkases of beastes in butchers stall.
        And in another corner wide were strowne
        The Antique ruins of the *Romanes* fall:
        Great *Romulus* the Grandsyre of them all,
        Proud *Tarquin,* and too lordly *Lentulus,*
        Stout *Scipio,* and stubborne *Hanniball,*
        Ambitious *Sylla,* and sterne *Marius,*
    High *Caesar,* great *Pompey,* and fiers *Antonius.*[6]

---

[1] Croesus is proverbial for wealth. Spenser mixes Biblical with classical figures.

[2] Antiochus is the king of Syria who desecrated the temple at Jerusalem in some manner (1 Macc. 1.20–25; 2 Macc. 6.4–5).

[3] **warrayd:** made war on. Nimrod was a "mighty hunter," which phrase the Geneva Bible glossed as "a cruel oppressour and tyrant" (Gloss *e*); one of his kingdoms was Babel, see Genesis 10.8–10 on which the Geneva gloss says "his tyrannie came into a proverbe." Always eager to denigrate "Nimrod and his companie" (Gloss *b*), this Bible comments on Gen. 11.4 that it was he who built the tower thereof, and that he was "moved with pride and ambition" (Gloss *e*). Genesis does not name the individuals who built the tower.

[4] Ninus founded Nineveh, a wicked city, in Jon. 1.1. T. Cooper's *Thesaurus* claims "he was the first that made warre." In II.ix 21.5–6 and 56.8, Spenser has Ninus, not Nimrod, as the one who built the Tower of Babel.

[5] Alexander the Great, who, scorning his own father, claimed to be the son of Jupiter Ammon (ACH). After this, T. Cooper says "he fell into such crueltie and pryde . . . that he became odious to his owne people . . . [and] was poisoned."

[6] "These men would be well known to any Elizabethan schoolboy. Most of the material is in T. Cooper and Plutarch" (ACH). All of them from Stanza 48 though 50 are in T. Cooper except the biblical examples Nimrod and Nebuchadnezzar. Lines 7 through 9 are organized in terms of enemies: Hannibal versus Scipio, Marius versus Sylla (or Sulla), and Caesar versus Pompey versus Antonius.

50　　Amongst these mightie men were wemen mixt,
　　　　Proud wemen, vaine, forgetfull of their yoke:[1]
　　　　The bold *Semiramis,* whose sides transfixt
　　　　With sonnes own blade, her fowle reproches spoke;[2]
　　　　Fayre *Sthenoboea,* that her selfe did choke
　　　　With wilfull chord, for wanting of her will;[3]
　　　　High minded *Cleopatra,* that with stroke
　　　　Of Aspes sting her selfe did stoutly kill:[4]
　　　And thousands moe the like, that did that dongeon fill.

51　　Besides the endlesse routes[5] of wretched thralles,
　　　　Which thether were assembled day by day,
　　　　From all the world after their wofull falles,
　　　　Through wicked pride, and wasted welthes decay.
　　　　But most of all, which in the Dongeon lay
　　　　Fell from high Princes courtes, or Ladies bowres,
　　　　Where they in ydle pomp, or wanton play,
　　　　Consumed had their goods, and thriftlesse howres,
　　　And lastly thrown themselves into these heavy stowres.[6]

52　　Whose case whenas the carefull Dwarfe had tould,[7]
　　　　And made ensample of their mournfull sight
　　　　Unto his maister, he no lenger would
　　　　There dwell in perill of like painefull plight,

---

[1] I.e., forgetful that they should remain subordinate to men—presumably that desiring rule was itself a sin of pride on their part, though by no means their only sin. The catalogue of women is from T. Cooper's *Thesaurus* and from Boccaccio, *De claris mulieribus.*

[2] Semiramis, the wife of Ninus, was most valiant and ruled well after her husband's death. Her honor was destroyed by her lasciviousness. She seduced her son, who later killed her (TPR).

[3] **will:** sexual desire. Sthenoboea loved a younger man, Bellerophon—not her husband Proetus, a king of Argos. When Bellerophon turned her down and then married someone else, she despaired and killed herself (M&P).

[4] Cleopatra, the queen of Egypt, and Mark Antony were lovers; she killed herself after Mark Antony's death, so that she would not be captured and made a public spectacle by her conqueror Julius Caesar.

[5] **routes:** crowds. Just what distinguishes the "murdred men" outside, other than their anonymity, from Pride's victims inside and the spirits in Hades is not clear. Pride's victims inside seem to be living a kind of half life, and the spirits in Hell are of course eternal.

[6] **stowres:** afflictions.

[7] The Dwarf's report is further evidence that he symbolizes or exemplifies worldly prudence.

But earely rose, and ere that dawning light
Discovered had the world to heaven wyde,
He by a privy Posterne[1] tooke his flight,
That of no envious eyes he mote be spyde:
For doubtlesse death ensewed, if any him descryde.

53　　Scarse could he footing find in that fowle way,
　　　　For many corses, like a great Lay-stall[2]
　　　　Of murdred men which therein strowed[3] lay,
　　　　Without remorse, or decent funerall:
　　　　Which al through that great Princesse pride did fall
　　　　And came to shamefull end. And them besyde
　　　　Forth ryding underneath the castell wall,
　　　　A Donghill of dead carcases he spyde,
　　The dreadfull spectacle of that sad house of *Pryde*.

---

[1] **Posterne:** the usually inconspicuous back
gate of a castle.

[2] **Lay-stall:** heap of trash or dung.

[3] **strowed:** strewn, cast at random.

Canto Six

From lawlesse lust by wondrous grace
fayre Una is releast:
Whom salvage nation does adore,
and learnes her wise beheast.

1   As when a ship, that flyes fayre under sayle,
An hidden rocke escaped hath unwares,
That lay in waite her wrack for to bewaile,[1]
The Marriner yet halfe amazed stares
At perill past, and yet in doubt ne dares
To joy at his foolhappie oversight:
So doubly is distrest twixt joy and cares
The dreadlesse corage of this Elfin knight,
Having escapt so sad ensamples in his sight.

2   Yet sad he was, that his too hastie speed
The fayre *Duess'* had forst him leave behind;
And yet more sad, that *Una* his deare dreed[2]
Her truth had staynd with treason so unkind;[3]
Yet cryme in her could never creature find,
But for his love, and for her owne selfe sake,
She wandred had from one to other *Ynd,*[4]
Him for to seeke, ne ever would forsake,
Till her unwares the fiers *Sansloy* did overtake.

3   Who after *Archimagoes* fowle defeat,
Led her away into a forest wilde,
And turning wrathfull fyre to lustfull heat,
With beastly sin thought her to have defilde,
And made the vassall of his pleasures vilde.

---

[1] Since a rock, even a personified one, is unlikely to bewail the shipwreck it has caused, this represents a forced usage or error by Spenser (OED, 3b).

[2] **deare dreed:** object both of love and of awe or reverence. OED cites this line.

[3] **unkind:** both in its modern sense and in its older sense of unnatural.

[4] **from one to other Ynd:** from the East Indies to the West Indies—a rhetorical exaggeration, since no mention is made of a ship.

Yet first he cast by treatie, and by traynes,[1]
Her to persuade, that stubborne fort to yilde:
For greater conquest of hard love he gaynes,
That workes it to his will, then he that it constraines.

4   With fawning wordes he courted her a while,
          And looking lovely, and oft sighing sore,
          Her constant hart did tempt with diverse guile:
          But wordes, and lookes, and sighes she did abhore,
          As rock of Diamond stedfast evermore.
          Yet for to feed his fyrie lustfull eye,
          He snatcht the vele, that hong her face before;
          Then gan her beautie shyne, as brightest skye,
And burnt his beastly hart t'efforce her chastitye.[2]

5   So when he saw his flatt'ring artes to fayle,
          And subtile engines bett from batteree,[3]
          With greedy force he gan the fort assayle,
          Whereof he weend possessed soone to bee,
          And win rich spoile of ransackt chastitee.
          Ah heavens, that doe this hideous act behold,
          And heavenly virgin thus outraged see,
          How can ye vengeance just so long withhold,
And hurle not flashing flames vpon that Paynim bold?

6   The pitteous mayden carefull[4] comfortlesse,
          Does throw out thrilling shriekes, and shrieking cryes,
          The last vaine helpe of wemens great distresse,
          And with loud plaintes importuneth the skyes,
          That molten starres doe drop like weeping eyes;
          And *Phoebus* flying so most shamefull sight,
          His blushing face in foggy cloud implyes,[5]
          And hydes for shame. What witt of mortall wight
Can now devise to quitt a thrall[6] from such a plight?

---

[1] **by treatie, and by traynes:** by pleading and by trickery.

[2] **t'efforce her chastitye:** to take her virginity by force.

[3] **engines bett from batteree:** war devices beaten down from their assault.

Spenser uses imagery of battle to describe the sexual contest (TPR).

[4] **carefull:** full of worry.

[5] **implyes:** enfolds.

[6] **thrall:** captive.

7   Eternall providence exceeding thought,
        Where none appeares can make her selfe a way:
        A wondrous way it for this Lady wrought,
        From Lyons clawes to pluck the gryped pray.
        Her shrill outcryes and shrieks so loud did bray,
        That all the woodes and forestes did resownd;
        A troupe of *Faunes* and *Satyres*[1] far a way
        Within the wood were dauncing in a rownd,
    Whiles old *Sylvanus*[2] slept in shady arber sownd.

8   Who when they heard that pitteous strained voice,
        In haste forsooke their rurall meriment,
        And ran towardes the far rebownded noyce,
        To weet, what wight so loudly did lament.
        Unto the place they come incontinent:[3]
        Whom when the raging Sarazin espyde,
        A rude, mishappen, monstrous rablement,
        Whose like he never saw, he durst not byde,
    But got his ready steed, and fast away gan ryde.

9   The wyld woodgods arrived in the place,
        There find the virgin doolfull desolate,
        With ruffled rayments, and fayre blubbred[4] face,
        As her outrageous foe had left her late,
        And trembling yet through feare of former hate;
        All stand amazed at so uncouth sight,
        And gin to pittie her unhappie state,
        All stand astonied[5] at her beautie bright,
    In their rude eyes unworthy of so wofull plight.

10   She more amazd, in double dread doth dwell;
        And every tender part for feare does shake:
        As when a greedy Wolfe through honger fell[6]
        A seely[7] Lamb far from the flock does take,
        Of whom he meanes his bloody feast to make,
        A Lyon spyes fast running towards him,

---

[1] Deities of the forest, human from the waist up and goat from the waist down.

[2] God of fauns and satyrs. Spenser's son by his first wife was named Sylvanus.

[3] **incontinent:** at once.

[4] **blubbred:** swollen from weeping.

[5] **astonied:** stunned.

[6] **fell:** ruthless.

[7] **seely:** innocent, synonymous with "silly" in its old sense of innocent.

The innocent pray in hast he does forsake,
Which quitt[1] from death yet quakes in every lim
With chaunge of feare, to see the Lyon looke so grim.

11   Such fearefull fitt assaid her trembling hart,
          Ne word to speake, ne joynt to move she had:
          The salvage[2] nation feele her secret smart,
          And read her sorrow in her count'nance sad;
          Their frowning forheades with rough hornes yclad,
          And rustick horror[3] all a syde doe lay,
          And gently grenning,[4] shew a semblance glad
          To comfort her, and feare to put away,
      Their backward bent knees teach her humbly to obay.[5]

12   The doubtfull Damzell dare not yet committ,
          Her single person to their barbarous truth,[6]
          But still twixt feare and hope amazd does sitt,
          Late learnd what harme to hasty trust ensu'th,[7]
          They in compassion of her tender youth,
          And wonder of her beautie soverayne,
          Are wonne with pitty and unwonted ruth,[8]
          And all prostrate upon the lowly playne,
      Doe kisse her feete, and fawne on her with count'nance fayne.[9]

13   Their harts she ghesseth by their humble guise,[10]
          And yieldes her to extremitie of time;
          So from the ground she fearelesse doth arise,

---

[1] **quitt:** here, released, usually with the overtone of "bought" or "redeemed."

[2] **salvage:** savage, Spenser's usual spelling. The word and concept are very important in this canto and in Book Six. Not necessarily derogatory; could be neutrally anthropological, as here. Sylvanus' attempt to identify Una with one of the classical deities represents an exercise in natural religion; it is more successful than that of the Satyrs he governs, but still not correct.

[3] **horror:** here roughness, hairiness. Presumably they shave, comb, or slick down their hair.

[4] **grenning:** grinning.

[5] The grammatical subject of this clause is they or all, referring back to "the salvage nation." "They teach their knees (bent backward like those of a goat) to kneel in humble obedience to her" (M&P). Word order is mixed up in order to arrange six strong and consonant-clogged syllables in a row, dramatizing 1) how difficult it is for an animal's back legs to kneel, and 2) the difficulty one experiences in learning and practicing Christian doctrine.

[6] **single:** solitary; **truth:** honesty.

[7] I.e., recently taught what harm comes from trusting someone too hastily.

[8] **unwonted ruth:** unaccustomed pity.

[9] **fayne:** happy, cheerful.

[10] **guise:** behavior.

And walketh forth without suspect of crime:
They all as glad, as birdes of joyous Pryme,[1]
Thence lead her forth, about her dauncing round,
Shouting, and singing all a shepheards ryme,
And with greene braunches strowing all the ground,
Do worship her, as Queene, with olive girlond cround.

14 And all the way their merry pipes they sound,
That all the woods with doubled Eccho ring,
And with their horned feet doe weare the ground,
Leaping like wanton kids in pleasant Spring.
So towards old *Sylvanus* they her bring;
Who with the noyse awaked, commeth out,
To weet the cause, his weake steps governing,
And aged limbs on Cypresse stadle[2] stout,
And with an yvie twyne his waste is girt about.

15 Far off he wonders, what them makes so glad,
Or *Bacchus* merry fruit they did invent,[3]
Or *Cybeles* franticke rites have made them mad;[4]
They drawing nigh, unto their God present
That flowre of fayth and beautie excellent:
The God himselfe vewing that mirrhour rare,[5]
Stood long amazd, and burnt in his intent;[6]
His owne fayre *Dryope* now he thinkes not faire,
And *Pholoe* fowle, when her to this he doth compaire.[7]

16 The woodborne people fall before her flat,
And worship her as Goddesse of the wood;
And old *Sylvanus* selfe bethinkes not, what
To thinke of wight so fayre, but gazing stood,
In doubt to deeme her borne of earthly brood;

---

[1] **Pryme:** early morning or springtime.

[2] **stadle:** staff.

[3] I.e., whether they had found some wine. Spenser often uses "or . . . or" where we would use "whether . . . or"; see II.ii.4.

[4] The priests of Cybele celebrated her rites with wild dances and music (TPR).

[5] **mirrhour rare:** mirror of God, goodness, and beauty, as in Proem 5.2 of Queen Elizabeth: "mirrour of grace and majesty divine"—ultimately a Platonic notion.

[6] **burnt in his intent:** not, as it turns out, in lust for her, but in intense gaze or observation.

[7] Dryope and Pholoe were wives of other sylvan gods whom Spenser may have conflated with Sylvanus. "The pun ('Pholoe fowle') may be what attracted Spenser to the latter" (TPR).

Sometimes Dame *Venus* selfe he seemes to see,
But *Venus* never had so sober mood;
Sometimes *Diana* he her takes to be,
But misseth bow, and shaftes, and buskins[1] to her knee.

17   By vew of her he ginneth to revive
      His ancient love, and dearest *Cyparisse*,[2]
      And calles to mind his pourtraiture alive,[3]
      How fayre he was, and yet not fayre to this,
      And how he slew with glauncing dart amisse
      A gentle Hynd, the which the lovely boy
      Did love as life, above all worldly blisse;
      For griefe whereof the lad n'ould after joy,[4]
But pynd away in anguish and selfewild annoy.[5]

18   The wooddy Nymphes, fayre *Hamadryades*[6]
      Her to behold do thether runne apace,
      And all the troupe of light-foot *Naiades*,[7]
      Flocke all about to see her lovely face:
      But when they vewed have her heavenly grace,
      They envy her in their malitious mind,
      And fly away for feare of fowle disgrace:
      But all the *Satyres* scorne their woody kind,[8]
And henceforth nothing faire, but her on earth they find.

19   Glad of such lucke, the luckelesse lucky mayd,[9]
      Did her content to please their feeble eyes,
      And long time with that salvage people stayd,
      To gather breath in many miseryes.

[1] **buskins:** boots. Diana needs such equipment because she is goddess of the hunt. She resembles Una and contrasts with Venus in her chastity.

[2] Because Sylvanus loved Cyparissus, he changed the lad into a cypress tree (Latin: *cyparissus*). Sylvanus ever after carried a cypress branch, which accounts for the "Cypresse stadle" of 14.8. Spenser follows Natalis Comes, *Mythologia*, 5.10; and Boccaccio, *Genealogia Deorum*, 13.17. In *Metamorphoses* (10.106ff), it was Apollo who loved the lad (TPR; M&P).

[3] I.e., his appearance when alive.

[4] **n'ould after joy:** the lad took no joy in anything thereafter.

[5] **selfewild annoy:** self-imposed suffering.

[6] *Hamadryades:* nymphs of individual trees.

[7] *Naiades:* nymphs of rivers or springs.

[8] **woody kind:** generally, inhabitants of the forest; esp. potential mates of the Satyrs' own species, or from among the nymphs.

[9] Oxymoron.

During which time her gentle wit she plyes,
　To teach them truth, which worshipt her in vaine,
　And made her th'Image of Idolatryes;
　But when their bootlesse[1] zeale she did restrayne
From her own worship, they her Asse would worship fayn.

20　It fortuned a noble warlike knight
　　By just occasion to that forrest came,
　　To seeke his kindred, and the lignage right,
　　From whence he tooke his weldeserved name:
　　He had in armes abroad wonne muchell fame,
　　And fild far landes with glorie of his might,
　　Plaine, faithfull, true, and enimy of shame,
　　And ever lov'd to fight for Ladies right,
　But in vaine glorious frayes he litle did delight.

21　A Satyres sonne yborne in forrest wyld,
　　By straunge adventure as it did betyde,
　　And there begotten of a Lady myld,
　　Fayre *Thyamis* the daughter of *Labryde*,[2]
　　That was in sacred bandes of wedlocke tyde
　　To *Therion*,[3] a loose unruly swayne;
　　Who had more joy to raunge the forrest wyde,
　　And chase the salvage beast with busie payne,[4]
　Then serve his Ladies love, and waste in pleasures vayne.

22　The forlorne mayd[5] did with loves longing burne,
　　And could not lacke her lovers company,
　　But to the wood she goes, to serve her turne,
　　And seeke her spouse, that from her still does fly,
　　And followes other game and venery:[6]
　　A Satyre chaunst her wandring for to finde,
　　And kindling coles of lust in brutish eye,
　　The loyall linkes of wedlocke did unbinde,
　And made her person thrall unto his beastly kind.

---

[1] **bootlesse:** useless because wrongly directed.

[2] **Thyamis:** Greek for "passion"; **Labryde:** Greek for "turbulent," "greedy."

[3] **Therion:** Greek for "wild beast."

[4] **busie payne:** careful industry.

[5] **mayd:** i.e., Thyamis. Spenser is digressing into Satyrane's biography.

[6] **venery:** hunting; with a pun on venery as the works of Venus, sexual activity.

23   So long in secret cabin there he held
            Her captive to his sensuall desyre,
            Till that with timely fruit her belly sweld,
            And bore a boy unto that salvage syre:
            Then home he suffred her for to retyre,
            For ransome leaving him the late-borne childe;
            Whom till to ryper yeares he gan aspyre,[1]
            He noursled up[2] in life and manners wilde,
        Emongst wild beastes and woods, from lawes of men exilde.

24   For all he taught the tender ymp[3] was but
            To banish cowardize and bastard feare;
            His trembling hand he would him force to put
            Upon the Lyon and the rugged Beare,
            And from the she Beares teats her whelps to teare;
            And eke wyld roring Buls he would him make
            To tame, and ryde their backes not made to beare;
            And the Robuckes in flight to overtake,
        That everie beast for feare of him did fly and quake.

25   Thereby so fearelesse, and so fell he grew,
            That his owne syre and maister of his guise
            Did often tremble at his horrid vew,
            And oft for dread of hurt would him advise,
            The angry beastes not rashly to despise,
            Nor too much to provoke: for he would learne[4]
            The Lyon stoup to him in lowly wise,
            (A lesson hard) and make the Libbard[5] sterne
        Leave roaring, when in rage he for revenge did earne.[6]

---

[1] **aspyre:** here, grow up; usually used in its modern, emotional sense.

[2] **noursled up:** reared; following the 1596 edition, frequent in Spenser. The 1590 variant "nousled" would be a Spenserian spelling of "nuzzled"—a word that Spenser applies only to moles.

[3] **ymp:** child. As Upton was the first to notice (*Var.*, 246), Satyrane's education is like that of Achilles, who was taught by the centaur Chiron; Spenser may have borrowed it from the education of Ruggiero, a major hero, by Atlantes (*OF,* 7.57). It is not certain what Satyrane symbolizes, but here he is clearly set above both the lion and the satyrs by his understanding of Christianity and the fact that he is three-fourths human.

[4] **learne:** teach.

[5] **Libbard:** leopard.

[6] **earne:** yearn.

26 And for to make his powre approved more,[1]
  Wyld beastes in yron yokes he would compell;
  The spotted Panther, and the tuskéd Bore,
  The Pardale[2] swift, and the Tigre cruell;
  The Antelope, and Wolfe both fiers and fell;
  And them constraine in equall teme to draw.[3]
  Such joy he had, their stubborne harts to quell,
  And sturdie courage tame with dreadfull aw,
That his beheast they feared, as a tyrans law.

27 His loving mother came upon a day
  Unto the woodes, to see her little sonne;
  And chaunst unwares to meet him in the way,
  After his sportes, and cruell pastime donne,
  When after him a Lyonesse did runne,
  That roaring all with rage, did lowd requere[4]
  Her children deare, whom he away had wonne:
  The Lyon whelpes she saw how he did beare,
And lull in rugged armes, withouten childish feare.

28 The fearefull Dame all quaked at the sight,
  And turning backe, gan fast to fly away,
  Untill with love revokt[5] from vaine affright,
  She hardly yet perswaded was to stay,
  And then to him these womanish words gan say;
  "Ah *Satyrane*, my dearling, and my joy,
  For love of me leave off this dreadfull play;
  To dally thus with death, is no fit toy,
Go find some other play-fellowes, mine own sweet boy."

29 In these and like delightes of bloody game
  He trayned was, till ryper yeares he raught,[6]
  And there abode, whylst any beast of name
  Walkt in that forrest, whom he had not taught,
  To feare his force: and then his courage haught[7]
  Desyrd of forreine foemen to be knowne,

---

[1] I.e., to prove his power the more.

[2] **Pardale:** panther or leopard.

[3] **equall teme to draw:** to pull together; the direct object, telling what they pulled, is left unstated.

[4] **requere:** variant spelling of "require."

[5] **revokt:** called back (Latin: *revocatus*).

[6] **raught:** variant form of "reached."

[7] **haught:** haughty.

And far abroad for straunge adventures sought:
In which his might was never overthrowne,
But through al Faery lond his famous worth was blown.

30   Yet evermore it was his maner faire,
    After long labours and adventures spent,
    Unto those native woods for to repaire,[1]
    To see his syre and ofspring[2] auncient.
    And now he thether came for like intent;
    Where he unwares the fairest *Una* found,
    Straunge Lady, in so straunge habiliment,[3]
    Teaching the Satyres, which her sat around
Trew sacred lore, which from her sweet lips did redound.

31   He wondred at her wisedome hevenly rare,
    Whose like in womens witt he never knew;
    And when her curteous deeds he did compare,
    Gan her admire, and her sad sorrowes rew,
    Blaming of Fortune, which such troubles threw,
    And joyd to make proofe of her cruelty
    On gentle Dame, so hurtlesse,[4] and so trew:
    Thenceforth he kept her goodly company,
And learnd her discipline of faith and verity.

32   But she all vowd unto the *Redcrosse* knight,
    His wandring perill closely[5] did lament,
    Ne in this new acquaintaunce could delight,
    But her deare heart with anguish did torment,
    And all her witt in secret counsels spent,
    How to escape. At last in privy wise
    To *Satyrane* she shewed her intent;
    Who glad to gain such favour, gan devise,
How with that pensive Maid he best might thence arise.[6]

33   So on a day when Satyres all were gone,
    To doe their service to *Sylvanus* old,
    The gentle virgin left behinde alone

---

[1] **repaire:** come or go; sometimes also used in the modern sense.

[2] **ofspring:** origin; see 20.3.

[3] **habiliment:** attire.

[4] **hurtlesse:** harmless.

[5] **closely:** secretly.

[6] **arise:** depart.

He led away with corage stout and bold.
Too late it was, to Satyres to be told,
Or ever hope recover her againe:
In vaine he seekes that having cannot hold.
So fast he carried her with carefull paine,
That they the woods are past, and come now to the plaine.

34   The better part now of the lingring day,
They traveild had, whenas they far espide
A weary wight forwandring[1] by the way,
And towards him they gan in hast to ride,
To weete of newes, that did abroad betide,
Or tidings of her knight of the *Redcrosse*.
But he them spying, gan to turne aside,
For feare as seemd, or for some feigned losse;
More greedy they of newes, fast towards him do crosse.

35   A silly[2] man, in simple weeds forworne,
And soild with dust of the long dried way;
His sandales were with toilsome travell torne,
And face all tand with scorching sunny ray,
As he had traveild many a sommers day,
Through boyling sands of *Arabie* and *Ynde;*
And in his hand a *Jacobs* staffe,[3] to stay
His weary limbs upon: and eke behind,
His scrip[4] did hang, in which his needments he did bind.

36   The knight approching nigh, of him inquerd
Tidings of warre, and of adventures new;
But warres, nor new adventures none he herd.
Then *Una* gan to aske, if ought he knew,
Or heard abroad of that her champion trew,
That in his armour bare a croslet[5] red.
"Ay me, Deare dame" (quoth he) "well may I rew
To tell the sad sight, which mine eies have red:
These eies did see that knight both living, and eke ded."

---

[1] **forwandring:** wandering far and wide, as if he had been wandering too long.

[2] **silly:** simple, unsophisticated.

[3] ***Jacobs* staffe:** pilgrim's staff.

[4] **scrip:** pilgrim's bag.

[5] **croslet:** little cross.

37   That cruell word her tender hart so thrild,[1]
           That suddein cold did ronne through every vaine,
           And stony horrour all her sences fild
           With dying fitt, that downe she fell for paine.
           The knight her lightly reared up againe,
           And comforted with curteous kind reliefe:
           Then wonne from death, she bad him tellen plaine
           The further processe[2] of her hidden griefe;
      The lesser pangs can beare, who hath endur'd the chief.[3]

38   Then gan the Pilgrim thus, "I chaunst this day,
           This fatall day, that shall I ever rew,
           To see two knights in travell on my way
           (A sory sight) arraung'd in batteill new,
           Both breathing vengeaunce, both of wrathfull hew:
           My fearefull flesh did tremble at their strife,
           To see their blades so greedily imbrew,[4]
           That dronke with blood, yet thristed after life:
      What more? the *Redcrosse* knight was slain with Paynim knife."

39   "Ah dearest Lord" (quoth she) "how might that bee,
           And he the stoutest knight, that ever wonne?"[5]
           "Ah dearest dame" (quoth hee) "how might I see
           The thing, that might not be, and yet was donne?"
           "Where is" (said *Satyrane*) "that Paynims sonne,
           That him of life, and us of joy hath refte?"[6]
           "Not far away" (quoth he) "he hence doth wonne[7]
           Foreby a fountaine, where I late him lefte
      Washing his bloody wounds, that through the steele were cleft."

40   Therewith the knight thence marched forth in hast,
           Whiles *Una* with huge heavinesse opprest,
           Could not for sorrow follow him so fast;
           And soone he came, as he the place had ghest,
           Whereas that *Pagan* proud him selfe did rest,

---

[1] **thrild:** pierced.

[2] **processe:** account.

[3] I.e., he who has endured the chief pang can bear the lesser ones. Una expresses the same courage in her reaction to the next "revelation" of Redcrosse's death (vii.25.5).

[4] **imbrew:** soak themselves in blood.

[5] **wonne:** engaged in battle (M&P).

[6] **refte:** bereaved, violently deprived; past tense of "reave."

[7] **wonne:** remain.

In secret shadow by a fountaine side:
Even he it was, that earst would have supprest[1]
Faire *Una:* whom when *Satyrane* espide,
With foule reprochfull words he boldly him defide.

41   And said, "Arise thou cursed Miscreaunt,
       That hast with knightlesse guile and trecherous train[2]
       Faire knighthood fowly shamed, and doest vaunt
       That good knight of the *Redcrosse* to have slain:
       Arise, and with like treason now maintain
       Thy guilty wrong, or els thee guilty yield."
       The Sarazin this hearing, rose amain,[3]
       And catching up in hast his three square[4] shield,
And shining helmet, soone him buckled to the field.

42   And drawing nigh him said, "Ah misborn Elfe,
       In evill houre thy foes thee hither sent,
       Anothers wrongs to wreak upon thy selfe:[5]
       Yet ill thou blamest me, for having blent[6]
       My name with guile and traiterous intent;
       That *Redcrosse* knight, perdie, I never slew,
       But had he beene, where earst his armes were lent,
       Th'enchaunter vaine his errour should not rew:[7]
But thou his errour shalt, I hope now proven trew."[8]

43   Therewith they gan, both furious and fell,[9]
       To thunder blowes, and fiersly to assaile
       Each other, bent his enimy to quell,
       That with their force they perst both plate and maile,

[1] **supprest:** raped.

[2] **knightlesse:** unknightly, unworthy of a knight; **train:** deceit.

[3] **amain:** at once.

[4] **three square:** triangular. In Book Three, Glauce, a good if limited character, has a shield of similar shape.

[5] I.e., "to draw upon yourself the consequences of another's wrongs" (M&P).

[6] **blent:** blemished.

[7] I.e., had Redcrosse been inside of his armor instead of Archimago, Archimago would not have been trounced as he was. Sansloy thinks that Archimago somehow acquired Redcrosse's armor, but the armor was just one of Archimago's illusions.

[8] I.e., "your experience at my hands shall now, I hope, confirm Archimago's foolishness in venturing to fight me" (M&P). Sansloy's witticism is cryptic, which may be why Satyrane proceeds to fight him despite his clearly expressed innocence of the charge.

[9] **fell:** ruthless.

And made wide furrowes in their fleshes fraile,
That it would pitty any living eie.[1]
Large floods of blood adowne their sides did raile;
But floods of blood could not them satisfie:
Both hongred after death: both chose to win, or die.

44   So long they fight, and fell[2] revenge pursue,
        That fainting each, themselves to breathen lett,[3]
        And ofte refreshed, battell oft renue:
        As when two Bores with rancling malice mett,
        Their gory sides fresh bleeding fiercely frett,
        Til breathlesse both them selves aside retire,
        Where foming wrath, their cruell tuskes they whett,
        And trample th'earth, the whiles they may respire;
    Then backe to fight againe, new breathed and entire.[4]

45   So fiersly, when these knights had breathed once,
        They gan to fight retourne, increasing more
        Their puissant force, and cruell rage attonce,
        With heaped strokes more hugely, then before,
        That with their drery[5] wounds and bloody gore
        They both deformed, scarsely could bee known.
        By this sad *Una* fraught with anguish sore,
        Led with their noise, which through the aire was thrown:
    Arriv'd, wher they in erth their fruitles blood had sown.

46   Whom all so soone as that proud Sarazin
        Espide, he gan revive the memory
        Of his leud lusts, and late attempted sin,
        And lefte the doubtfull[6] battell hastily,
        To catch her, newly offred to his eie:
        But *Satyrane* with strokes him turning, staid,
        And sternely bad him other businesse plie,
        Then hunt the steps of pure unspotted Maid:
    Wherewith he al enrag'd, these bitter speaches said.

---

[1] I.e., that it would move any living eye to pity.

[2] **fell:** ruthless.

[3] I.e., so that each one, feeling faint, lets himself take a breather.

[4] **entire:** whole, intact.

[5] **drery:** here, gory; often in almost the modern sense, but more intense.

[6] **doubtfull:** undecided.

47   "O foolish faeries sonne, what fury mad
       Hath thee incenst, to hast thy dolefull fate?
       Were it not better, I that Lady had,
       Then that thou hadst repented it too late?
       Most sencelesse man he, that himselfe doth hate,
       To love another. Lo then for thine ayd
       Here take thy lovers token on thy pate."
     So they to fight; the whiles the royall Mayd
  Fledd farre away, of that proud Paynim sore afrayd.[1]

48   But that false *Pilgrim*, which that leasing[2] told,
       Being in deed old *Archimage*, did stay
       In secret shadow, all this to behold,
       And much rejoyced in their bloody fray:
       But when he saw the Damsell passe away
       He left his stond,[3] and her pursewd apace,
       In hope to bring her to her last decay.[4]
     But for to tell her lamentable cace,
  And eke this battels end, will need another place.[5]

---

[1] The situation recalls *OF,* 1.16–19, in which Rinaldo and Ferraù fight over Angelica while she slips away.

[2] **leasing:** lie.

[3] **stond:** stand, place of ambush (ACH).

[4] Archimago catches up with Una only when she is reunited with Redcrosse and her family, and she exposes him (xii.24–36). In Book Two, we are told that he has given up on her and is seeking other victims such as Redcrosse (II.i.2).

[5] We never hear the end of this battle, or whether Sansloy or Satyrane won, although Sansloy appears again in II.ii.37 and Satyrane in III.vii.30. This may be Spenser's negligence, or it may be his way of saying that the battle was a draw because the two were evenly matched or perhaps even somewhat akin to one another; for a similar implication, see the unresolved battle between Redcrosse and Sansjoy in v.13–15.

Canto Seven

The Redcrosse knight is captive made
By Gyaunt proud opprest,
Prince Arthure meets with Una great-
ly with those newes distrest.

1   What man so wise, what earthly witt so ware,[1]
       As to discry the crafty cunning traine,[2]
       By which deceipt doth maske in visour[3] faire,
       And cast her coulours died deepe in graine,
       To seeme like truth, whose shape she well can faine,
       And fitting gestures to her purpose frame;
       The guiltlesse man with guile to entertaine?[4]
       Great maistresse of her art was that false Dame,
    The false *Duessa,* cloked with *Fidessaes* name.

2   Who when returning from the drery *Night,*
       She fownd not in that perilous hous of *Pryde,*
       Where she had left, the noble *Redcross* knight,
       Her hoped pray; she would no lenger byde,
       But forth she went, to seeke him far and wide.
       Ere long she fownd, whereas he wearie sate,
       To rest him selfe, foreby a fountaine syde,
       Disarmed all of yron-coted Plate,
    And by his side his steed the grassy forage ate.

3   Hee feedes upon the cooling shade, and bayes[5]
       His sweatie forehead in the breathing wynd,
       Which through the trembling leaves full gently playes
       Wherein the chearefull birds of sundry kynd
       Doe chaunt sweet musick, to delight his mynd,
       The witch approching gan him fayrely greet,

---

[1] **ware:** wary, wise.
[2] **traine:** here, trickery, scheme.
[3] **visour:** the headpiece of a helmet that can be lowered to cover the face.

[4] **to entertaine:** to treat in a specified manner, not always benevolently.
[5] **bayes:** bathes.

> And with reproch of carelesnes unkynd,
> Upbrayd, for leaving her in place unmeet,
> With fowle words tempring faire, soure gall with hony sweet.

4   Unkindnesse past, they gan of solace treat,[1]
> And bathe in pleasaunce of the joyous shade,
> Which shielded them against the boyling heat,
> And with greene boughes decking a gloomy glade,
> About the fountaine like a girlond made;
> Whose bubbling wave did ever freshly well,
> Ne ever would through fervent sommer fade
> The sacred Nymph, which therein wont to dwell,
> Was out of *Dianes* favor, as it then befell.

5   The cause was this: one day when *Phoebe* fayre[2]
> With all her band was following the chace,
> This Nymph, quite tyr'd with heat of scorching ayre
> Satt downe to rest in middest of the race:
> The goddesse wroth gan fowly her disgrace,
> And badd the waters, which from her did flow,
> Be such as she her selfe was then in place.
> Thenceforth her waters wexed dull and slow,
> And all that drinke thereof, do faint and feeble grow.[3]

6   Hereof this gentle knight unweeting was,
> And lying downe upon the sandie graile,[4]
> Dronke of the streame, as cleare as christall glas;
> Eftsoones his manly forces gan to fayle,
> And mightie strong was turnd to feeble frayle:
> His chaunged powres at first them selves not felt,

---

[1] I.e., they began to talk in ways that gave them pleasure.

[2] The goddess of the hunt, named both Diana and Phoebe.

[3] Redcrosse participates in the nymph's sloth, her sitting "down to rest in middest of the race," both by relaxing and by drinking of the nymph's enfeebling water. St. Paul pictures the Christian life as a race de-manding self-mastery in 1 Cor. 9.24—an analogue that imparts a spiritual dimension to Redcrosse's sloth. See the effeminating spring in the myth of Salmacis and Hermaphroditus in *Metamorphoses,* 4.285–388, esp. 286–7.

[4] **graile:** gravel; OED cites this line as the first instance, though not the only one: "Grail," 3.

Till crudled cold his corage[1] gan assayle,
And chearefull[2] blood in fayntnes chill did melt,
Which like a fever fit through all his body swelt.[3]

7   Yet goodly court he made still to his Dame,
     Pourd out in loosnesse on the grassy grownd,
     Both carelesse of his health,[4] and of his fame:
     Till at the last he heard a dreadfull sownd,
     Which through the wood loud bellowing, did rebownd,
     That all the earth for terror seemd to shake,
     And trees did tremble. Th'Elfe therewith astownd,[5]
     Upstarted lightly from his looser make,[6]
And his unready weapons gan in hand to take.

8   But ere he could his armour on him dight,[7]
     Or gett his shield, his monstrous enimy[8]
     With sturdie steps came stalking in his sight,
     An hideous Geaunt horrible and hye,
     That with his tallnesse seemd to threat the skye,
     The ground eke[9] groned under him for dreed;
     His living like saw never living eye,
     Ne durst behold: his stature did exceed
The hight of three the tallest sonnes of mortall seed.[10]

---

[1] **crudled   cold:** congealed coldness; **corage:** natural vigor (M&P).

[2] **chearefull:** lively, life-giving.

[3] **swelt:** raged, burned as with a fever (OED, 3b); to say that "fayntnes chill" does this is to say that fever causes chills as well as hotness. In a similar paradox, the cold curdles his vigor and at the same time melts his blood.

[4] **carelesse of his health:** implies penetration, so we know that this sexual act is consummated.

[5] **astownd:** confused.

[6] **looser   make:** sexually looser (or very loose) companion.

[7] **dight:** put on. That he hasn't time to do this, and esp. to grasp his shield, the shield of faith, is crucial. Cf. the prominence of Arthur's shield in his successful battle with Orgoglio in Canto Eight.

[8] Orgoglio is often read as a figure for presumption, "that form of pride most commonly paired with its opposite, despair, so explaining the placement of the Orgoglio and Despair episodes together" (TPR). He is "growen great . . . through presumption of his matchlesse might" (vii.10.1–3). Cf. x.1, a moralizing stanza occurring just after Redcrosse faces Despaire, which rejects the man who "boasts of fleshly might / And vaine assurance of mortalitie." There, "fleshly might" is said to include even one's "will" (x.1.9), so it is much more than strength of body. Like Redcrosse, Orgoglio too is said to boast—in this case of being sired by the "blustring" god Aeolus (vii.9.2).

[9] **eke:** moreover.

[10] The caesura-less alexandrine mimes his height.

9　　The greatest Earth his uncouth mother was,
　　　And blustring *Æolus* his boasted syre,[1]
　　　Who with his breath, which through the world doth pas,
　　　Her hollow womb did secretly inspyre,[2]
　　　And fild her hidden caves with stormie yre,
　　　That she conceiv'd;[3] and trebling the dew time,
　　　In which the wombes of wemen doe expyre,[4]
　　　Brought forth this monstrous masse of earthly slyme,
　　Puft up with emptie wynd, and fild with sinfull cryme.

10　　So growen great through arrogant delight
　　　Of th'high descent, whereof he was yborne,
　　　And through presumption of his matchlesse might,
　　　All other powres and knighthood he did scorne.
　　　Such now he marcheth to this man forlorne,
　　　And left to losse: his stalking steps are stayde
　　　Upon a snaggy Oke, which he had torne
　　　Out of his mothers bowelles, and it made
　　His mortall mace, wherewith his foemen he dismayde.

11　　That when the knight he spyde, he gan advaunce
　　　With huge force and insupportable mayne,[5]
　　　And towardes him with dreadfull fury praunce;
　　　Who haplesse, and eke hopelesse; all in vaine
　　　Did to him pace, sad battaile to darrayne,[6]
　　　Disarmd, disgraste, and inwardly dismayde,
　　　And eke so faint in every joynt and vayne,
　　　Through that fraile fountain, which him feeble made,
　　That scarsely could he weeld his bootlesse single blade.

12　　The Geaunt strooke so maynly[7] mercilesse,
　　　That could have overthrowne a stony towre,
　　　And were not hevenly grace, that him did blesse,

---

[1] Aeolus is the god of the winds, and the earth is here sufficiently personified to resemble Gaia, goddess of the earth, in bringing forth giants.

[2] **inspyre:** in its Latin meaning of "breathe into."

[3] Renaissance scientists thought earthquakes were explosions caused by wind in the inner passages of the earth; they were taken as monitory of the Last Judgment. To this extent, Orgoglio represents a punishment.

[4] **expyre:** breathe out, appropriate for a wind; loosely, give birth.

[5] **mayne:** might.

[6] **darrayne:** start a battle "in order to vindicate a claim (a legal term)" (ACH).

[7] **maynly:** mightily.

He had beene pouldred[1] all, as thin as flowre:
But he was wary of that deadly stowre,
And lightly lept from underneath the blow:
Yet so exceeding was the villeins powre
That with the winde it did him overthrow,
And all his sences stoond,[2] that still he lay full low.

13　　As when that divelish yron Engin[3] wrought
　　　In deepest Hell, and framd by *Furies*[4] skill,
　　　With windy Nitre and quick Sulphur fraught,
　　　And ramd with bollet[5] rownd, ordaind to kill,
　　　Conceiveth fyre, the heavens it doth fill
　　　With thundring noyse, and all the ayre doth choke,
　　　That none can breath, nor see, nor heare at will,
　　　Through smouldry cloud of duskish stincking smok,
　　That th'onely breath[6] him daunts, who hath escapt the stroke.

14　　So daunted when the Geaunt saw the knight,
　　　His heavie hand he heaved up on hye,
　　　And him to dust thought to have battred quight,
　　　Untill *Duessa* loud to him gan crye;
　　　"O great *Orgoglio,* greatest under skye,
　　　O hold thy mortall hand for Ladies sake,
　　　Hold for my sake, and doe him not to dye,
　　　But vanquisht thine eternall bondslave make,
　　And me thy worthy meed unto thy Leman[7] take."

15　　He hearkned, and did stay from further harmes,
　　　To gayne so goodly guerdon,[8] as she spake:
　　　So willingly she came into his armes,
　　　Who her as willingly to grace did take,

---

[1] **pouldred:** pulverized.

[2] **stoond:** stunned. Arthur will be able to withstand a similar maneuver from Orgoglio and turn it to his advantage; see viii.7–10.

[3] Many late-medieval and Renaissance writers deplored firearms in general and cannons in particular. See *OF,* 2.28–31, 88–91.

[4] *Furies:* usually spirits that arrange for retribution, though here the meaning is vaguer, something like spirits of evil. See iii.36.8.

[5] **bollet:** a variant spelling of "bullet," here in the now-obsolete sense of cannonball.

[6] **th'onely breath:** the blast alone, not the ball.

[7] **Leman:** female paramour.

[8] **guerdon:** reward; see also iii.40.3.

And was possessed of his newfound make.[1]
Then up he tooke the slombred sencelesse corse,
And ere he could out of his swowne awake,
Him to his castle brought with hastie forse,
And in a Dongeon deep him threw without remorse.

16   From that day forth *Duessa* was his deare,
       And highly honourd in his haughtie eye,
       He gave her gold and purple pall[2] to weare,
       And triple crowne set on her head full hye,
       And her endowd with royall majestye:[3]
       Then for to make her dreaded more of men,
       And peoples hartes with awfull terror tye,
       A monstrous beast ybredd in filthy fen
He chose, which he had kept long time in darksom den.

17   Such one it was, as that renowmed Snake
       Which great *Alcides*[4] in *Stremona* slew,
       Long fostred in the filth of *Lerna* lake,
       Whose many heades out budding ever new,
       Did breed him endlesse labor to subdew:[5]
       But this same Monster much more ugly was;
       For seven great heads out of his body grew,
       An yron brest, and back of scaly bras,
And all embrewd[6] in blood, his eyes did shine as glas.

---

[1] **make:** mate, match.

[2] **purple pall:** purple robe, symbol of royalty.

[3] Duessa already had significantly fancy clothes; see ii.13.1ff. and note ad loc. For her new clothes and equipment, see Rev. 17.3–4: "And I saw a woman sit upon a skarlet-coloured beast, full of names of blasphemie, which had seven heads and ten hornes. And the woman was arrayed in purple and skarlet,[b] and gilded with gold, and precious stones and pearls, and had a cup of gold in her hand, full of abominations and filthiness of her fornication." Geneva Bible's gloss *b:* "A skarlet colour, that is with a red and purple garment: and surely it was not without cause that the Romish clergie were so much delighted with this colour." The seven heads of the whore's beast symbolize, among other things, the seven hills of Rome; see Geneva gloss on Rev. 17.9: "The seven heads,[c] are seven mountaines whereon the woman sitteth." Gloss *c:* "Very children knowe, what that seven hilled citie is, which is so much spoken of."

[4] *Alcides:* Hercules, who slew the Lernean Hydra.

[5] **endlesse labor to subdew:** the Hydra kept sprouting new heads to replace the damaged ones.

[6] **embrewd:** thoroughly soaked.

18 His tayle was stretched out in wondrous length,
  That to the hous of hevenly gods it raught,[1]
  And with extorted powre, and borrow'd strength,
  The everburning lamps from thence it braught,
  And prowdly threw to ground, as things of naught;
  And underneath his filthy feet did tread,
  The sacred thinges, and holy heastes foretaught.[2]
  Upon this dreadfull Beast with sevenfold head
He sett the false *Duessa*, for more aw and dread.

19 The wofull Dwarfe, which saw his maisters fall,
  Whiles he had keeping of his grasing steed,
  And valiant knight become a caytive[3] thrall,
  When all was past, tooke up his forlorne weed,
  His mightie Armour, missing most at need;[4]
  His silver shield, now idle maisterlesse;
  His poynant[5] speare, that many made to bleed,
  The ruefull moniments of heavinesse,[6]
And with them all departes, to tell his great distresse.

20 He had not travaild long, when on the way
  He wofull Lady, wofull *Una* met,
  Fast flying from the Paynims greedy pray,[7]
  Whilest *Satyrane* him from pursuit did let:[8]
  Who when her eyes she on the Dwarf had set,
  And saw the signes, that deadly tydinges spake,
  She fell to ground for sorrowfull regret,
  And lively breath her sad brest did forsake,
Yet might her pitteous hart be seen to pant and quake.

21 The messenger of so unhappie newes,
  Would faine have dyde: dead was his hart within,
  Yet outwardly some little comfort shewes:

---

[1] **raught:** variant form of "reached"; see also vi.29.2.

[2] **heastes foretaught:** commandments taught long ago. The prehensile tail comes from a seven-headed dragon described in Rev. 12.3–4 and associated with the devil: "beholde a great red dragon, having seven heads and ten hornes, and seven crownes upon his heads: And his taile drew the third part of the starres of heaven, and cast them to the earth."

[3] **caytive:** captive; in a moral sense it can mean base, as in v.11.1.

[4] I.e., missing when most needed.

[5] **poynant:** sharp.

[6] **moniments of heavinesse:** reminders or memorials of a loss.

[7] **pray:** here, preying, predation.

[8] **let:** prevent.

At last recovering hart, he does begin
To rubb her temples, and to chaufe her chin,
And everie tender part does tosse and turne:
So hardly[1] he the flitted life does win,
Unto her native prison to retourne:
Then gins her grieved ghost[2] thus to lament and mourne.

22   "Ye dreary instruments of dolefull sight,
That doe this deadly spectacle behold,
Why do ye lenger feed on loathed light,
Or liking find to gaze on earthly mould,[3]
Sith cruell fates the carefull[4] threds unfould,
The which my life and love together tyde?[5]
Now let the stony dart of sencelesse cold
Perce to my hart, and pas through everie side,
And let eternall night so sad sight fro me hide.

23   "O lightsome day, the lampe of highest *Jove*,
First made by him, mens wandring wayes to guyde,
When darknesse he in deepest dongeon drove,
Henceforth thy hated face for ever hyde,
And shut up heavens windowes shyning wyde:
For earthly sight can nought but sorow breed,
And late repentance, which shall long abyde.
Mine eyes no more on vanitie shall feed,
But seeled up with death, shall have their deadly meed."

24   Then downe againe she fell unto the ground;
But he her quickly reared up againe:
Thrise did she sinke adowne in deadly swownd,
And thrise he her reviv'd with busie paine:
At last when life recover'd had the raine,[6]
And over-wrestled his strong enimy,

---

[1] **hardly:** with difficulty.

[2] **ghost:** spirit.

[3] **earthly mould:** material things.

[4] **sith:** since; **carefull:** burdened with cares.

[5] An elliptical metaphor. The fates spin everyone's life as a thread or, here, a cord of threads. In Una's cord, the thread of love is knotted to—i.e., essential to—the thread of life, so that she feels that if she were to lose her beloved, she must die. But now the fates are unfolding—i.e., untying—the two, forcing her to go on living without her love.

[6] **raine:** reign, one of several possible spellings.

With foltring tong, and trembling everie vaine,
"Tell on" (quoth she) "the wofull Tragedy,
The which these reliques sad present unto mine eye.

25   "Tempestuous fortune hath spent all her spight,
        And thrilling sorrow throwne his utmost dart;
        Thy sad tong cannot tell more heavy plight,
        Then that I feele, and harbour in mine hart:
        Who hath endur'd the whole, can beare ech part.
        If death it be, it is not the first wound,
        That launched hath my brest with bleeding smart.
        Begin, and end the bitter balefull stound;[1]
If lesse, then that I feare, more favour I have found."

26   Then gan the Dwarfe the whole discourse declare,
        The subtile traines of *Archimago* old;
        The wanton loves of false *Fidessa* fayre,
        Bought with the blood of vanquisht Paynim bold:
        The wretched payre transformd to treen mould;[2]
        The house of *Pryde,* and perilles round about;
        The combat, which he with *Sansjoy* did hould;
        The lucklesse conflict with the Gyaunt stout,
Wherein captiv'd, of life or death he stood in doubt.

27   She heard with patience all unto the end,
        And strove to maister sorrowfull assay,[3]
        Which greater grew, the more she did contend,
        And almost rent her tender hart in tway;
        And love fresh coles unto her fire did lay:
        For greater love, the greater is the losse.
        Was never Lady loved dearer day,
        Then she did love the knight of the *Redcrosse;*
For whose deare sake so many troubles her did tosse.

28   At last when fervent sorrow slaked was,
        She up arose, resolving him to find
        Alive or dead: and forward forth doth pas,
        All as the Dwarfe the way to her assynd:[4]

[1] **bitter balefull stound:** moment of sorrow; not that grief will cease, but that it will not hurt so much after the first moment.

[2] **treen mould:** the shape of trees.

[3] **assay:** trial.

[4] **All as:** just as; **assynd:** pointed out.

And evermore in constant carefull mind
She fedd her wound with fresh renewed bale;
Long tost with stormes, and bet[1] with bitter wind,
High over hills, and lowe adowne the dale,
She wandred many a wood, and measurd many a vale.

29   At last she chaunced by good hap to meet
A goodly knight, faire marching by the way[2]
Together with his Squyre, arayed meet:
His glitterand armour shined far away,
Like glauncing light of *Phoebus* brightest ray;
From top to toe no place appeared bare,
That deadly dint of steele endanger may:
Athwart his brest a bauldrick[3] brave he ware,
That shind, like twinkling stars, with stones most pretious rare.

30   And in the midst thereof one pretious stone
Of wondrous worth, and eke of wondrous mights,
Shapt like a Ladies head,[4] exceeding shone,
Like *Hesperus* emongst the lesser lights,[5]
And strove for to amaze the weaker sights;
Thereby his mortall blade full comely hong
In yvory sheath, ycarv'd with curious slights;[6]
Whose hilts were burnisht gold, and handle strong
Of mother perle, and buckled with a golden tong.[7]

31   His haughtie Helmet, horrid[8] all with gold,
Both glorious brightnesse, and great terrour bredd,
For all the crest a Dragon did enfold
With greedie pawes, and over all did spredd

[1] **bet:** beaten.

[2] This is the first appearance of Prince Arthur. He appears as a more perfect exemplar when the titular knight has lost control of a situation, here and in II.viii; he appears for other reasons in IV.viii, V.viii, and VI.vi.

[3] **bauldrick:** belt worn over the shoulder and diagonally across the chest to carry a sword.

[4] **Ladies head:** the head of Gloriana, the Faerie Queen, who is Arthur's beloved, as we learn in Canto Nine.

[5] *Hesperus:* the planet Venus; **lights:** stars.

[6] **curious slights:** elaborate designs. Spenser describes Arthur's armor at such length both because he represents magnificence ("Letter to Raleigh"), which, strictly defined, is the art of spending money well; and to contrast with Redcrosse's disarmed state when he approached Orgoglio.

[7] **tong:** tongue of the buckle.

[8] **horrid:** bristling.

His golden winges: his dreadfull hideous hedd
Close couched on the bever,[1] seemd to throw
From flaming mouth bright sparckles fiery redd,
That suddeine horrour to faint hartes did show;
And scaly tayle was stretcht adowne his back full low.[2]

32   Upon the top of all his loftie crest,
    A bounch of heares discolourd diversly,[3]
    With sprincled pearle, and gold full richly drest,
    Did shake, and seemd to daunce for jollity,
    Like to an Almond tree ymounted hye
    On top of greene *Selinis*[4] all alone,
    With blossoms brave bedecked daintily;
    Her tender locks do tremble every one
At everie little breath, that under heaven is blowne.[5]

33   His warlike shield all closely cover'd was,
    Ne might of mortall eye be ever seene;
    Not made of steele, nor of enduring bras,
    Such earthly mettals soone consumed beene:
    But all of Diamond perfect pure and cleene
    It framed was, one massy entire mould,[6]
    Hewen out of Adamant rocke[7] with engines keene,
    That point of speare it never percen could,
Ne dint of direfull sword divide the substance would.[8]

---

[1] This must mean the visor in the modern sense of that word. If its head were couched on the faceplate, the usual meaning of bever, then the faceplate could not be raised when necessary (see II.i.29.1–2).

[2] The caesura-less alexandrine mimes the trailing length of the tail (Kaske 1999, 37).

[3] **discolourd diversly:** of various colors. See ii.11.6, which describes the plume worn by Archimago when he is disguised as the Redcrosse Knight and hence, presumably, Redcrosse's plume as well.

[4] **green Selinis:** "from Virgil's *palmosa Selinus* (*Aeneid,* 3.705), the town of the victor's palm" (ACH). Since a tree is unlikely to be "on top of" a town, and "all alone" there, Spenser seems to have interpreted this town as a mountain.

[5] "Marlowe quotes these lines to describe Tamburlaine's triumphant appearance in *2 Tamburlaine* 4.3.119–24. See 'Marlowe' in *SE*" (ACH). Marlowe too thinks Selinus is a "celestial mount."

[6] **one massy entire mould:** shaped wholly of one single diamond, to render it more impenetrable.

[7] Diamond and adamant are two closely related stones, here treated as synonymous; the first is real, the second fictional, supposed to exceed all others in hardness.

[8] Arthur's shield is based on Raimondo's diamond shield in *GL,* 7.82, which Tasso himself glosses in his "Allegory of *Gerusalemme liberata*" as "The special custody of the Lord God" (158); on which also see Hankins, 1971, 32. See Ps. 84.11: "For the

34   The same to wight he never wont disclose,
      But when as monsters huge he would dismay,
      Or daunt unequall armies of his foes,[1]
      Or when the flying heavens he would affray:[2]
      For so exceeding shone his glistring ray,
      That *Phoebus* golden face it did attaint,
      As when a cloud his beames doth over-lay
      And silver *Cynthia* wexed pale and faynt,
As when her face is staynd with magicke arts constraint.[3]

35   No magicke arts hereof had any might,
      Nor bloody wordes of bold Enchaunters call,
      But all that was not such, as seemd in sight,
      Before that shield did fade, and suddeine fall:
      And when him list the raskall routes[4] appall,
      Men into stones therewith he could transmew,[5]
      And stones to dust, and dust to nought at all;
      And when him list the prouder lookes subdew
He would them gazing blind, or turne to other hew.

36   Ne let it seeme that credence this exceedes,
      For he that made the same, was knowne right well
      To have done much more admirable deedes.
      It *Merlin* was, which whylome did excell
      All living wightes in might of magicke spell:
      Both shield, and sword, and armour all he wrought
      For this young Prince, when first to armes he fell,
      But when he dyde, the Faery Queene it brought
To Faerie lond, where yet it may be seene, if sought.

Lord God is the sunne and shielde unto us." As such, it symbolizes God's answer to faith. Fidelia, or faith, works some of the same miracles as does this shield; see x.20 and note below. Faith is what Redcrosse's shield symbolizes, according to the "Letter to Raleigh," which cites Eph. 6.16, and, as we have seen, the Saracen Sansfoy affirms that the cross on it and on Redcrosse's breastplate magically protect Redcrosse.

[1] Faith has "turned to flight the armies of the aliantes [aliens]" (Heb. 11.34).

[2] In the Ptolemaic system, the visible heavens revolve around the earth and, given their size, were thought to go very fast. To affray them would be to damage them, for example, to make them stop or go backward.

[3] Magicians were believed to have the power to cause eclipses—i.e., to stain Cynthia (the moon) with "magicke arts." See VII.vi.16.5. Fidelia, or faith, by her explicitly Christian magic, can even make the sun stop or go backward; see x.20.2–3.

[4] **raskall routes:** crowds of lower-class people.

[5] **transmew:** transmute.

37   A gentle youth, his dearely loved Squire[1]
            His speare of heben[2] wood behind him bare,
            Whose harmful head, thrise heated in the fire,
            Had riven many a brest with pikehead square;
            A goodly person, and could menage[3] faire,
            His stubborne steed with curbed canon bitt,[4]
            Who under him did amble as the aire,[5]
            And chauft, that any on his backe should sitt;
        The yron rowels[6] into frothy fome he bitt.

38   Whenas this knight nigh to the Lady drew,
            With lovely court he gan her entertaine;
            But when he heard her aunswers loth, he knew
            Some secret sorrow did her heart distraine:[7]
            Which to allay and calme her storming paine,
            Faire feeling words he wisely gan display,
            And for her humor fitting purpose faine,[8]
            To tempt the cause it selfe for to bewray;[9]
        Wherewith emmovd, these bleeding words she gan to say.

39   "What worlds delight, or joy of living speach
            Can hart, so plungd in sea of sorrowes deep,
            And heaped with so huge misfortunes, reach?
            The carefull cold beginneth for to creep,
            And in my heart his yron arrow steep,[10]
            Soone as I thinke upon my bitter bale:
            Such helplesse harmes yts better hidden keep,
            Then rip up griefe, where it may not availe,
        My last left comfort is, my woes to weepe and waile."

---

[1] Arthur's squire is named Timias (Greek: "honoured"), and he reappears in Books Three, Four, and Six. He functions as a low-grade version of Arthur, an understudy, to whom calamities happen that might have happened to Arthur, had the latter been less outstanding than he is.

[2] **heben:** ebon, of ebony.

[3] **menage:** control, equestrian term.

[4] **curbed canon bitt:** smooth, round bit (M&P).

[5] The 1596 edition has "trample" in place of "amble," which befits the spirited nature of this horse, but does not accord with "as the aire." A case could be made for either one.

[6] **rowels:** ends of the bit.

[7] **distraine:** distress.

[8] **purpose:** topic of conversation; **faine:** here, a variant spelling of "feign," meaning contrive.

[9] **bewray:** manifest.

[10] **steep:** soak, allow to remain in one place for a long time.

40   "Ah Lady deare," quoth then the gentle knight,
       "Well may I ween, your grief is wondrous great;
       For wondrous great griefe groneth in my spright,
       Whiles thus I heare you of your sorrowes treat.
       But woefull Lady, let me you intrete,
       For to unfold the anguish of your hart:
       Mishaps are maistred by advice discrete,
       And counsell mitigates the greatest smart;
Found never help, who never would his hurts impart."

41   "O but" (quoth she) "great griefe will not be tould,
       And can more easily be thought, then said."
       "Right so" (quoth he) "but he, that never would,
       Could never: will to might gives greatest aid."
       "But griefe" (quoth she) "does greater grow displaid,
       If then it find not helpe, and breeds despaire."
       "Despaire breeds not" (quoth he) "where faith is staid."[1]
       "No faith so fast" (quoth she) "but flesh does paire."[2]
"Flesh may empaire" (quoth he) "but reason can repaire."

42   His goodly reason, and well guided speach
       So deepe did settle in her gracious thought,
       That her perswaded to disclose the breach,
       Which love and fortune in her heart had wrought,
       And said "faire Sir, I hope good hap hath brought
       You to inquere the secrets of my griefe,
       Or that your wisedome will direct my thought,
       Or that your prowesse can me yield reliefe:
Then heare the story sad, which I shall tell you briefe.

43   "The forlorne Maiden, whom your eies have seene
       The laughing stocke of fortunes mockeries,
       Am th'onely daughter of a King and Queene,
       Whose parents deare whiles equal destinies,
       Did ronne about, and their felicities
       The favourable heavens did not envy,

---

[1] **staid:** variant spelling of "stayed"; propped.

[2] **paire:** impair. This exchange is a stichomythia: a "dialogue in alternate lines, employed in sharp disputation, and characterized by antithesis and . . . taking up of the opponent's words" (OED).

Did spred their rule through all the territories,
Which *Phison* and *Euphrates* floweth by,
And *Gehons* golden waves doe wash continually.[1]

44   "Till that their cruell cursed enemy,
An huge great Dragon horrible in sight,
Bred in the loathly lakes of *Tartary*,[2]
With murdrous ravine, and devouring might
Their kingdome spoild, and countrey wasted quight:
Themselves, for feare into his jawes to fall,
He forst to castle strong to take their flight,
Where fast embard in mighty brasen wall,
He has them now fowr years besiegd to make them thrall.[3]

45   "Full many knights adventurous and stout
Have enterprizd that Monster to subdew;
From every coast that heaven walks about,
Have thither come the noble Martial crew,
That famous harde atchievements still pursew,
Yet never any could that girlond win,
But all still shronke, and still he greater grew:
All they for want of faith, or guilt of sin,
The pitteous pray of his fiers cruelty have bin.

46   "At last yled with far reported praise,
Which flying fame throughout the world had spred,
Of doughty knights, whom Fary land did raise,
That noble order hight of maidenhed,[4]
Forthwith to court of *Gloriane* I sped,
Of *Gloriane* great Queene of glory bright,

[1] Phison, Euphrates, and Gehon are three of the four rivers of Paradise, the fourth river being Hiddekel. See Gen. 2.10–4.

[2] *Tartary:* Tartarus, Hell.

[3] This is an account of the fall of mankind—a skewed one, in that it puts all the blame upon Satan and pictures his assault as physical. He, not God, expels Adam and Eve from Paradise into a brazen tower that resembles the gate of Hell and the gate of Hell's vestibule, Limbo—the place of the virtuous souls before Christ's redemption, as in the legend of the Harrowing of Hell.

[4] The Order of Maidenhead is the order of knights in Faerie Land, foreshadowing the Knights of the Garter, the highest order of knights in England. The emblem of the Knights of the Garter was a figure of St. George slaying the dragon. See II.ii.42; IV.iv 22–48 passim; and V.iv.29.

Whose kingdomes seat *Cleopolis*[1] is red,
There to obtaine some such redoubted knight,
That Parents deare from tyrants powre deliver might.

47   "Yt was my chaunce (my chaunce was faire and good)
       There for to find a fresh unproved knight,
       Whose manly hands imbrewd[2] in guilty blood
       Had never beene, ne ever by his might
       Had throwne to ground the unregarded[3] right:
       Yet of his prowesse proofe he since hath made
       (I witnes am) in many a cruell fight;
       The groning ghosts of many one dismaide
Have felt the bitter dint of his avenging blade.

48   "And ye the forlorne reliques of his powre,
       His biting sword, and his devouring speare,
       Which have endured many a dreadfull stowre,
       Can speake his prowesse, that did earst you beare,
       And well could rule: now he hath left you heare,
       To be the record of his ruefull losse,
       And of my dolefull disaventurous deare:[4]
       O heavie record of the good *Redcrosse*,
Where have yee left your lord, that could so well you tosse?[5]

49   "Well hoped I, and faire beginnings had,
       That he my captive languor should redeeme,[6]
       Till all unweeting, an Enchaunter bad
       His sence abusd, and made him to misdeeme
       My loyalty, not such as it did seeme
       That rather death desire, then such despight.
       Be judge ye heavens, that all things right esteeme,
       How I him lov'd, and love with all my might,
So thought I eke[7] of him, and think I thought aright.

---

[1] Meaning "fame-city," capital of Faerie Land.

[2] **imbrewd:** steeped or stained.

[3] **unregarded:** not respected.

[4] **disaventurous deare:** unlucky lover.

[5] **tosse:** wield, handle.

[6] I.e., that he should redeem or deliver me from the captivity in which I languished. This could mean that she was imprisoned along with her parents initially and somehow managed to sneak away, or else "captive languor" is just a metaphor for her state of mind.

[7] **eke:** also.

50   "Thenceforth me desolate he quite forsooke,
           To wander, where wilde fortune would me lead,
           And other bywaies he himselfe betooke,
           Where never foote of living wight did tread,
           That brought not backe the balefull body dead;
           In which him chaunced false *Duessa* meete,
           Mine onely foe, mine onely deadly dread,
           Who with her witchcraft and misseeming sweete,
       Inveigled him to follow her desires unmeete.[1]

51   "At last by subtile sleights she him betraid
           Unto his foe, a Gyaunt huge and tall,
           Who him disarmed, dissolute, dismaid,
           Unwares surprised, and with mighty mall[2]
           The monster mercilesse him made to fall,
           Whose fall did never foe before behold;
           And now in darkesome dungeon, wretched thrall,
           Remedilesse, for aie[3] he doth him hold;
       This is my cause of griefe, more great, then may be told."

52   Ere she had ended all, she gan to faint:
           But he her comforted, and faire bespake,
           "Certes, Madame, ye have great cause of plaint,
           That stoutest heart, I weene, could cause to quake.
           But be of cheare, and comfort to you take:
           For till I have acquitt your captive knight,
           Assure your selfe, I will you not forsake."
           His chearefull words reviv'd her chearelesse spright,
       So forth they went, the Dwarfe them guiding ever right.

---

[1] **unmeete:** inappropriate.   [3] **for aie:** for aye, forever.
[2] **mall:** club, the uprooted oak tree.

Canto Eight

Faire virgin to redeeme her deare
Brings Arthure to the fight:
Who slayes the Gyaunt, wounds the beast,
And strips Duessa quight.

1   Ay me, how many perils doe enfold
      The righteous man, to make him daily fall,
      Were not that heavenly grace doth him uphold,
      And stedfast truth acquite him out of all:
      Her love is firme, her care continuall,
      So oft as he thorough his own foolish pride,
      Or weaknes is to sinfull bands[1] made thrall:
      Els should this *Redcrosse* knight in bands have dyde,
For whose deliverance she this Prince doth thether guyd.[2]

2   They sadly traveild thus, untill they came
      Nigh to a castle builded strong and hye:
      Then cryde the Dwarfe, "lo yonder is the same,
      In which my Lord my liege doth lucklesse ly,
      Thrall to that Gyaunts hatefull tyranny:
      Therefore, deare Sir, your mightie powres assay."
      The noble knight alighted by and by
      From loftie steed, and badd the Ladie stay,
To see what end of fight should him befall that day.

---

[1] **bands:** bonds, here both physical and moral.

[2] Prov. 24.16: "For a just man falleth seven times, and riseth againe, but the wicked fall into mischief." This moralizing stanza confirms the identification of Una as Truth or the True Church, or, in a general way, the Christian God as active lover of human beings. By concluding with "this prince," it may identify Arthur with "heavenly grace," giving him yet another role besides magnificence or magnanimity ("Letter to Raleigh"). This meaning accords with his activities in Books One and Two, though not elsewhere, and combines well with the overtones of Christ about Arthur in this canto, e.g., the way he conquers by falling, and goes down "a deepe descent as dark as hell" to rescue Redcrosse (39.8).

3   So with his Squire, th'admirer of his might,
          He marched forth towardes that castle wall;
          Whose gates he fownd fast shutt, ne living wight
          To warde the same, nor answere commers call.
          Then tooke that Squire an horne of bugle small,[1]
          Which hong adowne his side in twisted gold,
          And tasselles gay. Wyde wonders over all
          Of that same hornes great vertues weren told,
      Which had approved[2] bene in uses manifold.

4   Was never wight, that heard that shrilling sownd,
          But trembling feare did feel in every vaine;
          Three miles it might be easy heard arownd,
          And Ecchoes three aunswerd it selfe againe:
          No false enchauntment, nor deceiptfull traine
          Might once abide the terror of that blast,
          But presently was void and wholly vaine:
          No gate so strong, no locke so firme and fast,
      But with that percing noise flew open quite, or brast.[3]

5   The same before the Geaunts gate he blew,
          That all the castle quaked from the grownd,
          And every dore of freewill open flew:
          The Gyaunt selfe dismaied with that sownd,
          Where he with his *Duessa* dalliaunce fownd,
          In hast came rushing forth from inner bowre,
          With staring countenance sterne, as one astownd,[4]
          And staggering steps, to weet, what suddein stowre,
      Had wrought that horror strange, and dar'd his dreaded powre.

6   And after him the proud *Duessa* came,
          High mounted on her many headed beast,[5]
          And every head with fyrie tongue did flame,
          And every head was crowned on his creast,
          And bloody mouthed with late cruell feast.
          That when the knight beheld, his mightie shild

---

[1] Literally, "bugle" is the entire horn of the wild ox, used as a hunting horn. Some critics allegorize the notes of the horn as the preaching of the gospel.

[2] **approved:** tested, proved by experience.

[3] **brast:** burst.

[4] **astownd:** stunned.

[5] For Duessa's beast, see note to vii.16.5.

Upon his manly arme he soone addrest,[1]
And at him fiersly flew, with corage fild,
And eger greedinesse through every member thrild.

7   Therewith the Gyant buckled him to fight,
     Inflamd with scornefull wrath and high disdaine,
     And lifting up his dreadfull club on hight,
     All armd with ragged snubbes[2] and knottie graine,
     Him thought[3] at first encounter to have slaine.
     But wise and wary was that noble Pere,
     And lightly leaping from so monstrous maine,[4]
     Did fayre avoide the violence him nere;
It booted nought, to thinke, such thunderbolts to beare.

8   Ne shame he thought to shonne so hideous might,
     The ydle[5] stroke, enforcing furious way,
     Missing the marke of his misaymed sight
     Did fall to ground, and with his heavy sway[6]
     So deepely dinted in the driven clay,
     That three yardes deepe a furrow up did throw:
     The sad earth wounded with so sore assay,
     Did grone full grievous underneath the blow,
And trembling with strange feare, did like an erthquake show.

9   As when almightie *Jove* in wrathfull mood,
     To wreake the guilt of mortall sins is bent,
     Hurles forth his thundring dart with deadly food,[7]
     Enrold in flames, and smouldring dreriment,
     Through riven cloudes and molten firmament;
     The fiers threeforked engin[8] making way,
     Both loftie towres and highest trees hath rent,
     And all that might his angry passage stay,
And shooting in the earth, castes up a mound of clay.

---

[1] **addrest:** made ready.

[2] **snubbes:** projecting bits of root; see also vii.10.7.

[3] **Him thought:** the verb is impersonal: it seemed to Orgoglio that he would slay Arthur at his first encounter.

[4] **maine:** power.

[5] **ydle:** ineffectual.

[6] **sway:** momentum.

[7] **food:** feud.

[8] **engin:** weapon, meaning the lightning.

10   His boystrous[1] club, so buried in the grownd,
    He could not rearen up againe so light,
    But that the knight him at advantage fownd,
    And whiles he strove his combred clubbe to quight,
    Out of the earth, with blade all burning bright
    He smott off his left arme, which like a block
    Did fall to ground, depriv'd of native might;
    Large streames of blood out of the truncked stock
Forth gushed, like fresh water streame from riven rocke.

11   Dismayed with so desperate deadly wound,
    And eke impatient of unwonted payne,
    He lowdly brayd with beastly yelling sownd,
    That all the fieldes rebellowed againe,
    As great a noyse, as when in Cymbrian plaine[2]
    An heard of Bulles, whom kindly rage doth sting,
    Doe for the milky mothers want complaine,
    And fill the fieldes with troublous bellowing,
The neighbor woods arownd with hollow murmur ring.

12   That when his deare *Duessa* heard, and saw
    The evill stownd, that daungerd her estate,
    Unto his aide she hastily did draw
    Her dreadfull beast, who swolne with blood of late
    Came ramping[3] forth with proud presumpteous gate,
    And threatned all his heades like flaming brandes.
    But him the Squire made quickly to retrate,
    Encountring fiers with single sword in hand,
And twixt him and his Lord did like a bulwarke stand.

13   The proud *Duessa* full of wrathfull spight,
    And fiers disdaine, to be affronted so,
    Enforst her purple beast with all her might
    That stop[4] out of the way to overthroe,
    Scorning the let[5] of so unequall foe:
    But nathemore[6] would that corageous swayne

---

[1] **boystrous:** rough and massive.

[2] The Cimbri were a savage Teutonic tribe occupying Denmark and Norway (M&P; ACH).

[3] **ramping:** rearing for attack, like the lion in iii.5.2.

[4] **that stop:** that obstacle; i.e., Timias.

[5] **the let:** the hindrance.

[6] **nathemore:** not for all that.

> To her yeeld passage, gainst his Lord to goe,
> But with outrageous strokes did him restraine,
> And with his body bard the way atwixt them twaine.

14 Then tooke the angrie witch her golden cup,
> Which still she bore, replete with magick artes;[1]
> Death and despeyre did many thereof sup,
> And secret poyson through their inner partes,
> Th'eternall bale of heavie wounded harts;
> Which after charmes and some enchauntments said,[2]
> She lightly sprinkled on his weaker partes;
> Therewith his sturdie corage soone was quayd,[3]
> And all his sences were with suddein dread dismayd.

15 So downe he fell before the cruell beast,
> Who on his neck his bloody clawes did seize,
> That life nigh crusht out of his panting brest:
> No powre he had to stirre, nor will to rize.
> That when the carefull knight gan well avise,
> He lightly left the foe, with whom he fought,
> And to the beast gan turne his enterprise;
> For wondrous anguish in his hart it wrought,
> To see his loved Squyre into such thraldom brought.

16 And high aduauncing his blood-thirstie blade,
> Stroke one of those deformed headed[4] so sore,
> That of his puissaunce proud ensample made;
> His monstrous scalpe downe to his teeth it tore,
> And that misformed shape misshaped more:
> A sea of blood gusht from the gaping wownd,

---

[1] This is Spenser's first mention of Duessa's golden cup, which recalls the gold cup of Revelation "full of abominations, and filthines of her fornication" (Rev. 17.4), which signifies, according to M&P, "the Catholic Mass and what Protestants thought the false and pseudomagical doctrine of transubstantiation," i.e., the doctrine that when the priest says the words of consecration, the bread and wine become Christ. Retrospectively this reveals Archimago's general association with magic—which at the time characterized him as merely the devil in his role as tempter—to be a Roman Catholic trait (i.36ff; ii.Arg.1). Cf. Fidelia's golden cup in x.13. For other portrayals of the Whore in this pose that Spenser must have known, see *SE*, "Theatre for Worldlings."

[2] Duessa's "charmes" and "enchauntments" symbolize the words of consecration.

[3] **quayd:** subdued.

[4] A literal echo of Rev. 13.3: "And I sawe one of his heads as it were wounded to death."

That her[1] gay garments staynd with filthy gore,
And overflowed all the field arownd;
That over shoes in blood he waded on the grownd.

17   Thereat he rored for exceeding paine,
That to have heard, great horror would have bred,
And scourging th'emptie ayre with his long trayne,
Through great impatience of his grieved hed
His gorgeous ryder from her loftie sted
Would have cast downe, and trodd in durty myre,
Had not the Gyaunt soone her succoured;
Who all enrag'd with smart and frantick yre,
Came hurtling in full fiers, and forst the knight retyre.

18   The force, which wont in two to be disperst,
In one alone left[2] hand he now unites,
Which is through rage more strong then both were erst;
With which his hideous club aloft he dites,[3]
And at his foe with furious rigor smites,
That strongest Oake might seeme to overthrow:
The stroke upon his shield so heavie lites,
That to the ground it doubleth him full low
What mortall wight could ever beare so monstrous blow?

19   And in his fall his shield, that covered was,[4]
Did loose his vele by chaunce, and open flew:
The light whereof, that hevens light did pas,
Such blazing brightnesse through the ayer threw,
That eye mote[5] not the same endure to vew.
Which when the Gyaunt spyde with staring eye,
He downe let fall his arme, and soft withdrew
His weapon huge, that heaved was on hye,
For to have slain the man, that on the ground did lye.

---

[1] I.e., Duessa's.

[2] **left:** both left as opposed to right and left as remaining; pun.

[3] **dites:** lifts, raises; an erroneous usage by Spenser (OED, 16).

[4] The action parallels that of Ruggiero's accidentally uncovered shield in *OF,* 22.84–7. Here, it symbolizes that God's grace shines out when the hero is at his weakest, suggesting the way Christ conquered through defeat and suffering.

[5] **mote:** might.

20   And eke the fruitfull-headed[1] beast, amazd
        At flashing beames of that sunshiny shield,
        Became stark blind, and all his sences dazd
        That downe he tumbled on the durtie field,
        And seemd himselfe as conquered to yield.
        Whom when his maistresse proud perceiv'd to fall,
        Whiles yet his feeble feet for faintnesse reeld,
        Unto the Gyaunt lowdly she gan call,
"O helpe *Orgoglio*, helpe, or els we perish all."

21   At her so pitteous cry was much amoov'd,
        Her champion stout, and for to ayde his frend,
        Againe his wonted angry weapon proov'd:[2]
        But all in vaine: for he has redd his end
        In that bright shield, and all their forces spend
        Them selves in vaine: for since that glauncing[3] sight,
        He hath no poure to hurt, nor to defend;
        As where th'Almighties lightning brond does light,
It dimmes the dazed eyen, and daunts the sences quight.

22   Whom when the Prince, to batteill new addrest,
        And threatning high his dreadfull stroke did see,
        His sparkling blade about his head he blest,[4]
        And smote off quite his right leg by the knee,
        That downe he tombled; as an aged tree,
        High growing on the top of rocky clift,
        Whose hartstrings with keene steele nigh hewen be,
        The mightie trunck halfe rent, with ragged rift
Doth roll adowne the rocks, and fall with fearefull drift.[5]

23   Or as a Castle reared high and round,
        By subtile engins and malitious slight[6]
        Is undermined from the lowest ground,
        And her foundation forst,[7] and feebled quight,
        At last downe falles, and with her heaped hight
        Her hastie ruine does more heavie make,

---

[1] **fruitfull-headed:** many-headed, suggesting fruits on a tree.

[2] **proov'd:** here, put to use.

[3] **glauncing:** flashing.

[4] **blest:** brandished.

[5] **drift:** momentum.

[6] **slight:** trick.

[7] **forst:** penetrated.

> And yields it selfe unto the victours might;
> Such was this Gyaunts fall, that seemd to shake
> The stedfast globe of earth, as it for feare did quake.

24   The knight then lightly leaping to the pray,
> With mortall steele him smot againe so sore,
> That headlesse his unweldy bodie lay,
> All wallowd in his owne fowle bloody gore,
> Which flowed from his wounds in wondrous store.
> But soone as breath out of his breast did pas,
> That huge great body, which the Gyaunt bore,
> Was vanisht quite, and of that monstrous mas
> Was nothing left, but like an emptie blader was.[1]

25   Whose grievous fall, when false *Duessa* spyde,
> Her golden cup she cast unto the ground,
> And crowned mitre[2] rudely threw asyde;
> Such percing griefe her stubborne hart did wound,
> That she could not endure that dolefull stound,
> But leaving all behind her, fled away:
> The light-foot Squyre her quickly turnd around,
> And by hard meanes enforcing her to stay,
> So brought unto his Lord, as his deserved pray.

26   The roiall Virgin, which beheld from farre,
> In pensive plight, and sad perplexitie,
> The whole atchievement of this doubtfull[3] warre,
> Came running fast to greet his victorie,
> With sober gladnesse, and myld modestie,
> And with sweet joyous cheare him thus bespake;
> "Fayre braunch of noblesse, flowre of chevalrie,
> That with your worth the world amazed make,
> How shall I quite[4] the paynes, ye suffer for my sake?

---

[1] Besides being a powerful image of the downfall of anyone who is proud (see *Colin Clout,* 715–8), this line suggests detumescence and hints that one of Orgoglio's many meanings is as an erect phallus, which is appropriate to Redcrosse's activity in the previous episode. In line with this, ACH explains that the name "Orgoglio" is Italian for "Pride," and the Greek verb that sounds like it means "to be swollen with lust," suggesting that he "is man 'rashly puft up with his fleshly minde' (Col. 2.18)." M&P give a similar interpretation and secondary sources in their survey of Orgoglio's many meanings at vii.9.

[2] **crowned mitre:** the triple tiara of the popes.

[3] **doubtfull:** hotly contested.

[4] **quite:** repay.

27   "And you[1] fresh budd of vertue springing fast,
            Whom these sad eyes saw nigh unto deaths dore,
            What hath poore Virgin for such perill past,
            Wherewith you to reward? Accept therefore
            My simple selfe, and service evermore:
            And he that high does sit, and all things see
            With equall eye, their merites to restore,
            Behold what ye this day have done for mee,
And what I cannot quite, requite with usuree.[2]

28   "But sith the heavens, and your faire handeling
            Have made you master of the field this day,
            Your fortune maister eke with governing,
            And well begonne end all so well, I pray,
            Ne let that wicked woman scape away;
            For she it is, that did my Lord bethrall,
            My dearest Lord, and deepe in dongeon lay,
            Where he his better dayes hath wasted all.
O heare, how piteous he to you for ayd does call."

29   Forthwith he gave in charge unto his Squyre,
            That scarlot whore to keepen carefully;
            Whyles he himselfe with greedie great desyre
            Into the Castle entred forcibly,
            Where living creature none he did espye;
            Then gan he lowdly through the house to call:
            But no man car'd to answere to his crye.
            There raignd a solemne silence over all,
Nor voice was heard, nor wight was seene in bowre or hall.

30   At last with creeping crooked pace forth came
            An old old man, with beard as white as snow,
            That on a staffe his feeble steps did frame,[3]
            And guyde his wearie gate both too and fro;
            For his eye sight him fayled long ygo,
            And on his arme a bounch of keyes he bore,

---

[1] I.e., Timias.

[2] **quite:** repay; **usuree:** interest. The distinction is unclear; perhaps to repay with usury means to repay with money.

[3] **frame:** manage to make.

The which unused rust did overgrow:
Those were the keyes of every inner dore,
But he could not them use, but kept them still in store.[1]

31   But very uncouth sight was to behold,
How he did fashion his untoward pace,
For as he forward moovd his footing old,
So backward still was turnd his wrincled face,
Unlike to men, who ever as they trace,
Both feet and face one way are wont to lead.[2]
This was the auncient keeper of that place,
And foster father of the Gyaunt dead;
His name *Ignaro* did his nature right aread.[3]

32   His reverend heares and holy gravitee
The knight much honord, as beseemed well,
And gently askt, where all the people bee,
Which in that stately building wont to dwell.
Who answerd him full soft, he could not tell.
Againe he askt, where that same knight was layd,
Whom great *Orgoglio* with his puissaunce fell
Had made his caytive thrall; againe he sayde,
He could not tell: ne ever other answere made.

33   Then asked he, which way he in might pas:
He could not tell, againe he answered.
Thereat the courteous knight displeased was,
And said, "Old syre, it seemes thou hast not red[4]
How ill it sits with that same silver hed,
In vaine to mocke, or mockt in vaine to bee:

---

[1] Ignaro and his useless keys are usually interpreted as the Catholic Church or clergy who have the keys to salvation—i.e., the scriptures, esp. the New Testament—but who do not know how to use or apply them because of ignorance.

[2] Ignaro's backward-looking head symbolizes the alleged Roman Catholic preoccupation with legalism and the Old Law, which was dismissed by Protestants as having been abrogated. The head symbolizes their insufficient appreciation of the radical newness of the New Testament (M&P), based as it is on spontaneous love. Ignaro's inability to say anything to the purpose links him to Abessa's utter speechlessness in Canto Three.

[3] **aread:** express. Ignaro's blindness relates him to Corceca in Canto Three; she too represents the ignorance of some Roman Catholics. For further details, see "Ignaro" in *SE*.

[4] **red:** learned.

> But if thou be, as thou art pourtrahed
> With natures pen,[1] in ages grave degree,
> Aread in graver wise, what I demaund of thee."

34   His answere likewise was, he could not tell.
    Whose sencelesse speach, and doted ignorance[2]
    When as the noble Prince had marked well,
    He ghest his nature by his countenance,
    And calmd his wrath with goodly temperance.
    Then to him stepping, from his arme did reach
    Those keyes, and made himselfe free enterance.[3]
    Each dore he opened without any breach;[4]
There was no barre to stop, nor foe him to empeach. [5]

35   There all within full rich arayd he found,
    With royall arras[6] and resplendent gold,
    And did with store of every thing abound,
    That greatest Princes presence might behold.
    But all the floore (too filthy to be told)
    With blood of guiltlesse babes, and innocents trew,
    Which there were slaine, as sheepe out of the fold,
    Defiled was, that dreadfull was to vew,
And sacred ashes over it was strowed new.[7]

---

[1] **pourtrahed with natures pen:** as your physical appearance indicates.

[2] **doted ignorance:** ignorance resulting from age, which has taken away his mind.

[3] The Scriptures, Spenser seems to be saying, must be appropriated forcibly by the laity, who had been forbidden to read them, not only by Catholics but, in one of his moods, even by Henry VIII.

[4] **breach:** forcing.

[5] **empeach:** oppose.

[6] **arras:** tapestries hung on walls to prevent drafts; they were often exceedingly beautiful and ornate.

[7] Referring to all who were killed on some religious charge. The babies suggest, among other things, the Slaughter of the Innocents in Matt. 2.16–8. The ashes suggests those martyrs who were burned, and the fact that they were scattered "new" suggests contemporaneous martyrdoms of Protestants by Catholics, esp. both in the St. Bartholomew's Day Massacre in Paris on August 24, 1572, and by the Spanish in the Netherlands, a subject treated in Book Five. See Rev. 6.9–10: "I saw under the altar the soules of them, that were killed for the worde of God, and for the testimonie which they maintained. And they cried with a lowde voyce, saying, How long, Lord, holie and true! doest not thou judge and avenge our blood on them that dwell on the earth?"

36   And there beside of marble stone was built
      An Altare, carv'd with cunning ymagery,
      On which trew Christians blood was often spilt,
      And holy Martyres often doen to dye,
      With cruell malice and strong tyranny:
      Whose blessed sprites from underneath the stone
      To God for vengeance cryde continually,
      And with great griefe were often heard to grone,
That hardest heart would bleede, to heare their piteous mone.

37   Through every rowme he sought, and everie bowr,
      But no where could he find that wofull thrall:
      At last he came unto an yron doore,
      That fast was lockt, but key found not at all
      Emongst that bounch, to open it withall;
      But in the same a little grate was pight,[1]
      Through which he sent his voyce, and lowd did call
      With all his powre, to weet, if living wight
Were housed therewithin, whom he enlargen might.[2]

38   Therewith an hollow, dreary, murmuring voyce
      These pitteous plaintes and dolours did resound;
      "O who is that, which bringes me happy choyce
      Of death, that here lye dying every stound,[3]
      Yet live perforce in balefull[4] darkenesse bound?
      For now three Moones have changed thrice their hew,
      And have beene thrice hid underneath the ground,
      Since I the heavens chearefull face did vew,
O welcome thou, that doest of death bring tydings trew."

39   Which when that Champion heard, with percing point
      Of pitty deare his hart was thrilled sore,
      And trembling horrour ran through every joynt,
      For ruth of gentle knight so fowle forlore:[5]
      Which shaking off, he rent that yron dore,
      With furious force, and indignation fell;

---

[1] **pight:** inset, installed.
[2] **enlargen might:** might set free.
[3] **stound:** hour.
[4] **balefull:** dire, deathlike.
[5] **forlore:** abandoned.

Where entred in, his foot could find no flore,
But all a deepe descent, as darke as hell,[1]
That breathed ever forth a filthie banefull smell.

40   But nether darkenesse fowle, nor filthy bands,
    Nor noyous[2] smell his purpose could withhold,
    (Entire affection hateth nicer[3] hands)
    But that with constant zele, and corage bold,
    After long paines and labors manifold,
    He found the meanes that Prisoner up to reare;
    Whose feeble thighes, unhable to uphold
    His pined corse,[4] him scarse to light could beare,
A ruefull spectacle of death and ghastly drere.[5]

41   His sad dull eies deepe sunck in hollow pits,
    Could not endure th'unwonted sunne to view;
    His bare thin cheekes for want of better bits,[6]
    And empty sides deceived of their dew,
    Could make a stony hart his hap to rew;
    His rawbone armes, whose mighty brawned bowrs[7]
    Were wont to rive steele plates, and helmets hew,
    Were clene consum'd, and all his vitall powres
Decayd, and al his flesh shronk up like withered flowres.

42   Whome when his Lady saw, to him she ran
    With hasty joy: to see him made her glad,
    And sad to view his visage pale and wan,
    Who earst in flowres of freshest youth was clad.
    Tho[8] when her well of teares she wasted had,
    She said, "Ah dearest Lord, what evill starre
    On you hath frownd, and pourd his influence bad,
    That of your selfe ye thus berobbed arre,
And this misseeming hew your manly looks doth marre?

---

[1] A suggestion of Christ's Harrowing of Hell, making Arthur a Christ figure. Other analogies are the low, dark, smelly place and the bursting of a metal door—both occasional features of accounts of Christ's Harrowing of Hell. See ACH note to stanzas 39 and 40, and "Hell" in *SE*.

[2] **noyous:** noxious.

[3] **nicer:** too fastidious. See also II.ii.3.1–3.

[4] **pined corse:** emaciated body.

[5] **drere:** wretchedness.

[6] **better bits:** proper food, suggesting mouthfuls to fill out his cheeks (ACH).

[7] **bowrs:** muscles. The picture suggests spiritual malaise.

[8] **Tho:** then.

43   "But welcome now my Lord, in wele or woe,
            Whose presence I have lackt too long a day;
            And fie on Fortune mine avowed foe,
            Whose wrathfull wreakes[1] them selves do now alay.
            And for these wronges shall treble penaunce[2] pay
            Of treble good: good growes of evils priefe."[3]
            The chearelesse man, whom sorow did dismay,
            Had no delight to treaten[4] of his griefe;
        His long endured famine needed more reliefe.

44   "Faire Lady, then said that victorious knight,
            The things, that grievous were to doe, or beare,
            Them to renew,[5] I wote, breeds no delight;
            Best musicke breeds delight in loathing eare:[6]
            But th'only good, that growes of passed feare,
            Is to be wise, and ware of like agein.
            This daies ensample hath this lesson deare
            Deepe written in my heart with yron pen,
        That blisse may not abide in state of mortall men.

45   "Henceforth Sir knight, take to you wonted strength,
            And maister these mishaps with patient might;
            Loe wher your foe lies stretcht in monstrous length,
            And loe that wicked woman in your sight,
            The roote of all your care, and wretched plight,
            Now in your powre, to let her live, or die."
            "To doe her die" (quoth *Una*) "were despight,
            And shame t'avenge so weake an enimy;
        But spoile[7] her of her scarlot robe, and let her fly."

---

[1] **wreakes:** calamities, without the usual sense of retribution.

[2] **penaunce:** satisfaction.

[3] **evils priefe:** testing by evil.

[4] **to treaten:** to discuss; "-en" is the sign of the infinitive in Middle English.

[5] **renew:** remember, recount.

[6] This line is a much-discussed puzzle. ACH tells us that older critics emended it, but more modest modern critics construe the text, as we have it, in one of two ways: 1) "music best breeds delight, not a recital of grievous matters," or 2) "only the best music, not a recital of grievous matters, may breed delight."

[7] **spoile:** despoile, strip. Spenser "carefully avoids bringing in the destruction of the Scarlet Whore" (Rev. 17.16). Nevertheless "her exit in nakedness and desolation" owes something to it (TPR on stanzas 46 and 50). This stripping symbolizes the full disclosure that Truth seeks; her vengeance goes no further. In external action, it echoes the revelation of Alcina deprived of her magical beauty aids to the rescued Ruggiero in *OF,* 7.70–74.

46   So as she bad, that witch they disaraid,
      And robd of roiall robes, and purple pall,[1]
      And ornaments that richly were displaid;
      Ne spared they to strip her naked all.
      Then when they had despoyld her tire and call,[2]
      Such as she was, their eies might her behold,
      That her misshaped parts did them appall,
      A loathly, wrinckled hag, ill favoured, old,
Whose secret filth good manners biddeth not be told.

47   Her crafty head was altogether bald,
      And as in hate of honorable eld,[3]
      Was overgrowne with scurfe and filthy scald;[4]
      Her teeth out of her rotten gummes were feld,
      And her sowre breath abhominably smeld;
      Her dried dugs, lyke bladders lacking wind,
      Hong downe, and filthy matter from them weld;
      Her wrizled[5] skin as rough, as maple rind,
So scabby was, that would have loathd all womankind.[6]

48   Her neather parts, the shame of all her kind,
      My chaster Muse for shame doth blush to write;[7]
      But at her rompe she growing had behind
      A foxes taile, with dong all fowly dight;[8]
      And eke her feete most monstrous were in sight;
      For one of them was like an Eagles claw,
      With griping talaunts[9] armd to greedy fight,
      The other like a beares uneven paw:
More ugly shape yet never living creature saw.

---

[1] **pall:** robe or cloak, usually purple.

[2] **tire and call:** attire and headdress; see the quotation from Isaiah below.

[3] **in hate of honorable eld:** such as would cause hatred for those whose old age would otherwise claim honor (ACH); an elliptical expression.

[4] **scurfe and filthy scald:** scabs and a scabby disease.

[5] **wrizled:** wrinkled.

[6] I.e., that would have been disgusting to all womankind.

[7] See Isaiah 3.17, 24: "Therefore shal the Lord make the heads of the daughters of Zion balde, and the Lord shal discover their secret partes. In that day shal the Lord take away . . . the calles, and the round tyres . . . And in stead of swete savour, there shalbe stinke, and in stead of a girdle, a rent, and in stead of dressing of the heere, baldnes . . . and burning in stead of beautie" (ACH).

[8] **dight:** dressed, arranged.

[9] **talaunts:** talons.

49   Which when the knights beheld, amazd they were,
           And wondred at so fowle deformed wight.
           "Such then" (said *Una*) "as she seemeth here,
           Such is the face of falshood, such the sight
           Of fowle *Duessa*, when her borrowed light
           Is laid away, and counterfesaunce knowne."
           Thus when they had the witch disrobed quight,
           And all her filthy feature open showne,
     They let her goe at will, and wander waies unknowne.

50   Shee flying fast from heavens hated face,
           And from the world that her discovered wide,
           Fled to the wastfull wildernesse apace,
           From living eies her open shame to hide,
           And lurkt in rocks and caves long unespide.
           But that faire crew of knights, and *Una* faire
           Did in that castle afterwards abide,
           To rest them selves, and weary powres repaire,
     Where store they fownd of al, that dainty was and rare.

Canto Nine

His loves and lignage Arthure tells
the knights knitt friendly hands:
Sir Trevisan flies from Despeyre,
Whom Redcros knight withstands.

1   O Goodly golden chayne, wherewith yfere[1]
      The vertues linked are in lovely wize:
      And noble mindes of yore allyed were,
      In brave poursuitt of chevalrous emprize,
      That none did others safety despize,
      Nor aid envy to him, in need that stands,[2]
      But friendly each did others praise devize,
      How to advaunce with favourable hands,
As this good Prince redeemd the *Redcrosse* knight from bands.[3]

2   Who when their powres empayrd through labor long,
      With dew repast they had recured well,[4]
      And that weake captive wight now wexed strong,
      Them list no lenger there at leasure dwell,
      But forward fare, as their adventures fell,
      But ere they parted, *Una* faire besought
      That straunger knight his name and nation tell;
      Least so great good, as he for her had wrought,
Should die unknown, and buried be in thankles thought.

3   "Faire virgin" (said the Prince) "yee me require
      A thing without[5] the compas of my witt:
      For both the lignage and the certein Sire,

---

[1] **yfere:** together as equals.

[2] I.e., nor begrudge aid to him who stands in need.

[3] Spenser's "Goodly golden chayne" is a horizontal chain and is used in a favorable sense, allied with the virtues of chivalry. Elsewhere, Spenser's vertical golden chain is used in a derogatory sense; see II.vii.46–47; so also Homer, *Iliad,* 8.18–27.

[4] **dew repast:** sufficient rest as well as food (ACH); **recured well:** well recovered. Redcrosse later proves himself to be less than fully recovered.

[5] **without:** outside.

From which I sprong, from mee are hidden yitt.[1]
For all so soone as life did me admitt
Into this world, and shewed hevens light,
From mothers pap I taken was unfitt:
And streight delivered to a Fary knight,
To be upbrought in gentle thewes[2] and martiall might.

4   "Unto old *Timon* he me brought bylive,[3]
Old *Timon,* who in youthly yeares hath beene
In warlike feates th'expertest man alive,
And is the wisest now on earth I weene;
His dwelling is low in a valley greene,
Under the foot of *Rauran* mossy hore,[4]
From whence the river *Dee* as silver cleene
His tombling billowes rolls with gentle rore:[5]
There all my daies he traind me up in vertuous lore.

5   "Thether the great magicien *Merlin* came,
As was his use, ofttimes to visitt mee
For he had charge my discipline[6] to frame,
And Tutors nouriture to oversee.
Him oft and oft I askt in privity,
Of what loines and what lignage I did spring.
Whose aunswere bad me still assured bee,
That I was sonne and heire unto a king,
As time in her just term the truth to light should bring."

6   "Well worthy impe,"[7] said then the Lady gent,
"And Pupill fitt for such a Tutors hand.
But what adventure, or what high intent

---

[1] In *Le Morte D'Arthur,* Book One, Malory gives the young Arthur to Sir Ector and keeps the former ignorant of his lineage for a short time; but Spenser never reveals Arthur's lineage to him in this poem as we have it. Arthur knows only that he is "sonne and heire unto a king" (5.8), though Spenser reveals everything to us over Arthur's head in II.x.68.

[2] **thewes:** manners as distinct from fighting ability. See also Redcrosse's praise of Guyon (II.i.33.9).

[3] **he:** presumably Merlin, who is mentioned later; **bylive:** immediately.

[4] **mossy hore:** hoary or grey with moss.

[5] Dee and Rauran are a river and a hill in Wales—a country originally and still, to some extent, inhabited by Britons or Celts, not Anglo-Saxons; and the country whence the Tudors originated.

[6] **discipline:** both instruction and practical training by reward and punishment. The "Letter to Raleigh" claims it to be the goal of the present poem: "to fashion a gentleman or noble person in vertuous and gentle discipline."

[7] **impe:** scion, offspring, with no sense of the modern "impish."

Hath brought you hether into Fary land,
Aread[1] Prince *Arthure,* crowne of Martiall band?"
"Full hard it is" (quoth he) "to read aright
The course of heavenly cause, or understand
The secret meaning of th'eternall might,
That rules mens waies, and rules the thoughts of living wight.

7   "For whether he[2] through fatal deepe foresight
       Me hither sent, for cause to me unghest,
       Or that fresh bleeding wound, which day and night
       Whilome doth rancle in my riven[3] brest,
       With forced fury following his behest,[4]
       Me hether brought by wayes yet never found,
       You to have helpt I hold my selfe yet blest."
"Ah courteous knight" (quoth she) "what secret wound
Could ever find, to grieve the gentlest hart on ground?"[5]

8   "Deare Dame" (quoth he) "you sleeping sparkes awake,
       Which troubled once, into huge flames will grow,
       Ne ever will their fervent fury slake,
       Till living moysture into smoke do flow,
       And wasted life doe lye in ashes low.
       Yet sithens[6] silence lesseneth not my fire,
       But told it flames, and hidden it does glow,
       I will revele, what ye so much desire:
Ah Love, lay down thy bow, the whiles I may respyre.

9   "It was in freshest flowre of youthly yeares,
       When corage[7] first does creepe in manly chest,
       Then first the cole of kindly heat appeares
       To kindle love in every living brest;
       But me had warnd old *Timons*[8] wise behest,

---

[1] **aread:** tell, explain.

[2] **he:** "th'eternall might" mentioned in previous stanza; a vague reference to God.

[3] **riven:** split open. Perfect passive participle of rive, meaning to split open.

[4] **his behest:** Love's command.

[5] **find, to:** contrive to; **on ground:** on the earth.

[6] **sithens:** since.

[7] **corage:** typically courage, but sometimes love or lust, as here; Spenser spells it this way to emphasize its derivation from the Latin word *cor,* "heart."

[8] Timon does not appear in the sources. 1590 edition has "Cleons," a name otherwise unattested in the poem, which was corrected to "Timons" in F.E., 1596. The error reveals Spenser's rationale for naming. It is etymological: both Cleon and Timon

Those creeping flames by reason to subdew,[1]
Before their rage grew to so great unrest,
As miserable lovers use to rew,
Which still wex old in woe, whiles wo stil wexeth new.

10   "That ydle name of love, and lovers life,
As losse of time, and vertues enimy
I ever scornd, and joyd to stirre up strife,
In middest of their mournfull Tragedy,
Ay wont to laugh, when them I heard to cry,
And blow the fire, which them to ashes brent:
Their God[2] himselfe, grievd at my libertie,
Shott many a dart at me with fiers intent,
But I them warded all with wary government.[3]

11   "But all in vaine: no fort can be so strong,
Ne fleshly brest can armed be so sownd,
But will at last be wonne with battrie[4] long,
Or unawares at disavantage fownd:
Nothing is sure, that growes on earthly grownd:
And who most trustes in arme of fleshly might,
And boastes, in beauties chaine not to be bownd,
Doth soonest fall in disaventrous[5] fight,
And yeeldes his caytive neck to victours most despight.[6]

12   "Ensample make of him your haplesse joy,
And of my selfe now mated,[7] as ye see;
Whose prouder vaunt that proud avenging boy
Did soone pluck downe, and curbd my libertee.
For on a day prickt forth with jollitee[8]

---

are based on Greek words for "fame, honor, and glory"—see Cleopolis and Timias—values that are the goal of Arthur's stated virtue of magnificence/magnanimity.

[1] So Glauce advises Britomart in the first throes of love; and again the advice proves impracticable (III.ii.46).

[2] I.e., Cupid.

[3] **government:** self-government, self-control; synonymous with governance.

[4] **battrie:** military attacks.

[5] **disaventrous:** disastrous.

[6] Redcrosse made the same error (i.12.9). "Fleshly might" (line 6) is not physical but moral, as the next line—"and boasts, in beauties chaine not to be bownd"—makes clear.

[7] **mated:** overcome, from "checkmated" in chess.

[8] The following story is based, perhaps remotely, on Celtic folktales of forward fairy mistresses. This interview disturbingly recalls the love offered to the dreaming Redcrosse by the false Una (i.43ff.). Chaucer tells a derisive version of this story in "The Tale of Sir Thopas"; see ACH ad loc.

Of looser life, and heat of hardiment,[1]
Raunging the forest wide on courser free,
The fields, the floods, the heavens with one consent
Did seeme to laugh on me, and favour mine intent.

13   "For wearied with my sportes, I did alight
    From loftie steed, and downe to sleepe me layd;
    The verdant gras my couch did goodly dight,
    And pillow was my helmett fayre displayd:
    Whiles every sence the humour sweet embayd,[2]
    And slombring soft my hart did steale away
    Me seemed, by my side a royall Mayd
Her daintie limbes full softly down did lay:
So fayre a creature yet saw never sunny day.

14   "Most goodly glee and lovely blandishment[3]
    She to me made, and badd me love her deare;
    For dearely sure her love was to me bent,
    As when just time expired should appeare.[4]
    But whether dreames delude, or true it were,
    Was never hart so ravisht with delight,
    Ne living man like wordes did ever heare,
    As she to me delivered all that night;
And at her parting said, She Queene of Faries hight.[5]

15   "When I awoke, and found her place devoyd,
    And nought but pressed gras where she had lyen,[6]
    I sorrowed all so much, as earst I joyd,
    And washed all her place with watry eyen.
    From that day forth I lov'd that face divyne;
    From that day forth I cast in carefull mynd,

---

[1] **looser:** very relaxed, almost too relaxed; **hardiment:** boldness.

[2] **humour:** moisture, the dews of night or of sleep; **embayd:** bathed, suffused.

[3] I.e., fine entertainment and loving flattery. Critics have debated not only "how far they went" (since fairy mistresses have looser morals than do humans), but also whether the entire incident was a delusion and whether it is so allegorical that it does not matter. The incident allegorizes how fame, honor, and glory seem to seek out certain people, whereas others who may seem equally meritorious cannot "get to first base."

[4] I.e., which would appear when an appropriate amount of time had expired.

[5] **hight:** was called.

[6] **lyen:** lain. Middle English form.

To seeke her out with labor, and long tyne,[1]
And never vowd to rest,[2] till her I fynd,
Nyne monethes I seek in vain yet ni'll that vow unbynd."[3]

16 Thus as he spake, his visage wexed pale,
  And chaunge of hew great passion did bewray;
  Yett still he strove to cloke his inward bale,[4]
  And hide the smoke, that did his fire display,
  Till gentle *Una* thus to him gan say;
  "O happy Queene of Faries, that hast fownd
  Mongst many, one that with his prowesse may
  Defend thine honour, and thy foes confownd:
True Loves are often sown, but seldom grow on grownd."

17 "Thine,[5] O then," said the gentle *Redcrosse* knight,
  "Next to that Ladies love, shalbe the place,[6]
  O fayrest virgin, full of heavenly light,
  Whose wondrous faith, exceeding earthly race,
  Was firmest fixt in myne extremest case.
  And you, my Lord, the Patrone of my life,
  Of that great Queene may well gaine worthie grace:
  For onely worthie you through prowes priefe[7]
Yf living man mote worthie be, to be her liefe."[8]

18 So diversly discoursing of their loves,
  The golden Sunne his glistring head gan shew,
  And sad remembraunce now the Prince amoves,
  With fresh desire his voyage to pursew:

---

[1] **tyne:** toil.

[2] **never vowd to rest:** vowed never to rest.

[3] Arthur's quest. Since everyone else knows where Gloriana is—i.e., in her capital city Cleopolis—and could easily inform him, his quest is less a matter of geographic knowledge than of proving his worthiness of her. Britomart's quest, too, is for a beloved seen in a special vision (III.ii).

[4] **bale:** pain, here psychological pain. See "balefull" in the Glossary.

[5] I.e., Una's.

[6] Stanza 17, lines 1 through 4 are difficult because they illustrate Spenser's characteristic indefinite pronoun reference. I.e., Una's love will be placed in Redcrosse's heart next to the love of Gloriana, his current ruler, and to his love of that glory and honor which she symbolizes. See Richard Lovelace's lyric: "I could not love thee, dear, so much, / Loved I not honour more" ("To Lucasta, Going to the Wars," Aldington, ed., 446–7).

[7] **prowes priefe:** the proof of prowess (which we have just seen).

[8] **liefe:** beloved.

Als *Una* earnd her traveill to renew.[1]
Then those two knights, fast frendship for to bynd,
And love establish each to other trew,
Gave goodly gifts, the signes of gratefull mynd,
And eke as pledges firme, right hands together joynd.

19   Prince *Arthur* gave a boxe of Diamond sure,
        Embowd with gold and gorgeous ornament,
        Wherein were closd few drops of liquor pure,
        Of wondrous worth, and vertue excellent,
        That any wownd could heale incontinent:[2]
        Which to requite, the *Redcrosse* knight him gave
        A booke, wherein his Saveours testament
        Was writt with golden letters rich and brave;
        A worke of wondrous grace, and hable soules to save.[3]

20   Thus beene they parted, *Arthur* on his way
        To seeke his love, and th'other for to fight
        With *Unaes* foe, that all her realme did pray.[4]
        But she now weighing the decayed plight,
        And shrunken synewes of her chosen knight,
        Would not a while her forward course pursew,
        Ne bring him forth in face of dreadfull fight,
        Till he recovered had his former hew:
        For him to be yet weake and wearie well she knew.

21   So as they traveild, lo they gan espy
        An armed knight towards them gallop fast,
        That seemed from some feared foe to fly,
        Or other griesly thing, that him agast.[5]
        Still as he fledd, his eye was backward cast,
        As if his feare still followed him behynd;

---

[1] **als *Una* earnd:** also Una yearned.

[2] **incontinent:** immediately.

[3] The gifts symbolize the givers, not the re-
cipients; the fanciness of the box expresses
the straightforward sense of Arthur's virtue,
magnificence, which is the ability to spend
money well. Critics debate what the "liquor
pure" symbolizes. Arthur keeps some liquor
for himself, for he uses this liquor to cure
the wounds of Amoret in IV.viii.20. The
book Redcrosse gives is the New Testa-
ment. To judge by their gifts, Redcrosse
belongs to the spiritual world, despite his
sins, whereas Arthur, by contrast, seems to
belong to the external material world in his
pervasive role, despite his temporary role in
Canto Eight and II.viii of a Christ figure
and a seemingly internal divine grace.

[4] **pray:** prey on.

[5] **that him agast:** that made him aghast.

Als flew his steed, as he his bandes had brast,[1]
And with his winged heeles did tread the wynd,
As he had beene a fole of *Pegasus* his kynd.[2]

22   Nigh as he drew, they might perceive his head
       To bee unarmd, and curld uncombed heares
       Upstaring stiffe, dismaid with uncouth dread;
       Nor drop of blood in all his face appeares
       Nor life in limbe: and to increase his feares,
       In fowle reproch of knighthoodes fayre degree,[3]
       About his neck an hempen rope he weares,
       That with his glistring armes does ill agree;
     But he of rope or armes has now no memoree.

23   The *Redcrosse* knight toward him crossed fast,
       To weet, what mister wight[4] was so dismayd:
       There him he findes all sencelesse and aghast,
       That of him selfe he seemd to be afrayd,
       Whom hardly he from flying forward stayd,
       Till he these wordes to him deliver might:
       "Sir knight, aread who hath ye thus arayd,
       And eke from whom make ye this hasty flight:
     For never knight I saw in such misseeming[5] plight."

24   He answerd nought at all, but adding new
       Feare to his first amazment, staring wyde
       With stony eyes, and hartlesse hollow hew,
       Astonisht stood, as one that had aspyde
       Infernall furies, with their chaines untyde.
       Him yett againe, and yett againe bespake
       The gentle knight, who nought to him replyde,
       But trembling every joynt did inly quake,
    And foltring tongue at last these words seemd forth to shake.

25   "For Gods deare love, Sir knight, doe me not stay;
       For loe he comes, he comes fast after mee."
       Eft[6] looking back would faine have runne away;
       But he him forst to stay, and tellen free
       The secrete cause of his perplexitie,

---

[1] I.e., as if he had just broken free.

[2] I.e., as if he had been a foal of Pegasus' species, and so winged.

[3] **degree:** rank, status.

[4] **what mister wight:** what kind of a person.

[5] **misseeming:** unseemly.

[6] **eft:** again.

Yet nathemore[1] by his bold hartie speach,
　Could his blood frosen hart emboldened bee,
　But through his boldnes rather feare did reach,
Yett forst, at last he made through silence suddein breach.

26　"And am I now in safetie sure" (quoth he)
　　"From him, that would have forced me to dye?
　　And is the point of death now turnd fro mee,
　　That I may tell this haplesse history?"
　　"Feare nought:" (quoth he) "no daunger now is nye."
　　"Then shall I you recount a ruefull cace,"
　　(Said he) "the which with this unlucky eye
　I late beheld, and had not greater grace
Me reft from it, had bene partaker of the place.[2]

27　"I lately chaunst (Would I had never chaunst)
　　With a fayre knight to keepen companee,
　　Sir *Terwin* hight, that well himselfe advaunst
　　In all affayres, and was both bold and free,
　　But not so happy as mote happy bee:
　　He lov'd, as was his lot, a Lady gent,
　　That him againe lov'd in the least degree:[3]
　For she was proud, and of too high intent,
And joyd to see her lover languish and lament.

28　"From whom retourning sad and comfortlesse,
　　As on the way together we did fare,
　　We met that villen (God from him me blesse)
　　That cursed wight, from whom I scapt whyleare,[4]
　　A man of hell, that calls himselfe *Despayre:*
　　Who first us greets; and after fayre areedes
　　Of tydinges straunge, and of adventures rare:
　So creeping close, as Snake in hidden weedes,
Inquireth of our states, and of our knightly deedes.

29　"Which when he knew, and felt our feeble harts
　　Embost with bale,[5] and bitter byting griefe,
　　Which love had launched with his deadly darts,

---

[1] **nathemore:** not for all this.

[2] I.e., if divine grace had not snatched me out of there, I would have shared the usual fate of those who are in that place.

[3] I.e., that reciprocated his love only a little.

[4] **whyleare:** a little while ago.

[5] **Embost with bale:** stricken with psychological pain. A hunting metaphor: the

With wounding words and termes of foule repriefe,
He pluckt from us all hope of due reliefe,
That earst us held in love of lingring life;
Then hopelesse hartlesse, gan the cunning thiefe
Perswade us dye, to stint[1] all further strife:
To me he lent this rope, to him a rusty knife.

30   "With which sad instrument of hasty death,
That wofull lover, loathing lenger light,
A wyde way made to let forth living breath.
But I more fearefull, or more lucky wight,
Dismayd with that deformed dismall sight,
Fledd fast away, halfe dead with dying feare;
Ne yet assur'd of life by you, Sir knight,
Whose like infirmity like chaunce may beare:[2]
But God you never let his charmed speaches heare."[3]

31   "How may a man" (said he) "with idle speach
Be wonne, to spoyle the Castle of his health?"
"I wote" (quoth he) "whom tryall late did teach,
That like would not for all this worldes wealth:[4]
His subtile tong, like dropping honny, mealt'th[5]
Into the heart, and searcheth every vaine,
That ere one be aware, by secret stealth
His powre is reft,[6] and weaknes doth remaine.
O never Sir desire to try his guilefull traine."

32   "Certes" (sayd he) "hence shall I never rest,
Till I that treachours art have heard and tryde;
And you Sir knight, whose name mote I request,
Of grace do me unto his cabin guyde."
"I that hight[7] *Trevisan*" (quoth he) "will ryde
Against my liking backe, to doe you grace:

---

quarry is embossed when it is so tired that it is flecked with foam and sweat.

[1] **stint:** stop.

[2] I.e., you who have the same weaknesses that my friend and I had and so may also be persuaded to suicide.

[3] I.e., may God keep you from ever hearing his magically persuasive speeches.

[4] I.e., I know, because recent experience has taught me, I who would not go through that experience again for all the wealth in the world.

[5] **mealt'th:** melts.

[6] **reft:** snatched away.

[7] **hight:** am called.

But nor for gold nor glee will I abyde
By you, when ye arrive in that same place;
For lever had I die,[1] then see his deadly face."

33   Ere long they come, where that same wicked wight
His dwelling has, low in an hollow cave,
Far underneath a craggy clift ypight,[2]
Darke, dolefull, dreary, like a greedy grave,
That still for carrion carcases doth crave:
On top whereof ay dwelt the ghastly Owle,
Shrieking his balefull note, which ever drave
Far from that haunt all other chearefull fowle;
And all about it wandring ghostes did wayle and howle.

34   And all about old stockes and stubs of trees,
Whereon nor fruite, nor leafe was ever seene,
Did hang upon the ragged rocky knees;[3]
On which had many wretches hanged beene,
Whose carcases were scattred on the greene,
And throwne about the cliffs. Arrived there,
That bare-head knight for dread and dolefull teene,[4]
Would faine have fled, ne durst approchen neare,
But th'other forst him staye, and comforted in feare.

35   That darkesome cave they enter, where they find
That cursed man, low sitting on the ground,
Musing full sadly in his sullein mind;
His griesie[5] lockes, long growen, and unbound,
Disordred hong about his shoulders round,
And hid his face; through which his hollow eyne
Lookt deadly dull, and stared as astound;
His raw-bone cheekes through penurie and pine,[6]
Were shronke into his jawes, as he did never dyne.

36   His garment nought but many ragged clouts,
With thornes together pind and patched was,
The which his naked sides he wrapt abouts;
And him beside there lay upon the gras

---

[1] **lever had I die:** I would rather die.

[2] **ypight:** placed.

[3] **knees:** crags.

[4] **teene:** sorrow.

[5] **griesie:** grey, filthy, hideous, or all of the above.

[6] Despaire didn't eat much because he was penurious, i.e., frugal; as a result he has pined away, i.e., gotten thin.

A dreary corse, whose life away did pas,
All wallowd in his own yet luke-warme blood,
That from his wound yet welled fresh alas;
In which a rusty knife fast fixed stood,
And made an open passage for the gushing flood.

37 Which piteous spectacle, approving trew
  The wofull tale, that *Trevisan* had told,
  When as the gentle *Redcrosse* knight did vew,
  With firie zeale he burnt in courage bold,
  Him to avenge, before his blood were cold,
  And to the villein sayd, "Thou damned wight,
  The authour of this fact,[1] we here behold,
  What justice can but judge against thee right,
With thine owne blood to price[2] his blood, here shed in sight."

38 "What franticke fit" (quoth he) "hath thus distraught
  Thee, foolish man, so rash a doome to give?
  What justice ever other judgement taught,
  But he should dye, who merites not to live?
  None els to death this man despayring drive,
  But his owne guiltie mind deserving death.
  Is then unjust to each his dew to give?[3]
  Or let him dye, that loatheth living breath?[4]
Or let him die at ease, that liveth here uneath?[5]

[1] **fact:** deed.

[2] **price:** pay for.

[3] Despaire pretends that Sir Terwin committed suicide out of guilt over some past misdeeds, because that is the motive for suicide which he plans to instill in Redcrosse. Actually, Sir Terwin committed suicide out of despair at ever winning his lady love—as his story shows. Despaire's small slip betrays his dishonesty, but Redcrosse does not seem to notice.

[4] After this foretaste of a temptation yet to come, Despaire moves into his hedonistic argument for suicide, which is aided by lulling rhetoric. The hedonistic arguments are drawn from those of classical Stoics for accepting death and even helping it along when it comes. Despaire assumes for the moment, and Redcrosse does not contradict him, that death is sleep, the end of consciousness—e.g., in stanza 40. Some of Despaire's arguments, as well as Redcrosse's and the ideal reader's responses, can be found in the treatment of despair and suicide in Chaucer's "Parson's Tale," in Montaigne's essay "To Flee from Sensual Pleasures at the Price of Life," and in Faustus' speeches at the end of Marlowe's *Dr. Faustus.* Despair and resulting suicide soon absorbed the interest of many writers: in Shakespeare there is Lucrece's reasoning in "The Rape of Lucrece"; Hamlet's famous soliloquy which begins, "To be or not to be," along with Horatio's intention to commit suicide at the end of that play; and the many suicides in his Roman plays. Other writers on this issue include John Donne in *Biathanatos,* and Robert Burton in *The Anatomy of Melancholy.*

[5] **uneath:** ill at ease, or with difficulty. Opposite of "eath," which means easy.

39   "Who travailes by the wearie wandring way,
        To come unto his wished home in haste,
        And meetes a flood, that doth his passage stay,
        Is not great grace to helpe him over past,
        Or free his feet, that in the myre sticke fast?
        Most envious man, that grieves at neighbours good,
        And fond, that joyest in the woe thou hast,
        Why wilt not let him passe, that long hath stood
Upon the bancke, yet wilt thy selfe not pas the flood?

40   "He there does now enjoy eternall rest
        And happy ease, which thou doest want and crave,
        And further from it daily wanderest:
        What if some little payne the passage have,
        That makes frayle flesh to feare the bitter wave?
        Is not short payne well borne, that brings long ease,
        And layes the soule to sleepe in quiet grave?
        Sleepe after toyle, port after stormie seas,
Ease after warre, death after life does greatly please."

41   The knight much wondred at his suddeine wit,
        And sayd, "The terme of life is limited,
        Ne may a man prolong, nor shorten it;
        The souldier may not move from watchfull sted,
        Nor leave his stand, untill his Captaine bed."[1]
        "Who life did limit by almightie doome,"
        (Quoth he)[2] "knowes best the termes established;
        And he, that points the Centonell his roome,
Doth license him depart at sound of morning droome.[3]

42   "Is not his deed, what ever thing is donne,
        In heaven and earth? did not he all create,
        To die againe? all ends that was begonne.
        Their times in his eternall booke of fate
        Are written sure, and have their certein date.
        Who then can strive with strong necessitie,

---

[1] Redcrosse cogently fends off Despaire's hedonistic arguments for suicide (stanzas 39–41) by saying that God, not man, must decide when it is time for the individual to die, and by implication that he personally has had no wound, illness, or societal ver- dict to indicate that now is the time for him to die. He echoes Cicero, *De Senectute,* 20.73, and perhaps Sidney, *Old Arcadia,* 294.

[2] I.e., Despaire.

[3] **droome:** drum.

That holds the world in his still chaunging state,
Or shunne the death ordaynd by destinie?
When houre of death is come, let none aske whence, nor why.[1]

43   "The lenger life, I wote the greater sin,[2]
     The greater sin, the greater punishment:
     All those great battels, which thou boasts to win,
     Through strife, and blood-shed, and avengement,
     Now praysd, hereafter deare thou shalt repent:
     For life must life, and blood must blood repay.
     Is not enough thy evill life forespent?[3]
     For he, that once hath missed the right way,
The further he doth goe, the further he doth stray.

44   "Then doe no further goe, no further stray,
     But here ly downe, and to thy rest betake,
     Th'ill to prevent, that life ensewen may.[4]
     For what hath life, that may it loved make,
     And gives not rather cause it to forsake?
     Feare, sicknesse, age, losse, labour, sorrow, strife,
     Payne, hunger, cold, that makes the hart to quake;
     And ever fickle fortune rageth rife,
All which, and thousands mo do make a loathsome life.[5]

45   "Thou wretched man, of death hast greatest need,
     If in true ballaunce thou wilt weigh thy state:
     For never knight, that dared warlike deed,
     More luckless dissaventures did amate:[6]
     Witnes the dungeon deepe, wherein of late
     Thy life shutt up, for death so oft did call;

---

[1] Despaire replies feebly that if you commit suicide, it will be God working through you, since God makes everything happen, but he does not answer Redcrosse's objection. That they both refer to God but not the afterlife is consistent with Stoicism.

[2] Without allowing Redcrosse to speak, Despaire moves into his second argument, the argument for moral despair (stanzas 43, 45–47); and this argument finally convinces Redcrosse.

[3] **forespent:** already spent.

[4] **that life ensewen may:** that may ensue in the rest of your life.

[5] Despaire resumes the hedonistic argument (stanzas 44–45), this time by derogating life; again, it would be valid if Redcrosse were already dying of some other cause and if, as is declared in 47.9, there is no afterlife.

[6] **amate:** frustrate, frighten.

And though good lucke prolonged hath thy date,[1]
Yet death then, would the like mishaps forestall,
Into the which hereafter thou maist happen fall.

46   "Why then doest thou, O man of sin, desire
      To draw thy dayes forth to their last degree?
      Is not the measure of thy sinfull hire
      High heaped up with huge iniquitee,
      Against the day of wrath,[2] to burden thee?
      Is not enough, that to this Lady mild
      Thou falsest hast thy faith with perjuree,
      And sold thy selfe to serve *Duessa* vild,
With whom in al abuse thou hast thy selfe defild?

47   "Is not he just, that all this doth behold
      From highest heven, and beares an equall[3] eie?
      Shall he thy sins up in his knowledge fold,
      And guilty be of thine impietie?[4]
      Is not his lawe, Let every sinner die:
      Die shall all flesh? what then must needs be donne,
      Is it not better to doe willinglie,
      Then linger, till the glas be all out ronne?
Death is the end of woes: die soone, O faries sonne."[5]

48   The knight was much enmoved with his speach,
      That as a swords poynt through his hart did perse,
      And in his conscience made a secrete breach,
      Well knowing true all, that he did reherse,

---

[1] I.e., postponed your destined death-day thus far.

[2] **day of wrath:** Doomsday.

[3] **equall:** impartial.

[4] Despaire's rhetorical question implies the answer "No," but a fully Christian answer would be "Yes," in the sense that God in Christ assumed and expiated mankind's guilt. This indicates that Despaire is employing half-truths; he is emphasizing one side, the negative side, of the Gospel message, God's justice, and omitting the positive side, God's mercy, as Una indicates in stanza 53.

[5] The moral arguments for suicide: in stanza 43, the longer you live, the more you will sin; in stanza 46, you have sinned flagrantly already and deserve to go to hell. In stanza 46, Despaire admits that there is an afterlife, but here he says that "Death is the end of woes." Cf. stanza 49, which contradictorily says that the afterlife will be unpleasant for Redcrosse given his infidelity to Una. This would seem to make a case against suicide and to favor staying alive as long as possible, but Despaire manages to twist the implications to his purpose.

And to his fresh remembraunce did reverse,[1]
The ugly vew of his deformed crimes,
That all his manly powres it did disperse,
As he were charmed with inchaunted rimes,
That oftentimes he quakt, and fainted oftentimes.

49   In which amazement, when the Miscreaunt
Perceived him to waver weake and fraile,
Whiles trembling horror did his conscience daunt,
And hellish anguish did his soule assaile,
To drive him to despaire, and quite to quaile,
He shewd him painted in a table[2] plaine,
The damned ghosts, that doe in torments waile,
And thousand feends that doe them endlesse paine
With fire and brimstone, which for ever shall remaine.

50   The sight whereof so throughly him dismaid,
That nought but death before his eies he saw,
And ever burning wrath before him laid,
By righteous sentence of th'Almighties law:[3]
Then gan the villein him to overcraw,[4]
And brought unto him swords, ropes, poison, fire,
And all that might him to perdition draw;
And bad him choose, what death he would desire:
For death was dew to him, that had provokt Gods ire.

51   But whenas none of them he saw him take,
He to him a dagger sharpe and keene,
And gave it him in hand: his hand did quake,
And tremble like a leafe of Aspin greene,
And troubled blood through his pale face was seene
To come, and goe with tidings from the heart,
As it a ronning messenger had beene.
At last resolv'd to worke his finall smart,
He lifted up his hand, that backe againe did start.[5]

---

[1] **reverse:** recall.

[2] **table:** picture.

[3] Despaire manages to attract Redcrosse to the punishments of hell by the fact that Redcrosse has deserved them and by the argument that he should cooperate with God and become his own executioner.

[4] **overcraw:** crow over, exult over.

[5] **that backe againe did start:** that, out of an instinct for self-preservation, refused to make the stabbing motion Redcrosse desired.

52   Which whenas *Una* saw, through every vaine
       The crudled cold ran to her well of life,[1]
       As in a swowne: but soone reliv'd[2] againe,
       Out of his hand she snatcht the cursed knife,
       And threw it to the ground, enraged rife,
       And to him said, "Fie fie, faint hearted knight,
       What meanest thou by this reprochfull strife?
       Is this the battaile, which thou vauntst to fight
    With that fire-mouthed Dragon, horrible and bright?[3]

53   "Come, come away, fraile, feeble, fleshly wight,
       Ne let vaine words bewitch thy manly hart,
       Ne divelish thoughts dismay thy constant spright.
       In heavenly mercies hast thou not a part?[4]
       Why shouldst thou then despeire, that chosen art?[5]
       Where justice growes, there grows eke greter grace,
       The which doth quench the brond of hellish smart,
       And that accurst hand-writing doth deface.[6]
    Arise, Sir knight arise, and leave this cursed place."

54   So up he rose, and thence amounted streight.
       Which when the carle[7] beheld, and saw his guest
       Would safe depart, for all his subtile sleight,
       He chose an halter from among the rest,
       And with it hong him selfe, unbid[8] unblest.
       But death he could not worke himselfe thereby;
       For thousand times he so him selfe had drest,
       Yet nathelesse it could not doe him die,
    Till he should die his last, that is eternally.

---

[1] I.e., a chill of bloodcurdling horror gripped her heart.

[2] **reliv'd:** brought back to life.

[3] With psychological insight, Una first physically grabs the dagger, then appeals to Redcrosse's ambition. Only then does she enter upon the theological refutation of Despaire's moral argument for suicide.

[4] I.e., will not God have mercy on you? Christian doctrine would add, "provided you repent," and Redcrosse has already taken the first step in that direction and admitted his guilt (48.4–6).

[5] Una invokes predestination, a doctrine common to all Christians but emphasized by Calvinists; see also "chosen" in x.57. Besides God, only the individual can know, and that only in some branches of Protestantism, that he is chosen or predestinated for heaven; this suggests that Una here represents the Holy Spirit within Redcrosse, bearing "witnesse with our spirit, that we are the children of God" (Rom. 8.16).

[6] **deface:** blot, i.e., erase, the justice of the old law that Despaire invoked—a paraphrase of Col. 2.14. It is now satisfied and made irrelevant by the mercy of Christ.

[7] **carle:** a large, crude, low-class fellow.

[8] **unbid:** without anyone urging him to.

Canto Ten

Her faithfull knight faire Una brings
To house of Holinesse,
Where he is taught repentaunce, and
The way to hevenly blesse.

1   What man is he, that boasts of fleshly might,
       And vaine assuraunce of mortality,
       Which all so soone, as it doth come to fight,
       Against spirituall foes,[1] yields by and by,
       Or from the fielde most cowardly doth fly?
       Ne let the man ascribe it to his skill,
       That thorough grace hath gained victory.
       If any strength we have, it is to ill,
    But all the good is Gods, both power and eke will.[2]

2   By that, which lately hapned, *Una* saw,
       That this her knight was feeble, and too faint;
       And all his sinewes woxen weake and raw,[3]
       Through long enprisonment, and hard constraint,
       Which he endured in his late restraint,
       That yet he was unfitt for bloody fight:

---

[1] In Redcrosse's case, Orgoglio and Despaire.

[2] See Una's teaching in ix.53: a person is not saved by works, but by God's grace in response to faith and prayer. Both statements are extremely Protestant, i.e., Calvinistic. The rest of the canto, however, with a few exceptions, is surprisingly Catholic, in that the individual has to do many things in order to merit heaven. There are many biblical analogues to x.1, esp. in the Pauline epistles, esp. Phil. 2.13: "it is God which worketh in you, bothe the wil and the dede." For Spenserian examples of the "man" (line 1) who makes this error, see Redcrosse's boast: "Vertue gives her self light, through darkenesse for to wade" (i.12.9); the description of Orgoglio discussed above (vii.9–10); Arthur's dismissal of the "arme of fleshly might" in ix.11.6. On the other hand, cf. II.i.33, which gives some role to the individual's will. This stanza resembles *Articles of Religion of the Church of England* (known as The 39 Articles, available in most older editions of The Book of Common Prayer), Articles 11 and 12.

[3] **raw:** unfit.

Therefore to cherish him with diets daint,[1]
She cast to bring him, where he chearen[2] might,
Till he recovered had his late decayed plight.[3]

3   There was an auncient house not far away,[4]
        Renowmd throughout the world for sacred lore,
        And pure unspotted life: so well they say
        It governd was, and guided evermore,
        Through wisedome of a matrone grave and hore;[5]
        Whose onely joy was to relieve the needes
        Of wretched soules, and helpe the helpelesse pore:
        All night she spent in bidding of her bedes,[6]
And all the day in doing good and godly deedes.

4   Dame *Caelia*[7] men did her call, as thought
        From heaven to come, or thether to arise,
        The mother of three daughters, well upbrought
        In goodly thewes,[8] and godly exercise:
        The eldest two most sober, chast, and wise,
        Fidelia and *Speranza* virgins were,
        Though spousd, yet wanting wedlocks solemnize;
        But faire *Charissa* to a lovely fere[9]
Was lincked, and by him had many pledges dere.[10]

---

[1] **daint:** dainty; last syllable omitted for the sake of the rhyme.

[2] **chearen:** in the modern sense of "cheer up" and also in the older sense of "become healthy."

[3] I.e., had gotten over his recently decayed health.

[4] The closest overall analogue to the House of Holiness is the illustrated description of two French religious processions, the King's and the Queen's, which took place in Paris in 1583 and 1584. Among many similarities, the Queen's ended at a real charitable institution called "The House of Love." See Yates, 174–91, 197–207; she makes the connection between all this and Spenser's House of Holiness on pp. 181–2. Plates showing contemporary drawings of these two processions are numbered 24 to 39.

[5] **hore:** hoary, gray with age; adjective.

[6] **bedes:** the rosary. Cf. Archimago's (i.30) and Corceca's (iii.13–14) uses of the rosary, which are satirized, presumably because the recital takes up too much of their time and because the prayers are counted on the beads, implying that the prayers are viewed as meritorious in themselves. Caelia does not divulge her numbers; her rosary seems just an aid to concentration, and she divides her time between saying the rosary and "doing good and godly deeds"—a balance of action and contemplation. See ACH note.

[7] *Caelia:* heavenly.

[8] **thewes:** manners, distinguished here from religious good deeds.

[9] **fere:** mate, here presumably Christ.

[10] Faith, Hope, and Charity or Love are the three theological virtues; see 1 Cor. 13.13. The rest of the House of Holiness evinces

5   Arrived there, the dore they find fast lockt;
         For it was warely watched night and day,
         For feare of many foes: but when they knockt,
         The Porter opened unto them straight way:
         He was an aged syre, all hory gray,
         With lookes full lowly cast, and gate full slow,
         Wont on a staffe his feeble steps to stay,
         Hight *Humiltá*. They passe in stouping low;
     For streight and narrow was the way,[1] which he did shew.

6   Each goodly thing is hardest to begin,
         But entred in a spatious court they see,
         Both plaine, and pleasaunt to be walked in,
         Where them does meete a francklin[2] faire and free,
         And entertaines with comely courteous glee,
         His name was *Zele*, that him right well became,
         For in his speaches and behaveour hee
         Did labour lively to expresse the same,
     And gladly did them guide, till to the Hall they came.

7   There fayrely them receives a gentle Squyre,
         Of myld demeanure, and rare courtesee,
         Right cleanly clad in comely sad attire;
         In word and deede that shewd great modestee,
         And knew his good[3] to all of each degree,
         Hight *Reverence*. He them with speaches meet
         Does faire entreat; no courting nicetee,
         But simple trew, and eke unfained sweet,
     As might become a Squyre so great persons to greet.

8   And afterwardes them to his Dame he leades,
         That aged Dame, the Lady of the place:
         Who all this while was busy at her beades:

---

agreement with this verse that "the chiefest
of these is love." Faith and esp. Hope are
merely "spousd"—i.e., engaged—to a
lovely fere," presumably to Christ, because
they, and esp. Hope, look to the future in
heaven. Charity is already married to him
and has borne many children, often fea-
tured in visual portrayals of her, because
while she too will be fulfilled in heaven, she
also works in this world.

[1] See Matt. 7.14.

[2] **francklin:** wealthy, non-noble landowner.

[3] **his good:** what was good to say to vari-
ous types of comers.

Which doen, she up arose with seemely grace,
And toward them full matronely did pace.
Where when that fairest *Una* she beheld,
Whom well she knew to spring from hevenly race,
Her heart with joy unwonted inly sweld,
As feeling wondrous comfort in her weaker eld.[1]

9   And her embracing said, "O happy earth,
Whereon thy innocent feet doe ever tread,
Most vertuous virgin borne of hevenly berth,
That to redeeme thy woefull parents head,
From tyrans rage, and ever-dying dread,
Hast wandred through the world now long a day;
Yett ceassest not thy weary soles[2] to lead,
What grace hath thee now hether brought this way?
Or doen thy feeble feet unweeting hether stray?

10   Strange thing it is an errant knight[3] to see
Here in this place, or any other wight,
That hether turnes his steps. So few there bee,
That chose the narrow path, or seeke the right:
All keepe the broad high way, and take delight
With many rather for to goe astray,
And be partakers of their evill plight,
Then with a few to walke the rightest way;
O foolish men, why hast ye to your owne decay?"

11   "Thy selfe to see, and tyred limbes to rest,
O matrone sage" (quoth she) "I hether came,
And this good knight his way with me addrest,[4]
Ledd with thy prayses and broad-blazed fame,
That up to heven is blowne." The auncient Dame,
Him goodly greeted in her modest guyse,
And enterteynd them both, as best became,
With all the court'sies, that she could devyse,
Ne wanted ought, to shew her bounteous or wise.

---

[1] **eld:** old age.

[2] **soles:** soles of feet or shoes, with a pun on "souls," i.e., converts such as Redcrosse. The line pictures Truth wandering the earth throughout history along with her few converts.

[3] **errant knight:** a knight on a quest, wandering. Could carry some moral ambiguity.

[4] **addrest:** directed.

12   Thus as they gan of sondrie thinges devise,[1]
          Loe two most goodly virgins came in place,
          Ylinked arme in arme in lovely wise,
          With countenance demure, and modest grace,
          They numbred even steps and equall pace:
          Of which the eldest, that *Fidelia* hight,
          Like sunny beames threw from her Christall face,
          That could have dazd the rash beholders sight,
And round about her head did shine like hevens light.

13   She was araied all in lilly white,[2]
          And in her right hand bore a cup of gold,
          With wine and water fild up to the hight,
          In which a Serpent did himselfe enfold,
          That horrour made to all, that did behold;[3]
          But she no whitt did change her constant mood:
          And in her other hand she fast did hold
          A booke that was both signd and seald with blood,
Wherein darke things were writt, hard to be understood.[4]

14   Her younger Sister, that *Speranza* hight,
          Was clad in blew,[5] that her beseemed well;
          Not all so chearefull seemed she of sight,
          As was her sister; whether dread did dwell,
          Or anguish in her hart, is hard to tell:
          Upon her arme a silver anchor[6] lay,
          Whereon she leaned ever, as befell:
          And ever up to heven, as she did pray,
Her stedfast eyes were bent, ne swarved other way.

---

[1] **devise:** can mean talk.

[2] The traditional color of faith.

[3] The golden cup is a traditional attribute of faith, symbolizing the Eucharistic cup, as Spenser's wine and water makes clear. Cf. Duessa's golden cup, which causes "Death and despeyre" (viii.14). On the distinction between good and bad cups, see 1 Cor. 10.21 and ACH note. The serpent in the cup recalls the serpent of Num. 21.8–9, the healing property of which, when it was raised on a pole and gazed upon, Christ compares to his own when he shall be crucified (John 3.14). The cup and serpent cause "horrour," one's emotion on considering that God died and we eat him—a salvific horror.

[4] The Bible. The New Testament is particularly "signd and seald" with the blood of Christ, but the Old Testament will soon be said to be written "With bloody letters" (53.7) and so must be included as well. See Peter on Paul's epistles: "among the which some things are hard to be understood" (2 Pet. 3.16).

[5] Blue, traditional color of hope.

[6] The anchor is the traditional emblem of hope. Hope includes anxiety as faith does not.

15   They seeing *Una,* towardes her gan wend,
        Who them encounters with like courtesee;
        Many kind speeches they betweene them spend,
        And greatly joy each other for to see:
        Then to the knight with shamefast[1] modestie
        They turne them selves, at *Unaes* meeke request,
        And him salute with well beseeming glee;
        Who faire them quites,[2] as him beseemed best,
And goodly gan discourse of many a noble gest.[3]

16   Then *Una* thus: "But she your sister deare,
        The deare *Charissa* where is she become?
        Or wants she health, or busie is elswhere?"
        "Ah no," said they, "but forth she may not come:
        For she of late is lightned of her wombe,
        And hath encreast the world with one sonne more,
        That her to see should be but troublesome."
        "Indeed" (quoth she) "that should her trouble sore,
But thankt be God, and her encrease so evermore."

17   Then saide the aged *Caelia,* "Deare dame,
        And you good Sir, I wote[4] that of your toyle,
        And labors long, through which ye hether came,
        Ye both forwearied[5] be: therefore a whyle
        I read you rest, and to your bowres recoyle."
        Then called she a Groome, that forth him ledd
        Into a goodly lodge, and gan despoile[6]
        Of puissant armes, and laid in easie bedd;
His name was meeke *Obedience* rightfully aredd.

18   Now when their wearie limbes with kindly rest,
        And bodies were refresht with dew repast,
        Fayre *Una* gan *Fidelia* fayre request,
        To have her knight into her schoolehous plaste,
        That of her heavenly learning he might taste,
        And heare the wisedom of her wordes divine.

---

[1] **shamefast:** in a weak sense, and hence favorable: humble and chaste.

[2] **quites:** replies in the same vein.

[3] **gest:** deed of arms.

[4] **wote:** know; sometimes spelled "wot"; similar to "weet(e)" and "wit."

[5] **forwearied:** very wearied.

[6] **despoile:** undress, disrobe.

She graunted, and that knight so much agraste,[1]
That she him taught celestiall discipline,
And opened his dull eyes, that light mote in them shine.

19   And that her sacred Booke, with blood ywritt,
        That none could reade, except she did them teach,
        She unto him disclosed every whitt,
        And heavenly documents thereout did preach,
        That weaker witt of man could never reach,
        Of God, of grace, of justice, of free will,[2]
        That wonder was to heare her goodly speach:
        For she was hable, with her wordes to kill,
And rayse againe to life the hart, that she did thrill.[3]

20   And when she list poure out her larger spright,
        She would commaund the hasty Sunne to stay,
        Or backward turne his course from hevens hight,
        Sometimes great hostes of men she could dismay,
        [Dry-shod to passe, she parts the flouds in tway;][4]
        And eke huge mountaines from their native seat
        She would commaund, themselves to beare away,
        And throw in raging sea with roaring threat.
Almightie God her gave such powre, and puissaunce great.[5]

21   The faithfull knight now grew in litle space,
        By hearing her, and by her sisters lore,
        To such perfection of all hevenly grace;
        That wretched world he gan for to abhore,
        And mortal life gan loath, as thing forlore,[6]

---

[1] **agraste:** agraced, showed favor to.

[2] Fidelia teaches fundamental doctrinal topics for intellectual assent. Spenser does not say what Fidelia taught about any of them, much less about free will. This line is a chiasmus: grace and justice are opposed and complementary forces in salvation, as we saw in the preceding canto, and God and free will are opposed and complementary forces in good deeds, as we are seeing in this canto.

[3] **thrill:** pierce, but also with some of its modern meaning.

[4] In 1590 line 5 was missing, yielding an eight-line stanza; I have therefore put it in brackets. It was added only in 1609, ten years after Spenser's death, yet it sounds Spenserian.

[5] Fidelia's abilities illustrate the *fides miraculorum,* "the faith of miracles." For analogues to these miraculous feats, see the following: for line 2, Josh. 10.12–3; for line 3, 2 Kings 20.10; for line 4, Judg. 7.19–22; for line 5, Exod. 14.21–31, and the present canto 53.2–5; for lines 6–8, Matt. 21.21.

[6] **forlore:** abandoned, here in a good sense.

Greevd with remembrance of his wicked wayes,
And prickt with anguish of his sinnes so sore,
That he desirde, to end his wretched dayes:
So much the dart of sinfull guilt the soule dismayes.[1]

22   But wise *Speranza* gave him comfort sweet,
          And taught him how to take assured hold
          Upon her silver anchor, as was meet;
          Els had his sinnes so great, and manifold
          Made him forget all, that *Fidelia* told.
          In this distressed doubtfull agony,
          When him his dearest *Una* did behold,
          Disdeining life, desiring leave to dye,
She found her selfe assayld with great perplexity.

23   And came to *Caelia* to declare her smart,
          Who well acquainted with that commune plight,
          Which sinfull horror workes in wounded hart,
          Her wisely comforted all, that she might,
          With goodly counsell and advisement right;
          And streightway sent with carefull diligence,
          To fetch a Leach,[2] the which had great insight
          In that disease of grieved conscience,
And well could cure the same; His name was *Patience*.

24   Who comming to that sowle-diseased knight,[3]
          Could hardly him intreat, to tell his grief:
          Which knowne, and all that noyd his heavie spright,
          Well searcht, eftsoones he gan apply relief,
          Of salves and med'cines, which had passing prief,[4]
          And there to added wordes of wondrous might:

---

[1] Again, as with Despaire, Redcrosse is moved by guilt to commit suicide. Here it is the result of Fidelia's presumably truthful teachings. On the former occasion, Una stepped in to prevent suicide (ix.53); this time, Speranza does. To grasp the anchor of hope might symbolize those arguments that Una used on the previous occasion—God's mercy and his intention for Redcrosse to go to heaven.

[2] **Leach:** doctor. Catholics would expect Penance in this role, but he occurs only later and in a subordinate role as disciplinarian.

[3] Patience initiates some but not all of the traditional steps in repentance, utilized chiefly by Catholics: confession, illustrated in stanza 24; amendment; and satisfaction, reparation, or paying God back by suffering, illustrated in stanzas 26–8.

[4] **had passing prief:** had been thoroughly tested.

By which to ease he him recured brief,
And much aswag'd the passion of his plight,
That he his paine endur'd, as seeming now more light.

25   But yet, the cause and root of all his ill,
          Inward corruption, and infected sin,
          Not purg'd nor heald, behind remained still,
          And festring sore did ranckle yett within,
          Close creeping twixt the marow and the skin.
          Which to extirpe,[1] he laid him privily
          Downe in a darksome lowly place far in,
          Whereas he meant his corrosives[2] to apply,
And with straight diet[3] tame his stubborne malady.

26   In ashes and sackcloth he did array
          His daintie corse, proud humors to abate,
          And dieted with fasting every day,[4]
          The swelling of his woundes to mitigate,
          And made him pray both earely and eke late:
          And ever as superfluous flesh did rott
          Amendment readie still at hand did wayt,
          To pluck it out with pincers fyrie whott,[5]
That soone in him was lefte no one corrupted jott.

27   And bitter *Penaunce* with an yron whip,
          Was wont him once to disple[6] every day:
          And sharpe *Remorse* his hart did prick and nip,
          That drops of blood thence like a well did play;
          And sad *Repentance* used to embay,[7]
          His blamefull body in salt water sore,
          The filthy blottes of sin to wash away.
          So in short space they did to health restore
The man that would not live, but erst lay at deathes dore.

---

[1] **extirpe:** extirpate.

[2] **corrosives:** "meter requires 'corsives'. . . . The term signifies both a corrosive drug and a caustic remedy" (ACH).

[3] **straight diet:** strict, restricted lifestyle.

[4] Redcrosse's mortification resembles Corceca's (iii.14.3), except that his is for specific sins, for a limited time, and for a psychological effect.

[5] **whott:** hot.

[6] **disple:** to subject to bodily punishment, esp. as a religious practice (OED). Flagellation was a Catholic practice, and one so ancient that it was seldom employed even by them in Spenser's time, but see the hints of flagellation in Yates's account of penitential confraternities (176 and 197).

[7] **embay:** bathe.

28   In which his torment often was so great,
        That like a Lyon he would cry and rore,
        And rend his flesh, and his owne synewes eat.
        His owne deare *Una* hearing evermore
        His ruefull shriekes and gronings, often tore
        Her guiltlesse garments, and her golden heare,
        For pitty of his payne and anguish sore;
        Yet all with patience wisely she did beare;
    For well she wist, his cryme could els be never cleare.[1]

29   Whom thus recover'd by wise Patience,
        And trew *Repentaunce* they to *Una* brought;
        Who joyous of his cured conscience,
        Him dearely kist, and fayrely eke besought
        Himselfe to chearish, and consuming thought
        To put away out of his carefull brest.
        By this *Charissa,* late in child-bed brought,
        Was woxen strong, and left her fruitfull nest;
    To her fayre *Una* brought this unacquainted guest.

30   She was a woman in her freshest age,
        Of wondrous beauty, and of bounty[2] rare,
        With goodly grace and comely personage,
        That was on earth not easie to compare;
        Full of great love, but *Cupids* wanton snare
        As hell she hated, chaste in worke and will;[3]
        Her necke and brests were ever open bare,
        That ay thereof her babes might sucke their fill;
    The rest was all in yellow robes arayed still.

31   A multitude of babes about her hong,
        Playing their sportes, that joyd her to behold,
        Whom still she fed, whiles they were weak and young,
        But thrust them forth still, as they wexed old:
        And on her head she wore a tyre[4] of gold,
        Adornd with gemmes and owches[5] wondrous fayre,

---

[1] A clear indication that his suffering is meant not just as therapy but as reparation or restitution, part of the Catholic sacrament of penance.

[2] **bounty:** not just generosity, but goodness in general.

[3] The sanctified love between Redcrosse and Una, though it has a physical component, is never ascribed to Cupid. Arthur's love for Gloriana is (Proem 3.3; ix.8.9).

[4] **tyre:** here a headdress.

[5] **owches:** ornaments.

Whose passing price uneath was to be told;
And by her syde there sate a gentle payre
Of turtle doves, she sitting in an yvory chayre.[1]

32   The knight and *Una* entring, fayre her greet,
And bid her joy of that her happy brood;
Who them requites with court'sies seeming meet,
And entertaynes with friendly chearefull mood.
Then *Una* her besought, to be so good,
As in her vertuous rules to schoole her knight,
Now after all his torment well withstood,
In that sad[2] house of *Penaunce,* where his spright
Had past the paines of hell, and long enduring night.

33   She was right joyous of her just request,
And taking by the hand that Faeries sonne,
Gan him instruct in everie good behest,
Of love, and righteousnes, and well to donne,
And wrath, and hatred warely to shonne,[3]
That drew on men Gods hatred,[4] and his wrath,
And many soules in dolours had fordonne:[5]
In which when him she well instructed hath,
From thence to heaven she teacheth him the ready path.[6]

34   Wherein his weaker wandring steps to guyde,
An auncient matrone she to her does call,
Whose sober lookes her wisedome well descryde:[7]
Her name was *Mercy,* well knowne over all,
To be both gratious, and eke liberall:
To whom the carefull charge of him she gave,
To leade aright, that he should never fall
In all his waies through this wide worldes wave,
That Mercy in the end his righteous soule might save.

---

[1] Charissa's attributes are traditional except for her unexplained yellow clothes (Charity's clothes are usually red or rose colored) and her turtle doves, which are attributes of Venus.

[2] **sad:** solemn.

[3] **warely to shonne:** warily to shun.

[4] I.e., hatred can send one to hell, implying that its opposite, love, can get one to heaven—an Augustinian doctrine.

[5] I.e., had ruined in the pains (of hell).

[6] The first unequivocal statement that Charity, not Faith, gets one into heaven; see 51.3 about Mercy.

[7] **descryde:** allowed to be descried, manifested.

35   The godly Matrone by the hand him beares
       Forth from her presence, by a narrow way,
       Scattred with bushy thornes, and ragged breares,
       Which still before him she remov'd away,
       That nothing might his ready passage stay:
       And ever when his feet encombred were,
       Or gan to shrinke, or from the right to stray,
       She held him fast, and firmely did upbeare,
   As carefull Nourse her child from falling oft does reare.

36   Eftsoones unto an holy Hospitall,
       That was fore by the way, she did him bring,
       In which seven Bead-men[1] that had vowed all
       Their life to service of high heavens king
       Did spend their daies in doing godly thing:
       There gates to all were open evermore,
       That by the wearie way were traveiling,
       And one sate wayting ever them before,
   To call in commers by, that needy were and pore.

37   The first of them that eldest was, and best,
       Of all the house had charge and governement,
       As Guardian and Steward of the rest:
       His office was to give entertainement
       And lodging, unto all that came, and went:
       Not unto such, as could him feast againe,
       And double quite,[2] for that he on them spent,
       But such, as want of harbour[3] did constraine:
   Those for Gods sake his dewty was to entertaine.

---

[1] The seven Bead-men in this good society personify the Seven Corporal Works of Mercy or the Seven Good Deeds, balancing in a general way the Seven Deadly Sins in the bad society, the House of Pride (Canto Four). For the first six, see Matt. 25.35–6; for the burial of the dead and the care of widows and orphans, see James 1.27. Besides appearing in multitudinous medieval and Catholic sources, visual and written, including the two processions discussed by Yates (174–91, 197–207), these seven appeared, says TPR, in the Protestant Heinrich Bullinger's *Decades,* translated as *Fiftie godlie sermons.* The name "Bead(s)-men" implies that they spend their lives praying (whether on rosary beads or otherwise), but these men are active. Apparently Spenser called them by this seemingly inappropriate name to indicate that, like Caelia, they have a contemplative side to them, which they, like Caelia, exercise at night.

[2] **quite:** requite, repay.

[3] **harbour:** place to live.

38   The second was as Almner[1] of the place,
          His office was, the hungry for to feed,
          And thrifty give to drinke, a worke of grace:
          He feard not once him selfe to be in need,
          Ne car'd to hoord for those, whom he did breede:[2]
          The grace of God he layd up still in store,
          Which as a stocke he left unto his seede;
          He had enough, what need him care for more?
      And had he lesse, yet some he would give to the pore.

39   The third had of their wardrobe custody,
          In which were not rich tyres,[3] nor garments gay,
          The plumes of pride, and winges of vanity,
          But clothes meet to keepe keene cold away,
          And naked nature seemely to aray;
          With which bare wretched wights he dayly clad,
          The images of God in earthly clay;
          And if that no spare clothes to give he had,
      His owne cote he would cut, and it distribute glad.

40   The fourth appointed by his office was,
          Poore prisoners to relieve with gratious ayd,
          And captives to redeeme with price of bras,[4]
          From Turkes and Sarazins, which them had stayd;[5]
          And though they faulty were, yet well he wayd,
          That God to us forgiveth every howre
          Much more then that, why they in bands were layd,
          And he that harrowd hell[6] with heavie stowre,
      The faulty soules from thence brought to his heavenly bowre.

41   The fift had charge sick persons to attend,
          And comfort those, in point of death which lay;
          For them most needeth comfort in the end,

[1] **Almner:** distributor of alms.

[2] **whom he did breede:** his children. Evidently this beads-man is married—a Protestant touch.

[3] **tyres:** attire.

[4] **price of bras:** brass coins.

[5] **stayd:** detained in prison, arrested.

[6] The Apostle's Creed says, on the basis of hints in scripture, that Christ "descended into hell." The Gospel of Nicodemus elaborates these hints into a story of Christ descending into hell and fighting devils to rescue virtuous persons who could not have known him because they lived before him. This explicit reference confirms interpretations of Arthur (Canto Eight) and Redcrosse (Canto Eleven) as reenacting this rescue.

When sin, and hell, and death doe most dismay
The feeble soule departing hence away.
All is but lost, that living we bestow,[1]
If not well ended at our dying day.
O man have mind of that last bitter throw;[2]
For as the tree does fall, so lyes it ever low.

42   The sixt had charge of them now being dead,
        In seemly sort their corses to engrave,[3]
        And deck with dainty flowres their brydall bed,
        That to their heavenly spouse[4] both sweet and brave
        They might appeare, when he their soules shall save.
        The wondrous workmanship of Gods owne mould,
        Whose face he made, all beastes to feare, and gave
        All in his hand, even dead we honour should.
Ah dearest God me graunt, I dead be not defould.

43   The seventh now after death and buriall done,
        Had charge the tender Orphans of the dead
        And wydowes ayd, least they should be undone:
        In face of judgement he their right would plead,
        Ne ought the powre of mighty men did dread
        In their defence, nor would for gold or fee
        Be wonne their rightfull causes downe to tread:
        And when they stood in most necessitee,
He did supply their want, and gave them ever free.[5]

44   There when the Elfin knight arrived was,
        The first and chiefest of the seven, whose care
        Was guests to welcome, towardes him did pas:
        Where seeing *Mercie*, that his steps upbare,

[1] **bestow:** give to charity, which in itself is a meritorious act; but it won't get one to heaven if one falls into mortal sin on one's death bed—a Catholic emphasis.

[2] **throw:** throe, i.e., the agony of death.

[3] **engrave:** put into the grave.

[4] Picturing the soul's entry into heaven as a marriage with Christ, and fancifully picturing her entering with her body and her material accoutrements. The next reason given is doctrinally serious: to honor God's image in and special creation of mankind; see Gen. 1.26–7.

[5] **free:** freely. Redcrosse and Guyon together perform the last four of the seven works of mercy, Redcrosse's being release of prisoners (Canto Eleven), and Guyon's comforting the dying, burying the dead, and caring for widows and orphans (II.i.35–ii.11).

And alwaies led, to her with reverence rare
He humbly louted[1] in meeke lowlinesse,
And seemely welcome for her did prepare:
For of their order she was Patronesse,
Albe *Charissa* were their chiefest founderesse.[2]

45   There she awhile him stayes, him selfe to rest,
That to the rest more hable[3] he might bee:
During which time, in every good behest
And godly worke of Almes and charitee
Shee him instructed with great industree;
Shortly therein so perfect he became,
That from the first unto the last degree,
His mortall life he learned had to frame
In holy righteousnesse, without rebuke or blame.

46   Thence forward by that painfull way they pas,
Forth to an hill, that was both steepe and hy;
On top whereof a sacred chappell was,
And eke a litle Hermitage thereby.
Wherein an aged holy man did lie,
That day and night said his devotion,
Ne other worldly busines did apply;
His name was hevenly *Contemplation;*
Of God and goodnes was his meditation.

47   Great grace that old man to him given had;
For God he often saw from heavens hight,
All[4] were his earthly eien both blunt and bad,
And through great age had lost their kindly sight,
Yet wondrous quick and persaunt[5] was his spright,
As Eagles eie, that can behold the Sunne:
That hill they scale with all their powre and might,
That his[6] fraile thighes nigh weary, and fordonne
Gan faile, but by her helpe the top at last he wonne.

---

[1] **louted:** bowed.

[2] Charity founded the hospital of the beadsmen, and Mercy, Charity's outward expression, is her deputy.

[3] **hable:** able.

[4] **All:** although.

[5] **persaunt:** piercing. The bestiaries tell us that only the eagle can look straight at the sun, which makes him an emblem of contemplation as well as of St. John, whose gospel emphasizes Christ's divine side.

[6] I.e., Redcrosse's.

48 Where they doe finde that godly aged Sire,
        With snowy lockes adowne his shoulders shed,
        As hoary frost with spangles doth attire
        The mossy branches of an Oke halfe ded.
        Each bone might through his body well be red,
        And every sinew seene through his long fast:
        For nought he car'd his carcas long unfed;
        His mind was full of spirituall repast,
    And pyn'd[1] his flesh, to keepe his body low and chast.

49 Who when these two approching he aspide,
        At their first presence grew agrieved sore,
        That forst him lay his hevenly thoughts aside;
        And had he not that Dame respected more,
        Whom highly he did reverence and adore,
        He would not once have moved for the knight.
        They him saluted standing far afore;
        Who well them greeting, humbly did requight,
    And asked, to what end they clomb[2] that tedious hight.

50 "What end" (quoth she) "should cause us take such paine,
        But that same end, which every living wight
        Should make his marke,[3] high heaven to attaine?
        Is not from hence the way, that leadeth right
        To that most glorious house, that glistreth bright
        With burning starres, and everliving fire,
        Whereof the keies are to thy hand behight[4]
        By wise *Fidelia?* shee doth thee require,
    To shew it to this knight, according his desire."

51 "Thrise happy man, said then the father grave,
        Whose staggering steps thy steady hand doth lead,
        And shewes the way, his sinfull soule to save.[5]
        Who better can the way to heaven aread,
        Then thou thy selfe, that was both borne and bred
        In hevenly throne, where thousand Angels shine?

---

[1] **pyn'd:** starved.

[2] **clomb:** climbed.

[3] **marke:** goal.

[4] **behight:** designated.

[5] This passage and 33.9 state unequivocally that human works of mercy get one into heaven; many other passages either imply it while equivocating on God's mercy (34.9) or state a compromise, that they earn grace (38).

Thou doest the praiers of the righteous sead[1]
Present before the majesty divine,
And his avenging wrath to clemency incline.

52   "Yet since thou bidst, thy pleasure shalbe donne.
          Then come thou man of earth,[2] and see the way,
          That never yet was seene of Faries sonne,[3]
          That never leads the traveiler astray,
          But after labors long, and sad delay,
          Bring them to joyous rest and endlesse blis.
          But first thou must a season fast and pray,
          Till from her bands the spright assoiled[4] is,
And have her strength recur'd[5] from fraile infirmitis."

53   That done, he leads him to the highest Mount;
          Such one, as that same mighty man of God,[6]
          That blood-red billowes like a walled front
          On either side disparted with his rod,
          Till that his army dry-foot through them yod,[7]
          Dwelt forty daies upon; where writt in stone
          With bloody letters by the hand of God,
          The bitter doome of death and balefull mone
He did receive, whiles flashing fire about him shone.[8]

54   Or like that sacred hill, whose head full hie,
          Adornd with fruitfull Olives all arownd,
          Is, as it were for endlesse memory
          Of that deare Lord, who oft theron was fownd,

---

[1] **sead:** seed, as in the expression "the seed of Abraham"; offspring. See Night's grumbling about how God favors "the sonnes of day" (v.25.7).

[2] Etymologizing Redcrosse's name, George, from *Ge* (Greek for earth), which the Hermit knows and will soon tell him.

[3] Elves and Fairies (except for Guyon) cannot see or go to heaven; only humans can.

[4] **assoiled:** absolved, in the technical, theological sense, with an etymological pun on "cleaned from soil."

[5] **recur'd:** a combination of cured and recovered.

[6] Moses.

[7] **yod:** went; past tense of "yede," go; also spelled "yode"—an archaism.

[8] The Ten Commandments were written in stone. They are pictured as threatening because, according to Protestants, no one could fulfill them, so their penalties were unavoidable. See also the identification of law with punishment in Despaire's arguments. In Scripture, the letters were not literally bloody, as here; Spenser's imagery opens the door to seeing Fidelia's book as the entire Bible.

For ever with a flowring girlond crownd:[1]
Or like that pleasaunt Mount, that is for ay
Through famous Poets verse each where renownd,
On which the thrise three learned Ladies play
Their hevenly notes, and make full many a lovely lay.[2]

55   From thence, far off he unto him did shew
A litle path, that was both steepe and long,
Which to a goodly Citty led his vew;
Whose wals and towres were builded high and strong
Of perle and precious stone, that earthly tong
Cannot describe, nor wit of man can tell;
Too high a ditty[3] for my simple song:
The Citty of the greate king hight it well,
Wherein eternall peace and happinesse doth dwell.

56   As he thereon stood gazing, he might see
The blessed Angels to and fro descend[4]
From highest heven, in gladsome companee,
And with great joy into that Citty wend,
As commonly as frend does with his frend.
Whereat he wondred much, and gan enquere,
What stately building durst so high extend
Her lofty towres unto the starry sphere,
And what unknowen nation there empeopled[5] were.

57   "Faire knight" (quoth he) "*Hierusalem* that is,
The new *Hierusalem,* that God has built
For those to dwell in, that are chosen his,
His chosen people purg'd from sinful guilt,
With piteous blood, which cruelly was spilt

[1] The flowering garland is from the Garden of Gethsemane, which was on the Mount of Olives (Matt. 26.30, 36).

[2] The pleasant mount is Parnassus, where the nine Muses dwell; the three mountains correspond to the three epochs of Nature (Parnassus), Law (Sinai), and Grace (Mount of Olives). Cf. the simile of the Well of Life to springs that are of the Old Testament, of the New Testament, or contemporary (xi.30). The triad implies an equality, per-haps as forms of vision, between Parnassus and the scriptural mountains. See ACH note ad loc; and Phillips.

[3] **ditty:** subject; the topos of authorial modesty again, perhaps justified in dealing with a theological subject.

[4] From Jacob's dream of angels ascending and descending between earth and heaven (Gen. 28.12).

[5] **empeopled:** installed as citizens.

On cursed tree, of that unspotted lam,
That for the sinnes of al the world was kilt:
Now are they Saints all in that Citty sam,[1]
More dear unto their God, then younglings to their dam."[2]

58   "Till now," said then the knight, "I weened well,
That great *Cleopolis,* where I have beene,
In which that fairest *Fary Queene* doth dwell
The fairest Citty was, that might be seene;
And that bright towre all built of christall clene,
Panthea,[3] seemd the brightest thing, that was:
But now by proofe all otherwise I weene;
For this great Citty that does far surpas,
And this bright Angels towre quite dims that towre of glas."

59   "Most trew," then said the holy aged man;
"Yet is *Cleopolis* for earthly frame,
The fairest peece, that eie beholden can:
And well beseemes all knights of noble name,
That covet in th'immortall booke of fame
To be eternized, that same to haunt,[4]
And doen their service to that soveraigne Dame,
That glory does to them for guerdon graunt:
For she is hevenly borne, and heaven may justly vaunt.[5]

60   "And thou faire ymp, sprong out from English race,
How ever now accompted[6] Elfins sonne,
Well worthy doest thy service for her grace,

---

[1] **sam:** together.

[2] Spenser here reverts to Protestantism again and says that one gets to heaven by God's arbitrary choice and by forgiveness through the blood of Christ. Perhaps this represents the view from the perspective of eternity. Christ as the sacrificial "Lamb of God" (John 1.29) harmonizes with the image in line 9 of all the saints as lambs.

[3] Derives from the Pantheon in Rome, which is a temple dedicated to all the gods—presumably here a temple to those who achieved earthly fame; perhaps an analogue of Westminster Abbey.

[4] **that same to haunt:** to hang around Cleopolis, to frequent it.

[5] The longest description of Cleopolis (fame-city), the Faerie capital, and Gloriana that we ever get in the poem as we have it. Spenser says of Gloriana, with less justification than of Una, that she is heavenly born; he equivocates on "glory"—heavenly or earthly?—in order to assimilate fame to salvation.

[6] **accompted:** counted as, assumed to be.

To aide a virgin desolate foredonne.
But when thou famous victory hast wonne,
And high emongst all knights hast hong thy shield,
Thenceforth the suitt[1] of earthly conquest shonne,
And wash thy hands from guilt of bloody field:
For blood can nought but sin, and wars but sorrows yield.

61   "Then seek this path, that I to thee presage,
       Which after all to heaven shall thee send;
       Then peaceably thy painefull pilgrimage
       To yonder same *Hierusalem* doe bend,
       Where is for thee ordaind a blessed end:
       For thou emongst those Saints, whom thou doest see,
       Shalt be a Saint, and thine owne nations frend
       And Patrone: thou Saint *George* shalt called bee,
Saint George of mery England, the signe of victoree."[2]

62   "Unworthy wretch" (quoth he) "of so great grace,
       How dare I thinke such glory to attaine?"
       "These that have it attaynd, were in like cace
       As wretched men, and lived in like paine."
       "But deeds of armes must I at last be faine,[3]
       And Ladies love to leave so dearely bought?"
       "What need of armes, where peace doth ay remaine,"
       (Said he) "and bitter battailes all are fought?
As for loose loves they'are vaine, and vanish into nought."[4]

---

[1] **suitt:** pursuit.

[2] Although Protestants had officially downgraded all saints, and both Protestants and Catholics alike doubted St. George's historical existence, he was immensely popular in England and had been for centuries. He was the patron saint of the royal Order of the Garter. The standard source is the *Legenda aurea,* or Golden Legend, of Jacobus de Voragine, a collection of saint's-lives, translated and published by Caxton in 1483 (TPR). Here and only here—i.e., in slaying the dragon to save the princess and her lamb (and, by implication, when he is in heaven being invoked by the English warriors)—does Redcrosse become like St. George. Their careers are otherwise quite

different, e.g., St. George is not interested in marrying the princess. As indicated above, Redcrosse could not have seen the New Jerusalem or become a Saint if he were truly an Elf.

[3] **faine:** content to leave.

[4] ACH outlines the difficult part of the debate thusly: Redcrosse's second question (5–6) has two parts: "Must I abandon arms and must I abandon love?" The first is parried by a double rhetorical question (7–8), and the second dismissed with a reproof (9), namely that loves vanish—presumably because "in the resurrection they nether marie wives, nor wives are bestowed in marriage" (Matt. 22.30).

63   "O let me not" (quoth he) "then turne againe
       Backe to the world, whose joyes so fruitlesse are,
       But let me heare for aie in peace remaine,
       Or straight way on that last long voyage fare,
       That nothing may my present hope empare."[1]
       "That may not be" (said he) "ne maist thou yitt
       Forgoe that royal maides bequeathed care,
       Who did her cause into thy hand committ,
  Till from her cursed foe thou have her freely quitt."

64   "Then shall I soone," (quoth he) "so God me grace,
       Abett that virgins cause disconsolate,
       And shortly back returne unto this place,
       To walke this way in Pilgrims poore estate.[2]
       But now aread, old father, why of late
       Didst thou behight[3] me borne of English blood,
       Whom all a Fairies sonne doen nominate?"[4]
       "That word shall I" (said he) "avouchen good,
  Sith to thee is unknowne the cradle of thy brood.

65   "For well I wote, thou springst from ancient race
       Of *Saxon* kinges, that have with mightie hand
       And many bloody battailes fought in place
       High reard their royall throne in *Britans* land
       And vanquisht them, unable to withstand:
       From thence a Faery thee unweeting reft,[5]
       There as thou slepst in tender swadling band,
       And her base Elfin brood there for thee left.
  Such men do Chaungelings call, so chaungd by Faeries theft.

66   "Thence she thee brought into this Faery lond,
       And in an heaped furrow did thee hyde,
       Where thee a Ploughman all unweeting fond,

---

[1] **empare:** impair.

[2] In Canto Twelve, Redcrosse reveals another reason why he cannot go to heaven now, the same as his reason for deferral of marriage to Una (an event that comes to seem like the equivalent of heaven)—his duty to Gloriana. Christians often are reluctant to go back to the world after a mystical experience and see their time on earth as a pointless deferral of heaven. The Hermit curiously motivates him to do so by the pursuit of fame, which reinforces his duty to Gloriana (see stanza 59).

[3] **behight:** call.

[4] **nominate:** denominate.

[5] **reft:** snatched away, took away violently; past tense of "reave."

As he his toylesome teme that way did guyde,
And brought thee up in ploughmans state to byde,[1]
Whereof *Georgos* he thee gave to name;[2]
Till prickt with courage, and thy forces pryde,
To Fary court thou cam'st to seeke for fame,
And prove thy puissaunt armes, as seemes thee best became."[3]

67   "O holy Sire" (quoth he) "how shall I quight[4]
The many favours I with thee have fownd,
That hast my name and nation redd aright,
And taught the way that does to heaven bownd?"
This saide, adowne he looked to the grownd,
To have returnd, but dazed were his eyne,
Through passing brightnes, which did quite confound
His feeble sence, and too exceeding shyne.
So darke are earthly thinges compard to things divine.

68   At last whenas himselfe he gan to fynd,
To *Una* back he cast him to retyre;
Who him awaited still with pensive mynd.
Great thankes and goodly meed[5] to that good syre,
He thens departing gave for his paynes hyre.
So came to *Una,* who him joyd to see,
And after litle rest, gan him desyre,
Of her adventure myndfull for to bee.
So leave they take of *Caelia,* and her daughters three.

---

[1] **byde:** remain.

[2] ACH quotes directly from Barclay's early modern translation of *The Golden Legend:* "George is sayd of geos which is as moche to saye as erthe and orge that is tilyenge so george is to say as tilyenge the erthe that is his flesshe," etc., with other etymologies.

[3] Once again, the Hermit affirms worldly values. Apparently fame can be renounced only after it has been won.

[4] **quight:** requite.

[5] **meed:** money or other worldly goods as recompense.

Canto Eleven

The knight with that old Dragon[1] fights
two dayes incessantly:
The third him overthrowes, and gayns
most glorious victory.

1   High time now gan it wex for *Una* fayre,
          To thinke of those her captive Parents deare,
          And their forwasted kingdom to repayre:
          Whereto whenas they now approched neare,
          With hartie wordes her knight she gan to cheare,
          And in her modest maner thus bespake;
          "Deare knight, as deare, as ever knight was deare,
          That all these sorrowes suffer for my sake,
      High heven behold the tedious toyle, ye for me take.

2   "Now are we come unto my native soyle,
          And to the place, where all our perilles dwell;
          Here hauntes that feend, and does his dayly spoyle,
          Therefore henceforth bee at your keeping well,[2]
          And ever ready for your foeman fell.
          The sparke of noble corage now awake,
          And strive your excellent selfe to excell;
          That shall ye evermore renowmed make,
      Above all knights on earth, that batteill undertake."

3   And pointing forth, "lo yonder is" (said she)
          "The brasen towre in which my parents deare
          For dread of that huge feend emprisond be
          Whom I from far, see on the walles appeare
          Whose sight my feeble soule doth greatly cheare:
          And on the top of all I do espye
          The watchman wayting tydings glad to heare,
          That O my parents might I happily
      Unto you bring, to ease you of your misery."[3]

---

[1] Citing Rev. 20.2: "the dragon that old serpent, which is the devil and Satan."

[2] I.e., be on your guard.

[3] In 1590, this entire stanza was missing; see Textual Notes.

4   With that they heard a roaring hideous sownd,
       That all the ayre with terror filled wyde,
       And seemd uneath[1] to shake the stedfast ground.
       Eftsoones that dreadfull Dragon they espyde,
       Where stretcht he lay upon the sunny side,
       Of a great hill, himselfe like a great hill.
       But all so soone, as he from far descryde
       Those glistring armes, that heven with light did fill,
   He rousd himselfe full blyth, and hastned them untill.[2]

5   Then badd the knight his Lady yede[3] aloof,
       And to an hill her selfe withdraw asyde,
       From whence she might behold that battailles proof
       And eke be safe from daunger far descryde:
       She him obayd, and turnd a litle wyde,[4]
       Now O thou sacred Muse, most learned Dame,[5]
       Fayre ympe of *Phoebus* and his aged bryde,[6]
       The Nourse of time, and everlasting fame,
   That warlike handes ennoblest with immortall name;

6   O gently come into my feeble brest,
       Come gently, but not with that mightie rage,
       Wherewith the martiall troupes thou doest infest,
       And hartes of great Heroes doest enrage,
       That nought their kindled corage may aswage,
       Soone as thy dreadfull trompe begins to sownd;

---

[1] **uneath:** almost; see ACH note ad loc.

[2] I.e., he raised himself most blithely and hastened unto them—like an eager host.

[3] **yede:** go—an archaism.

[4] **wyde:** off to one side.

[5] Spenser frequently calls his muse sacred. TPR identifies this one as Calliope, Muse of epic poetry; M&P identify her as Clio, Muse of history; ACH remains undecided. Clio is invoked at III.iii.4, and both Clio and Calliope at VII.vi.37. It is a long-standing problem in Spenser criticism. Perhaps he did not mean to be specific.

[6] Spenser's Muse is "Faiyre ympe of *Phoebus*," following Natalis Comes, whose quotation from *Metamorphoses* (1.516–17) seems to make Phoebus Apollo the father of the Muses (*Mythologiae,* 4.10), not Jove, as in Hesiod (*Theogony,* 56–62), and indeed even as in *The Faerie Queene,* IV.xi.10, VII.vi.37, VII.vii.1 (TPR; M&P; Roche 1989, 162–6; *SE* "Muse"). The Muse's mother is Phoebus' "aged bride" Mnemosyne, goddess of memory, pictured as old, and mother of the Muses by all accounts. 1590 has a comma after "Phoebus," which I delete in order to obviate the implication that the Muse is also the aged bride of Phoebus.

The God of warre with his fiers equipage[1]
Thou doest awake, sleepe never he so sownd,
And scared nations doest with horror sterne astownd.

7   Fayre Goddesse lay that furious fitt[2] asyde,
           Till I of warres and bloody *Mars* doe sing,[3]
           And Bryton fieldes with Sarazin blood bedyde,
           Twixt that great faery Queene and Paynim king,
           That with their horror heven and earth did ring,
           A worke of labour long, and endlesse prayse:
           But now a while lett downe that haughtie string,[4]
           And to my tunes thy second tenor rayse,[5]
           That I this man of God his godly armes may blaze.[6]

8   By this the dreadfull Beast drew nigh to hand,
           Halfe flying, and halfe footing in his haste,
           That with his largenesse measured much land,
           And made wide shadow under his huge waste;[7]
           As mountaine doth the valley overcaste.
           Approching nigh, he reared high afore

---

[1] **equipage:** equipment.

[2] **fitt:** mood.

[3] Possibly an allusion to Spenser's intended epic "of politicke virtues in [Arthur's] person, after that hee came to be king" ("Letter to Raleigh"), or to the projected Book Twelve of the present poem. Later Redcrosse reveals his promise to serve in what sounds like this same final, climactic battle "Gainst that proud Paynim king, that works her teene" (xii.18.8). See ACH for the critical debate.

[4] **haughtie string:** lofty strain. Spenser calls for a lower mode, perhaps alluding to Plato's notion that certain musical modes are appropriate for certain subjects and audiences.

[5] With "second tenor," Spenser inexplicably belittles the subject of this canto, a religious one (see Introduction, 4), in favor of that of the projected Book Twelve, presumably a secular one (though warring against Paynims was then considered a reli-

gious act). The invocation itself emphasizes the episode, even as the content deemphasizes it. However that may be, this invocation represents a valuable foreshadowing of how the poem would have ended had Spenser lived to complete it; it would have resembled Arthur's conquest of Rome in the "Arthur and Lucius" section of Malory's *Le Morte D'Arthur* in which the Paynim King would allegorize the Pope, and it would have lent to the poem a now-missing epic dimension. Nevertheless, in the poem as we have it, the dragon fight receives the longest treatment of any battle (55 stanzas), so it does not take second place to anything.

[6] **blaze:** proclaim. Like Proem 1.5–9, this is a rewriting of *Aeneid's* "Arma virumque cano," "I sing of arms and the man." Here Spenser claims to sing of "his godly armes" rather than of the man (ACH).

[7] **waste:** waist, synecdoche for his entire torso.

His body monstrous, horrible, and vaste,
Which to increase his wondrous greatnes more,
Was swoln with wrath, and poyson, and with bloody gore.

9   And over, all with brasen scales was armd,
        Like plated cote of steele, so couched neare,
        That nought mote perce, ne might his corse bee harmd
        With dint of swerd, nor push of pointed speare,
        Which as an Eagle, seeing pray appeare,
        His aery plumes doth rouze, full rudely dight,[1]
        So shaked he, that horror was to heare,
        For as the clashing of an Armor bright,
Such noyse his rouzed scales did send unto the knight.

10   His flaggy winges when forth he did display,
        Were like two sayles, in which the hollow wynd
        Is gathered full, and worketh speedy way:
        And eke the pennes, that did his pineons[2] bynd,
        Were like mayne-yardes, with flying canvas lynd,
        With which whenas him list the ayre to beat,
        And there by force unwonted passage fynd,
        The clowdes before him fledd for terror great,
And all the hevens stood still amazed with his threat.

11   His huge long tayle wownd up in hundred foldes,
        Does overspred his long bras-scaly back,
        Whose wreathed boughtes[3] when ever he unfoldes,
        And thick entangled knots adown does slack,
        Bespotted as with shieldes of red and blacke,
        It sweepeth all the land behind him farre,
        And of three furlongs does but litle lacke;
        And at the point two stinges in fixed arre,
Both deadly sharp, that sharpest steele exceeden farr.

12   But stinges and sharpest steele did far exceed[4]
        The sharpnesse of his cruel rending clawes;
        Dead was it sure, as sure as death in deed,

---

[1] **full rudely dight:** all ruffed out.

[2] **pennes:** feathers; **pineons:** in this context, wings (OED).

[3] **boughtes:** coils.

[4] **steele did far exceed:** direct object before subject; i.e., the sharpness of his cruel, rending claws did far exceed that of stings and sharpest steel.

What ever thing does touch his ravenous pawes,
Or what within his reach he ever drawes.
But his most hideous head my tongue to tell,
Does tremble: for his deepe devouring jawes
Wyde gaped, like the griesly mouth of hell,
Through which into his darke abysse all ravin[1] fell.

13   And that[2] more wondrous was, in either jaw
Threeranckes of yron teeth enraunged were,
In which yett trickling blood and gobbets raw
Of late devoured bodies did appeare,
That sight thereof bredd cold congealed feare:
Which to increase, and all atonce to kill,
A cloud of smoothering smoke and sulphure seare[3]
Out of his stinking gorge forth steemed still,
That all the ayre about with smoke and stench did fill.

14   His blazing eyes, like two bright shining shieldes,
Did burne with wrath, and sparkled living fyre;
As two broad Beacons, sett in open fieldes,
Send forth their flames far off to every shyre,
And warning give, that enimies conspyre,
With fire and sword the region to invade;
So flam'd his eyne with rage and rancorous yre:
But far within, as in a hollow glade,
Those glaring lampes were sett, that made a dreadfull shade.

15   So dreadfully he towardes him did pas,
Forelifting up a loft his speckled brest,
And often bounding on the brused gras,
As for great joyaunce of his newcome guest.
Eftsoones he gan advaunce his haughty crest,
As chauffed Bore his bristles doth upreare,
And shoke his scales to battaile ready drest;
That made the *Redcrosse* knight nigh quake for feare,
As bidding bold defyaunce to his foeman neare.

---

[1] **ravin:** prey.
[2] **that:** what.
[3] **seare:** burning.

16 The knight gan fayrely couch[1] his steady speare,
   And fiersely ran at him with rigorous might:
   The pointed steele arriving rudely theare,
   His harder hyde would nether perce, nor bight,
   But glauncing by foorth passed forward right;
   Yet sore amoved with so puissaunt push,
   The wrathfull beast about him turned light,[2]
   And him so rudely passing by, did brush
  With his long tayle, that horse and man to ground did rush.

17 Both horse and man up lightly rose againe,
   And fresh encounter towardes him addrest:
   But th'ydle stroke yet backe recoyld in vaine,
   And found no place his deadly point to rest.
   Exceeding rage enflam'd the furious beast,
   To be avenged of so great despight;[3]
   For never felt his imperceable brest
   So wondrous force, from hand of living wight;
  Yet had he prov'd[4] the powre of many a puissant knight.

18 Then with his waving wings displayed wyde,
   Himselfe up high he lifted from the ground,
   And with strong flight did forcibly divyde
   The yielding ayre, which nigh too feeble found
   Her flitting parts,[5] and element unsound,
   To beare so great a weight: he cutting way
   With his broad sayles, about him soared round:
   At last low stouping with unweldy sway,
  Snatcht up both horse and man, to beare them quite away.

19 Long he them bore above the subject[6] plaine,
   So far as Ewghen[7] bow a shaft may send,
   Till struggling strong did him at last constraine,
   To let them downe before his flightes end:

---

[1] **couch:** bring down from its vertical position and lay horizontally in the rest.

[2] **about him turned light:** either turned himself quickly about (as he would have to do to strike him with his tail) or turned quickly around Redcrosse.

[3] **despight:** insult.

[4] **prov'd:** tested by experience; synomous with approved.

[5] **flitting parts:** moving particles.

[6] **subject:** lying below, from the Latin word *subicere.*

[7] **Ewghen:** made of yew.

As hagard hauke[1] presuming to contend
With hardy fowle, above his hable might,[2]
His wearie pounces all in vaine doth spend,
To trusse[3] the pray too heavy for his flight;
Which comming down to ground, does free it selfe by fight.

20   He so disseized of his gryping grosse,[4]
The knight his thrillant speare againe assayd
In his bras-plated body to embosse,[5]
And three mens strength unto the stroake he layd;
Wherewith the stiffe beame quaked, as affrayd,
And glauncing from his scaly necke, did glyde
Close under his left wing, then broad displayd.
The percing steele there wrought a wound full wyde,
That with the uncouth smart the Monster lowdly cryde.

21   He cryde, as raging seas are wont to rore,
When wintry storme his wrathful wreck does threat,
The rolling billowes beat the ragged shore,
As they the earth would shoulder from her seat,
And greedy gulfe does gape, as he would eat
His neighbour element[6] in his revenge:
Then gin the blustring brethren[7] boldly threat,
To move the world from off his stedfast henge,[8]
And boystrous battaile make, each other to avenge.

22   The steely head stuck fast still in his flesh,
Till with his cruell clawes he snatcht the wood,
And quite a sunder broke. Forth flowed fresh
A gushing river of blacke gory blood,
That drowned all the land, whereon he stood;
The streame thereof would drive a water-mill.

---

[1] **hagard hauke:** a mature and wild hawk, in contrast to the young "Eyas hauke" (34.6) to which the knight is compared (ACH).

[2] **hable might:** what he was able to lift.

[3] **trusse:** carry conveniently.

[4] **gryping grosse:** heavy gripful (TPR; M&P). Syntax is unclear as to whether the knight or the dragon motivates the release from the dragon's grip.

[5] **embosse:** plunge, encase; apparently coined by Spenser (OED).

[6] **neighbour element:** earth.

[7] **blustring brethren:** the winds.

[8] **henge:** variant spelling of "hinge," referring to the poles.

Trebly augmented was his furious mood
With bitter sence of his deepe rooted ill,
That flames of fire he threw forth from his large nosethril.

23   His hideous tayle then hurled he about,
      And therewith all enwrapt the nimble thyes
      Of his froth-fomy steed, whose courage stout
      Striving to loose the knott, that fast him tyes,
      Himselfe in streighter bandes too rash implyes,[1]
      That to the ground he is perforce constraynd
      To throw his ryder: who can[2] quickly ryse
      From off the earth, with durty blood distaynd,[3]
For that reprochfull fall right fowly he disdaynd.

24   And fercely tooke his trenchand[4] blade in hand,
      With which he stroke so furious and so fell,
      That nothing seemd the puissaunce could withstand:
      Upon his crest the hardned yron fell,
      But his more hardned crest was armd so well,
      That deeper dint therein it would not make;
      Yet so extremely did the buffe him quell,
      That from thenceforth he shund the like to take,
But when he saw them come, he did them still forsake.[5]

25   The knight was wroth to see his stroke beguyld,
      And smot againe with more outrageous might;
      But backe againe the sparcling steele recoyld,
      And left not any marke, where it did light;
      As if in Adamant rocke it had beene pight,[6]
      The beast impatient of his smarting wound,
      And of so fierce and forcible despight,
      Thought with his winges to stye[7] above the ground;
But his late wounded wing unserviceable found.

26   Then full of griefe and anguish vehement,
      He lowdly brayd, that like was never heard,
      And from his wide devouring oven sent

[1] **implyes:** entangles.
[2] **can:** did.
[3] **distaynd:** stained.
[4] **trenchand:** sharp.

[5] **forsake:** get out of the way of.
[6] **Adamant:** a mythical substance proverbial for its hardness; **pight:** securely placed.
[7] **stye:** ascend.

A flake of fire,[1] that flashing in his beard,
Him all amazd, and almost made afeard:
The scorching flame sore swinged[2] all his face,
And through his armour all his body seard,
That he could not endure so cruell cace,
But thought his armes to leave, and helmet to unlace.[3]

27   Not that great Champion of the antique world,[4]
      Whom famous Poetes verse so much doth vaunt,
      And hath for twelve huge labours high extold,
      So many furies and sharpe fits did haunt,
      When him the poysoned garment did enchaunt
      With *Centaures* blood, and bloody verses charmd,
      As did this knight twelve thousand dolours[5] daunt,
      Whom fyrie steele now burnt, that erst him armd,
      That erst him goodly armd, now most of all him harmd.

28   Faynt, wearie, sore, emboyled, grieved, brent[6]
      With heat, toyle, wounds, armes, smart, and inward fire[7]
      That never man such mischiefes did torment;
      Death better were, death did he oft desire,
      But death will never come, when needes require.
      Whom so dismayd when that his foe beheld,

---

[1] **A flake of fire:** a spark, symbolizing, according to Kaske (1969, 616–20), concupiscence in general and, in particular, temptation—the first stage or zero grade of sin; e.g., shrinking from pain.

[2] **swinged:** singed.

[3] In view of past experience (Canto Seven), this thought must be a sin. Worse still, "thought to" in Elizabethan English can mean not just "considered whether to" but "planned to" (OED, "think," 7, 8). That Redcrosse should sink so low and that he stands in need of baptism (see below) indicate that he is underachieving on this first day and thus represents mankind in some darker period before Christianity, probably in the age of law. It could be argued that the paradoxically harmful armor symbolizes law.

[4] I.e., Hercules, who also suffered such agony that he committed suicide because he was burned by a magical garment (*Metamorphoses*, 9.152–272).

[5] **dolours:** discomforts; from the Latin word *dolor,* meaning pain.

[6] **emboyled:** boiled or seared within his armor; **brent:** variant form of burnt.

[7] *Versus correlativi,* or parallel verses, in which each word in the first line has a word in the following line that appropriately matches it, e.g., faint . . . with heat, wearie . . . with toyle, etc. The frequent spondees express both pain and resistance to pain.

He cast to suffer him no more respire,
But gan his sturdy sterne about to weld,[1]
And him so strongly stroke, that to the ground him feld.[2]

29 It fortuned (as fayre it then befell,)
Behynd his backe unweeting, where he stood,
Of auncient time there was a springing well,
From which fast trickled forth a silver flood,
Full of great vertues, and for med'cine good.
Whylome, before that cursed Dragon got
That happy land, and all with innocent blood
Defyld those sacred waves, it rightly hot[3]
The well of life,[4] ne yet his vertues had forgot.

30 For unto life the dead it could restore,
And guilt of sinfull crimes cleane wash away,
Those that with sicknesse were infected sore,
It could recure, and aged long decay
Renew, as one were borne that very day.
Both *Silo* this, and *Jordan* did excell,
And th'English *Bath,* and eke the german *Spau,*
Ne can *Cephise,* nor *Hebrus* match this well:[5]
Into the same the knight back overthrowen, fell.

31 Now gan the golden *Phoebus* for to steepe
His fierie face in billowes of the west,
And his faint steedes watred in Ocean deepe,
Whiles from their journall[6] labours they did rest,
When that infernall Monster, having kest[7]
His wearie foe into that living well,

---

[1] **weld:** wield, so spelled for the sake of the rhyme.

[2] Being knocked down by the dragon or the devil symbolizes being overcome by sin, in this case probably the sin of deciding to take his armor off and whatever that may symbolize.

[3] **hot:** past tense of hight, meaning "was called."

[4] See Rev. 22.1–2. Probably a symbol of baptism here, because of 36.2–4; cf. 46.9, 34.9, and 29.9. Probably the same as the "living well" anticipated by Fradubio in ii.43.

[5] There are six comparisons: two to biblical bodies of water, then two to contemporary, then two to classical; cf. the comparisons to Old-Testament, New-Testament, and classical mountains in x.53–54 and note. See Phillips.

[6] **journall:** daily.

[7] **kest:** cast; variant spelling for sake of rhyme.

Can high advaunce his broad discoloured brest,
Above his wonted pitch, with countenance fell,
And clapt his yron wings, as victor he did dwell.[1]

32   Which when his pensive Lady saw from farre,
    Great woe and sorrow did her soule assay,
    As weening that the sad end of the warre,
    And gan to highest God entirely pray,
    That feared chaunce from her to turne away;
    With folded hands and knees full lowly bent
    All night shee watcht, ne once adowne would lay
    Her dainty limbs in her sad dreriment,
But praying still did wake, and waking did lament.

33   The morrow next gan earely to appeare,
    That *Titan*[2] rose to runne his daily race;
    But carely ere the morrow next gan reare
    Out of the sea faire *Titans* deawy face,[3]
    Up rose the gentle virgin from her place,
    And looked all about, if she might spy
    Her loved knight to move his manly pace:
    For she had great doubt of his safety,
Since late she saw him fall before his enimy.

34   At last she saw, where he upstarted brave
    Out of the well, wherein he drenched lay;
    As Eagle fresh out of the Ocean wave,[4]
    Where he hath lefte his plumes all hory gray,
    And deckt himselfe with fethers youthly gay,
    Like Eyas[5] hauke up mounts unto the skies,
    His newly budded pineons to assay,
    And merveiles at him selfe, stil as he flies:[6]
So new this new-borne knight to battell new did rise.[7]

---

[1] **dwell:** remain.

[2] **That *Titan*:** when the sun.

[3] Titan, the sun, rises out of the sea as does the renewed eagle (34.3) and the knight "Out of the well" (34.2; ACH).

[4] See Ps. 103.5: "Thy youth is renewed like the egles." "It was supposed that the eagle, when old, would fly into the sun, burn off his old feathers, and then dive into a pool to renew his youth" (TPR).

[5] **Eyas:** young.

[6] I.e., and as he flies he keeps marveling at himself.

[7] On this middle day of the battle, Redcrosse performs as a godly-baptized Christian ideally would, holding his own against the devil without and pieces of him within, and falling not because he has sinned (cf. xi.26), but out of physical weakness.

35   Whom when the damned feend so fresh did spy,
        No wonder, if he wondred at the sight,
        And doubted, whether his late enimy
        It were, or other new supplied knight.
        He, now to prove his late renewed might,
        High brandishing his bright deaw-burning blade,
        Upon his crested scalp so sore did smite,
        That to the scull a yawning wound it made:
  The deadly dint his dulled sences all dismaid.

36   I wote not, whether the revenging steele
        Were hardned with that holy water dew,
        Wherein he fell, or sharper edge did feele,
        Or his baptized hands now greater grew;
        Or other secret vertue did ensew;
        Els never could the force of fleshly arme,
        Ne molten mettall in his blood embrew:[1]
        For till that stownd could never wight him harme,
  By subtilty, nor slight, nor might, nor mighty charme.

37   The cruell wound enraged him so sore,
        That loud he yelded[2] for exceeding paine;
        As hundred ramping Lions seemd to rore,
        Whom ravenous hunger did thereto constraine:
        Then gan he tosse aloft his stretched traine,
        And therewith scourge the buxome[3] aire so sore,
        That to his force to yielden it was faine;
        Ne ought his sturdy strokes might stand afore,
  That high trees overthrew, and rocks in peeces tore.

38   The same advauncing high above his head,
        With sharpe intended[4] sting so rude him smott,
        That to the earth him drove, as stricken dead,
        Ne living wight would have him life behott:[5]
        The mortall sting his angry needle shott
        Quite through his shield, and in his shoulder seasd,

---

[1] **embrew:** plunge.
[2] **yelded:** yelled.
[3] **buxome:** yielding.

[4] **intended:** extended and aimed.
[5] I.e., no one in the world would have thought him to be alive.

Where fast it stucke, ne would thereout be gott:
The griefe thereof him wondrous sore diseasd,
Ne might his rancling paine with patience be appeasd.

39 But yet more mindfull of his honour deare,
  Then of the grievous smart, which him did wring,
  From loathed soile he can him lightly reare,
  And strove to loose the far infixed sting:
  Which when in vaine he tryde with struggeling,
  Inflam'd with wrath, his raging blade he hefte,[1]
  And strooke so strongly, that the knotty string
  Of his huge taile he quite a sonder clefte,
 Five joints[2] thereof he hewd, and but the stump him lefte.

40 Hart cannot thinke, what outrage, and what cries,
  With fowle enfouldred[3] smoake and flashing fire,
  The hell-bred beast threw forth unto the skies,
  That all was covered with darknesse dire:
  Then fraught with rancour, and engorged yre,
  He cast at once him to avenge for all,
  And gathering up himselfe out of the mire,
  With his uneven wings did fiercely fall,
 Upon his sunne-bright shield, and grypt it fast withall.

41 Much was the man encombred with his hold,
  In feare to lose his weapon in his paw,
  Ne wist yett, how his talaunts[4] to unfold;
  Nor harder was from *Cerberus*[5] greedy jaw
  To plucke a bone, then from his cruell claw
  To reave by strength, the griped gage[6] away:
  Thrise he assayd it from his foote to draw,
  And thrise in vaine to draw it did assay,
 It booted nought to thinke, to robbe him of his pray.

---

[1] **hefte:** past tense of "heave," synonymous with heaved.

[2] Symbolizing the five senses, the usual entry points of sin, and hence an outpost of the devil carried around by all mankind. See the five senses among the besiegers of Alma's castle in II.xi.7–13.

[3] **enfouldred:** "black as a thundercloud" (OED).

[4] **talaunts:** talons.

[5] *Cerberus:* the dog that guards the gate to hell. I.e., "it would be harder to pluck a bone from Cerberus' jaw than. . ."

[6] **reave:** snatch away; **gage:** pledge, prize.

42   Tho[1] when he saw no power might prevaile,
      His trusty sword he cald to his last aid,
      Wherewith he fiersly did his foe assaile,
      And double blowes about him stoutly laid,
      That glauncing fire out of the yron plaid;
      As sparckles from the Andvile use to fly,
      When heavy hammers on the wedg are swaid;[2]
      Therewith at last he forst him to unty
One of his grasping feete, him to defend thereby.

43   The other foote, fast fixed on his shield,
      Whenas no strength, nor stroks mote him constraine
      To loose, ne yet the warlike pledg to yield,
      He smott thereat with all his might and maine,
      That nought so wondrous puissaunce might sustaine;
      Upon the joint the lucky steele did light,
      And made such way, that hewd it quite in twaine;[3]
      The paw yett missed not his minisht[4] might,
But hong still on the shield, as it at first was pight.

44   For griefe thereof, and divelish despight,
      From his infernall fournace forth he threw
      Huge flames, that dimmed all the hevens light,
      Enrold in duskish smoke and brimstone blew;
      As burning *Aetna* from his boyling stew
      Doth belch out flames, and rockes in peeces broke,
      And ragged ribs of mountaines molten new,
      Enwrapt in coleblacke clowds and filthy smoke,
That al the land with stench, and heven with horror choke.

45   The heate whereof, and harmefull pestilence
      So sore him noyd,[5] that forst him to retire
      A litle backeward for his best defence,
      To save his body from the scorching fire,
      Which he from hellish entrailes did expire.

---

[1] **tho:** then.

[2] **swaid:** swung and struck.

[3] Heb. 4.12: "For the worde of God is . . . sharper then anie two edged sworde, and entreth through, even unto the dividing asonder . . . of the joynts." Again, a piece of the devil is lodged within the godly Everyman, and again he refuses to be controlled by it.

[4] **minisht:** diminished, prefix omitted for sake of alliteration.

[5] **noyd:** annoyed.

It chaunst (eternall God that chaunce did guide)
As he recoiled backeward, in the mire
His nigh foreweried feeble feet did slide,
And downe he fell, with dread of shame sore terrifide.

46   There grew a goodly tree him faire beside,
    Loaden with fruit and apples rosy redd,
    As they in pure vermilion had beene dide,
    Whereof great vertues over all were redd:[1]
    For happy life to all, which thereon fedd,
    And life eke everlasting did befall:
    Great God it planted in that blessed stedd[2]
    With his Almighty hand, and did it call
The tree of life, the crime of our first fathers fall.[3]

47   In all the world like was not to be fownd,
    Save in that soile, where all good things did grow,
    And freely sprong out of the fruitfull grownd,
    As incorrupted Nature did them sow,
    Till that dredd Dragon all did overthrow.
    Another like faire tree[4] eke grew thereby,
    Whereof who so did eat, eftsoones did know
    Both good and ill: O mournfull memory:
That tree through one mans fault hath doen us all to dy.

48   From that first tree forth flowd, as from a well,
    A trickling streame of Balme, most soveraine
    And dainty deare, which on the ground still fell,
    And overflowed all the fertile plaine,
    As it had deawed bene with timely raine:
    Life and long health that gracious ointment gave,
    And deadly wounds could heale, and reare againe
    The sencelesse corse appointed for the grave.[5]
Into that same he fell: which did from death him save.

---

[1] **over all were redd:** far and wide were known.

[2] **stedd:** place, stead.

[3] See Gen. 3.22. "Spenser is not suggesting that the tree of life is the cause of Adam's fall" (TPR); rather, "it was a cause of reproach, or accusation (Lat. *crimen*), against Adam" (ACH); "his 'crime' is responsibility for the consequent denial of this tree (mentioned again in Rev. 22.2) to all human kind" (M&P). It is a Latinate ellipsis.

[4] The tree of knowledge of good and evil (Gen. 2.17, 3.3–7, 11–3).

[5] For the "Balme" and "ointment," see Rev. 22.2 and 2 Esd. 2.12: "They shal have at wil the tre of life, smelling of ointement:

49 For nigh thereto the ever damned Beast
  Durst not approch, for he was deadly made,
  And al that life preserved, did detest:
  Yet he it oft adventur'd[1] to invade.
  By this the drouping day-light gan to fade,
  And yield his rowme to sad succeeding night,
  Who with her sable mantle gan to shade
  The face of earth, and wayes of living wight,
 And high her burning torch set up in heaven bright.

50 When gentle *Una* saw the second fall
  Of her deare knight, who weary of long fight,
  And faint through losse of blood, moov'd not at all,
  But lay as in a dreame of deepe delight,
  Besmeard with pretious Balme, whose vertuous might
  Did heale his woundes, and scorching heat alay,
  Againe she stricken was with sore affright,
  And for his safetie gan devoutly pray;
 And watch the noyous[2] night, and wait for joyous day.

51 The joyous day gan early to appeare,
  And fayre *Aurora*[3] from the deawy bed
  Of aged *Tithone* gan her selfe to reare,
  With rosy cheekes, for shame as blushing red;
  Her golden locks for hast were loosely shed
  About her eares, when *Una* her did marke
  Clymbe to her charet,[4] all with flowers spred;
  From heven high to chace the chearelesse darke;
 With mery note her lowd salutes the mounting larke.

---

they shall nether labour nor be weary." In the indubitably apocryphal *Gospel of Nicodemus,* Seth is promised oil from the tree of life that will heal the dying Adam (for this and other sources, see ACH). Given its deifying effect (see Kaske 1969, 634–6), and given that the well symbolizes baptism, this tree probably symbolizes Holy Communion, but the resemblance is not close. Weatherby (26, 39–43, 169) interprets it as, among other things, the chrism or cross of oil applied right after baptism.

[1] **adventur'd:** tried.

[2] **noyous:** harmful.

[3] Goddess of the dawn. Aurora loved Tithonus and persuaded the gods to give him immortality, but she forgot to ask them to give him eternal youth as well, so he lived on but kept on getting older and older.

[4] **charet:** chariot, cart.

52   Then freshly up arose the doughty[1] knight,
            All healed of his hurts and woundes wide,
            And did himselfe to battaile readie dight;
            Whose early foe awaiting him beside
            To have devourd, so soone as day he spyde,
            When now he saw himselfe so freshly reare,
            As if late fight had nought him damnifyde,
            He woxe dismaid, and gan his fate to feare;
        Nathlesse with wonted rage he him advaunced neare.

53   And in his first encounter, gaping wyde,
            He thought attonce him to have swallowd quight,
            And rusht upon him with outragious pryde;
            Who him rencountring fierce, as hauke in flight,
            Perforce rebutted backe. The weapon bright
            Taking advantage of his open jaw,
            Ran through his mouth with so importune might,
            That deepe emperst his darksom hollow maw,
        And back retyrd, his life blood forth with all did draw.[2]

54   So downe he fell, and forth his life did breath,
            That vanisht into smoke and cloudes swift;
            So downe he fell, that th'earth him underneath
            Did grone, as feeble so great load to lift;
            So downe he fell, as an huge rocky clift,
            Whose false[3] foundacion waves have washt away,
            With dreadfull poyse[4] is from the mayneland rift,
            And rolling downe, great *Neptune*[5] doth dismay;
        So downe he fell, and like an heaped mountaine lay.[6]

---

[1] **doughty:** formidable. At this point, according to most critics, Redrosse becomes or starts to symbolize Christ in his death and Harrowing of Hell; he suffers no setbacks and is instantly victorious; moreover, it is the dawn of the third day.

[2] I.e., when the weapon pulled back, it drew forth the dragon's life blood.

[3] **false:** outwardly solid but internally fragile.

[4] **poyse:** hovering, as if it were falling in slow motion, as in a film.

[5] God of the sea.

[6] Anaphora—beginning two or more phrases with the same word or words—a figure perhaps inspired by the twofold repetition, "It has fallen, it has fallen, Babylon" (Rev. 18.2). In each colon or member, one of the four elements is mentioned: air, earth, and water, excluding fire; fire he had once, but no longer.

55   The knight him selfe even trembled at his fall,
      So huge and horrible a masse it seemd;
      And his deare Lady, that beheld it all,
      Durst not approch for dread, which she misdeemd,
      But yet at last, whenas the direfull feend
      She saw not stirre, off-shaking[1] vaine affright,
      She nigher drew, and saw that joyous end:
      Then God she praysd, and thankt her faithfull knight,
That had atchievde so great a conquest by his might.[2]

---

[1] **off-shaking:** forcing herself to shed.

[2] Antecedent of "his" hovers ambiguously between "knight" and "God" (see Introduction, 12), representing a problem for religious people: "If I do something good, is it I who deserve the credit, or God who worked through me?" Cf. II.i.33–34.

Canto Twelve

Fayre Una to the Redcrosse knight
betrouthed is with joy:
Though false Duessa it to barre
Her false sleightes doe imploy.

1 Behold I see the haven nigh at hand,
   To which I meane my wearie course to bend;
   Vere the maine shete, and beare up with[1] the land,
   The which afore is fayrly to be kend,[2]
   And seemeth safe from storms, that may offend;
   There this fayre virgin wearie of her way
   Must landed bee, now at her journeyes end:
   There eke my feeble barke[3] a while may stay,
Till mery wynd and weather call her thence away.

2 Scarsely had *Phoebus* in the glooming East
   Yett harnessed his fyrie-footed teeme,
   Ne reard above the earth his flaming creast,[4]
   When the last deadly smoke aloft did steeme,
   That signe of last outbreathed life did seeme,
   Unto the watchman on the castle wall;
   Who thereby dead that balefull Beast did deeme,
   And to his Lord and Lady lowd gan call,
To tell, how he had seene the Dragons fatall fall.

3 Uprose with hasty joy, and feeble speed
   That aged Syre, the Lord of all that land,
   And looked forth, to weet, if trew indeed
   Those tydinges were, as he did understand,

---

[1] **vere:** let it out so that the sail holds less wind; **beare up with:** steer toward.

[2] **fayrly to be kend:** seems fair. The image of writing a poem as sailing a ship occurs frequently in classical poetry: in Dante, in Chaucer, in Ariosto, and at the end of this canto. See ACH note and *SE*, "Ship-imagery."

[3] **barke:** boat.

[4] This is the same dawn as that which precedes the defeat of the dragon, as described in xi.51.

Which whenas trew by tryall he out fond,[1]
He badd to open wyde his brasen gate,
Which long time had beene shut, and out of hond[2]
Proclaymed joy and peace through all his state;
For dead now was their foe, which them forrayed[3] late.

4   Then gan triumphant Trompets sownd on hye,
That sent to heven the ecchoed report
Of their new joy, and happie victory
Gainst him, that had them long opprest with tort,[4]
And fast imprisoned in sieged fort.
Then all the people, as in solemne feast,
To him assembled with one full consort,
Rejoycing at the fall of that great beast,
From whose eternall bondage now they were releast.

5   Forth came that auncient Lord and aged Queene,
Arayd in antique robes downe to the grownd,
And sad habiliments right well beseene;[5]
A noble crew about them waited rownd
Of sage and sober Peres, all gravely gownd;
Whom far before did march a goodly band
Of tall young men, all hable armes to sownd,[6]
But now they laurell braunches bore in hand;
Glad signe of victory and peace in all their land.

6   Unto that doughtie Conquerour they came,
And him before themselves prostrating low,
Their Lord and Patrone loud did him proclame,
And at his feet their lawrell boughs did throw.
Soone after them all dauncing on a row
The comely virgins came, with girlands dight,
As fresh as flowres in medow greene doe grow,
When morning deaw upon their leaves doth light:
And in their handes sweet Timbrels[7] all upheld on hight.

[1] **by tryall he out fond:** he found out by looking for himself.

[2] **out of hond:** immediately.

[3] **forrayed:** ravaged.

[4] **with tort:** wrongfully.

[5] **sad:** sober; **well beseene:** can mean appropriate, which seems to befit the aged parents here, or attractive, as in xii.8.8.

[6] **armes to sownd:** to wield weapons, alluding to the fact that knights clash their shields, making a sound; see iv.40.3 and xi.9.8 (ACH).

[7] **timbrels:** tambourines.

7 And them before, the fry[1] of children yong
  Their wanton sportes and childish mirth did play,
  And to the Maydens sownding tymbrels song
  In well attuned notes, a joyous lay,[2]
  And made delightfull musick all the way,
  Untill they came, where that faire virgin stood;
  As fayre *Diana* in fresh sommers day,
  Beholdes her Nymphes, enraung'd in shady wood,
Some wrestle, some do run, some bathe in christall flood.[3]

8 So she beheld those maydens meriment
  With chearefull vew; who when to her they came,
  Themselves to ground with gracious humblesse bent
  And her ador'd by honorable name,
  Lifting to heven her everlasting fame:
  Then on her head they sett a girlond greene,
  And crowned her twixt earnest and twixt game;
  Who in her self-resemblance well beseene,[4]
Did seeme such, as she was, a goodly maiden Queene.

9 And after all the raskall many[5] ran,
  Heaped together in rude rablement,
  To see the face of that victorious man:
  Whom all admired, as from heaven sent,
  And gazd upon with gaping wonderment,
  But when they came, where that dead Dragon lay,
  Stretcht on the ground in monstrous large extent,
  The sight with ydle feare did them dismay,
Ne durst approach him nigh, to touch, or once assay.

10 Some feard, and fledd; some feard and well it faynd;
  One that would wiser seeme, then all the rest,
  Warnd him not touch, for yet perhaps remaynd
  Some lingring life within his hollow brest,

---

[1] **fry:** crowd.

[2] **lay:** song.

[3] Another use of classical images in a favorable sense—rare in Book One. The alexandrine expresses a panoramic view of Diana's triathlon—a cinematographic moment.

[4] I.e., with her leafy crown, attractively resembling what she really was, the heir of the kingdom, as opposed to Duessa, who usually resembles someone else.

[5] **raskall many:** the lower classes. This episode represents a comedy of social class. Also it restores the dragon's size, which Spenser had shrunk during the battle to allow Redcrosse to reach the base of his wing (xi.20) and the top of his head (xi.24).

Or in his wombe might lurke some hidden nest
Of many Dragonettes, his fruitfull seede;
Another saide, that in his eyes did rest
Yet sparckling fyre, and badd therof take heed;
Another said, he saw him move his eyes indeed.

11   One mother, whenas her foolehardy chyld
      Did come to neare, and with his talants play
      Halfe dead through feare, her litle babe revyld,
      And to her gossibs[1] gan in counsell say;
      "How can I tell, but that his talents may
      Yet scratch my sonne, or rend his tender hand."
      So diversly them selves in vaine they fray;
      Whiles some more bold, to measure him nigh stand,
To prove how many acres he did spred of land.[2]

12   Thus flocked all the folke him rownd about,
      The whiles that hoarie king, with all his traine,[3]
      Being arrived, where that champion stout
      After his foes defeasaunce[4] did remaine,
      Him goodly greetes, and fayre does entertayne,
      With princely gifts of yvory and gold,
      And thousand thankes him yeeldes for all his paine.
      Then when his daughter deare he does behold,
Her dearely doth imbrace, and kisseth manifold.

13   And after to his Pallace he them bringes,
      With shaumes,[5] and trompets, and with Clarions sweet;
      And all the way the joyous people singes,
      And with their garments strowes the paved street
      Whence mounting up, they fynd purveyaunce meet[6]
      Of all, that royall Princes court became,
      And all the floore was underneath their feet
      Bespredd with costly scarlott of great name,[7]
On which they lowly sitt, and fitting purpose[8] frame.

---

[1] **gossibs:** women friends.

[2] The caesura-less alexandrine expresses the dragon's length.

[3] **traine:** retinue.

[4] **defeasaunce:** defeat; unique in the poem; one suspects Spenser lengthened the word for the sake of the meter.

[5] **shaumes:** oboes.

[6] **purveyaunce meet:** suitable living conditions.

[7] **scarlott of great name:** scarlet cloth of high quality or price.

[8] **purpose:** topic of conversation.

14   What needes me tell their feast and goodly guize,[1]
         In which was nothing riotous nor vaine?
      What needes of dainty dishes to devize,[2]
         Of comely services, or courtly trayne?[3]
      My narrow leaves cannot in them contayne
      The large discourse of roiall Princes state.
         Yet was their manner then but bare and playne:
      For th'antique world excesse and pryde did hate;
   Such proud luxurious pompe is swollen up but late.

15   Then when with meates and drinkes of every kinde
         Their fervent appetites they quenched had,
      That auncient Lord gan fit occasion finde,
         Of straunge adventures, and of perils sad,
      Which in his travell him befallen had,
      For to demaund of his renowmed guest:
         Who then with utt'rance grave, and count'nance sad,
      From poynt to poynt, as is before exprest,
   Discourst his voyage long, according his request.

16   Great pleasure mixt with pittifull regard,
         That godly King and Queene did passionate,[4]
      Whyles they his pittifull adventures heard,
         That oft they did lament his lucklesse state,
      And often blame the too importune[5] fate,
      That heapd on him so many wrathfull wreakes:[6]
         For never gentle knight, as he of late,
      So tossed was in fortunes cruell freakes;[7]
   And all the while salt teares bedeawd the hearers cheaks.

17   Then sayd that royall Pere in sober wise;
         "Deare Sonne, great beene the evils, which ye bore
      From first to last in your late enterprise,
         That I note,[8] whether praise, or pitty more:

---

[1] **guize:** behavior. This stanza is one of many indications that the world within the poem, while fallen, is as yet relatively uncorrupted—a silver age.

[2] **devize:** talk; so also in 17.9, 18.2.

[3] **trayne:** retinue.

[4] **passionate:** if "King and Queene" is the subject, it means "express with feeling." If

"Great pleasure . . ." is the subject, then it means "make passionate."

[5] **importune:** grievous, severe, assiduous.

[6] **wreakes:** calamities, here apparently without the idea of vengeance.

[7] **freakes:** here, whims.

[8] **note:** don't know; contraction of "ne wot."

For never living man, I weene, so sore
In sea of deadly daungers was distrest;
But since now safe ye seised[1] have the shore,
And well arrived are, (high God be blest)
Let us devize of ease and everlasting rest."

18   "Ah dearest Lord," said then that doughty knight,
      "Of ease or rest I may not yet devize;
      For by the faith, which I to armes have plight,
      I bownden am streight after this emprize,
      As that your daughter can ye well advize,
      Backe to retourne to that great Faery Queene,
      And her to serve six yeares in warlike wize,
      Gainst that proud Paynim king, that works her teene:[2]
Therefore I ought crave pardon, till I there have beene."[3]

19   "Unhappy falls that hard necessity,"
      (Quoth he) "the troubler of my happy peace,
      And vowed foe of my felicity;
      Ne I against the same can justly preace:[4]
      But since that band ye cannot now release,
      Nor doen undoe; (for vowes may not be vayne)
      Soone as the terme of those six yeares shall cease,
      Ye then shall hether backe retourne agayne,
The marriage to accomplish vowd betwixt you twayn.

20   "Which for my part I covet to performe,
      In sort as[5] through the world I did proclame,
      That who so kild that monster most deforme,
      And him in hardy battayle overcame,
      Should have mine onely daughter to his Dame,[6]
      And of my kingdome heyre apparaunt bee:

---

[1] **seised:** reached.

[2] **teene:** sorrow.

[3] This deferral of the wedding in order to serve Gloriana comes as a surprise to us as well as to Una's family, though we received hints of it before (see ix.17.1–3) and apparently Una knew about it. Its duration of six years resembles the six years that Jacob was forced to serve to win Leah, his first wife, before he could marry Rachel, the girl he really wanted. Medievals interpreted Leah as the active life and Rachel as the contemplative life, thus arguing the chronological priority of the active life; see Gen. 29.17–30. Gloriana is clearly an aspect of the active life and Una, as religious truth, is an aspect of the contemplative life.

[4] **preace:** press.

[5] **In sort as:** according to what.

[6] **to his Dame:** for his wife.

> Therefore since now to thee perteynes the same,
> By dew desert of noble chevalree,
> Both daughter and eke kingdome, lo I yield to thee."[1]

21   Then forth he called that his daughter fayre,
> The fairest *Un'* his onely daughter deare,
> His onely daughter, and his only hayre;
> Who forth proceeding with sad sober cheare,[2]
> As bright as doth the morning starre appeare
> Out of the East, with flaming lockes bedight,
> To tell that dawning day is drawing neare,
> And to the world does bring long wished light;
> So faire and fresh that Lady shewd her selfe in sight.

22   So faire and fresh, as freshest flowre in May;
> For she had layd her mournefull stole aside,
> And widow-like sad wimple[3] throwne away,
> Wherewith her heavenly beautie she did hide,
> Whiles on her wearie journey she did ride;
> And on her now a garment she did weare,
> All lily white, withoutten spot, or pride,[4]
> That seemd like silke and silver woven neare,[5]
> But neither silke nor silver therein did appeare.

23   The blazing brightnesse of her beauties beame,
> And glorious light of her sunshyny face[6]
> To tell, were as to strive against the streame.
> My ragged rimes are all too rude and bace,
> Her heavenly lineaments for to enchace.[7]
> Ne wonder; for her own deare loved knight,
> All were she[8] daily with himselfe in place,
> Did wonder much at her celestiall sight:
> Oft had he seene her faire, but never so faire dight.

---

[1] A formulaic romance situation.

[2] **sad sober cheare:** serious, sober countenance.

[3] **wimple:** veil. In her new gown, she symbolizes the spotless bride of the Lamb in Rev. 19.7–8, 21.2, and 11. Accordingly, Redcrosse now typifies Christ as the Bridegroom, the Lamb.

[4] **pride:** ostentatious ornament.

[5] **neare:** closely.

[6] Una's brightness here links her to the Woman Clothed with the Sunne (Rev. 12.1), of whom she is sometimes seen as a type.

[7] I.e., to be a setting for her lineaments.

[8] **all were she:** although she was.

24   So fairely dight, when she in presence came,
        She to her Syre made humble reverence,
        And bowed low, that her right well became,
        And added grace unto her excellence:
        Who with great wisedome, and grave eloquence
        Thus gan to say. But eare he thus had sayd,[1]
        With flying speede, and seeming great pretence,
        Came running in, much like a man dismayd,
     A Messenger with letters, which his message sayd.

25   All in the open hall amazed stood,
        At suddeinnesse of that unwary[2] sight,
        And wondred at his breathlesse hasty mood.
        But he for nought would stay his passage right,[3]
        Till fast[4] before the king he did alight;
        Where falling flat, great humblesse he did make,
        And kist the ground, whereon his foot was pight;
        Then to his handes that writt he did betake,
     Which he disclosing, read thus, as the paper spake.[5]

26   "To thee, most mighty king of *Eden* fayre,[6]
        Her greeting sends in these sad lines addrest,
        The wofull daughter, and forsaken heyre
        Of that great Emperour of all the West;
        And bids thee be advised for the best,
        Ere thou thy daughter linck in holy band
        Of wedlocke to that new unknowen guest:
        For he already plighted his right hand
     Unto another love, and to another land.

[1] Anacoluthon, or breaking off in the middle of a sentence. As 36.6–7 makes clear, Una's father is about to "bid" the banns of marriage when he is interrupted.

[2] **unwary:** unexpected.

[3] **right:** direct.

[4] **fast:** close.

[5] I.e., Archimago presents the letter to the king, who unfolds it and reads it aloud. Duessa's letter exaggerates the seriousness of her relationship with Redcrosse: though he did sleep with her—a fact that has apparently been concealed from Una's parents up to now—Redcrosse never promised her anything; there was no altar, no betrothal, and no vow that we know of, and Duessa is not likely to have required one. See 32.9 and note.

[6] This confirms our impression from vii.44 that Una's parents symbolize, and in a sense are, Adam and Eve.

27   "To me sad mayd, or rather widow sad,
      He was affyaunced long time before,
      And sacred pledges he both gave, and had,
      False erraunt knight, infamous, and forswore:
      Witnesse the burning Altars, which[1] he swore,
      And guilty heavens of his bold perjury,
      Which though he hath polluted oft of yore,
      Yet I to them for judgement just doe fly,
  And them conjure t'avenge this shamefull injury.[2]

28   "Therefore since mine he is, or[3] free or bond,
      Or false or trew, or living or else dead,
      Withhold, O soverayne Prince, your hasty hond
      From knitting league with him, I you aread;
      Ne weene my right with strength adowne to tread,
      Through weakenesse of my widowhed, or woe:
      For truth is strong, her rightfull cause to plead,
      And shall finde friends, if need requireth soe.
  So bids thee well to fare, Thy neither friend, nor foe, *Fidessa*."

29   When he these bitter byting wordes had red,
      The tidings straunge did him abashed make,
      That still he sate long time astonished
      As in great muse, ne word to creature spake.
      At last his solemne silence thus he brake,
      With doubtfull eyes fast fixed on his guest;
      "Redoubted knight, that for myne only sake
      Thy life and honor late adventurest,
  Let nought be hid from me, that ought to be exprest.

30   "What meane these bloody vowes, and idle threats,
      Throwne out from womanish impatient mynd?
      What hevens? what altars? what enraged heates
      Here heaped up with termes of love unkynd,
      My conscience cleare with guilty bands would bynd?
      High God be witnesse, that I guiltlesse ame.

---

[1] **which:** on which.

[2] I.e., I fly for just judgment to the altars and the heavens by which he swore (to marry me), although he has been untrue to his vow before, and I entreat them to avenge this shameful injury.

[3] **or:** whether.

But if your selfe, Sir knight, ye faulty fynd,
Or wrapped be in loves of former Dame,
With cryme doe not it cover, but disclose the same."

31   To whom the *Redcrosse* knight this answere sent,
        "My Lord, my king, be nought hereat dismayd,
        Till well ye wote by grave intendiment,[1]
        What woman, and wherefore doth me upbrayd
        With breach of love, and loialty betrayd.
        It was in my mishaps, as hitherward
        I lately traveild, that unwares I strayd
        Out of my way, through perils straunge and hard;
    That day should faile me, ere I had them all declard.

32   "There did I find, or rather I was fownd
        Of this false woman, that *Fidessa* hight,
        Fidessa hight the falsest Dame on grownd,
        Most false *Duessa,* royall richly dight,
        That easy was t'inveigle[2] weaker sight:
        Who by her wicked arts, and wiely skill,
        Too false and strong for earthly skill or might,
        Unwares me wrought unto her wicked will,
    And to my foe betrayd, when least I feared ill."[3]

33   Then stepped forth the goodly royall Mayd,
        And on the ground her selfe prostrating low,
        With sober countenaunce thus to him sayd;
        "O pardon me, my soveraine Lord, to sheow
        The secret treasons, which of late I know
        To have bene wrought by that false sorceresse.
        Shee onely she it is, that earst did throw
        This gentle knight into so great distresse,
    That death him did awaite in daily wretchednesse.

---

[1] **intendiment:** consideration.

[2] **t'inveigle:** to deceive.

[3] Redcrosse claims that Duessa was conspiring with Orgoglio all along—something we have not heard before. Duessa seems to have been totally absent from Redcrosse's supposedly complete autobiography (stanzas 15–16). Una did not intervene. This omission represents a sin, which is why Spenser arranges to expose him—but a venial sin, for apparently children can legitimately lie to parents and keep them in the dark about love affairs. See Priscilla's lies, engineered by Calidore, to her father about what she was up to in the forest (VI.iii.16–19), and, for a source, ACH note ad loc.

34   "And now it seemes, that she suborned hath
            This crafty messenger with letters vaine,
            To worke new woe and improvided scath,[1]
            By breaking of the band betwixt us twaine;
            Wherein she used hath the practicke paine[2]
            Of this false footman, clokt with simplenesse,
            Whome if ye please for to discover plaine,
            Ye shall him *Archimago* find, I ghesse,
        The falsest man alive; who tries shall find no lesse."

35   The king was greatly moved at her speach,
            And all with suddein indignation fraight,[3]
            Bad on that Messenger rude hands to reach.
            Eftsoones the Gard, which on his state did wait,
            Attacht that faytor[4] false, and bound him strait:
            Who seeming sorely chauffed at his band,
            As chained beare, whom cruell dogs doe bait,
            With ydle force did faine them to withstand,
        And often semblaunce made to scape out of their hand.

36   But they him layd full low in dungeon deepe,
            And bound him hand and foote with yron chaines.
            And with continual watch did warely keepe;
            Who then would thinke, that by his subtile trains
            He could escape fowle death or deadly pains?[5]
            Thus when that Princes wrath was pacifide,
            He gan renew the late forbidden bains,[6]
            And to the knight his daughter deare he tyde,
        With sacred rites and vowes for ever to abyde.

37   His owne two hands the holy knotts did knitt,
            That none but death for ever can divide;
            His owne two hands, for such a turne most fitt,

---

[1] **improvided scath:** unforeseen harm.

[2] **practicke paine:** cunning efforts.

[3] **fraight:** filled.

[4] **attacht that faytor:** arrested that impostor.

[5] His foretold escape is modeled on Rev. 20.2–3, the imprisonment and subsequent escape of the dragon or Satan before he is finally consigned to the lake of fire (Rev.

20.7–10). See ACH note. Here it is prophesied that Archimago will do something that the dragon does in Rev., and he does it; see II.i.1ff.

[6] **bains:** banns of marriage; the repeated announcements, for the purpose of allowing time for any objections to be raised, that so-and-so will marry so-and-so at a specific time.

The housling[1] fire did kindle and provide,
And holy water thereon sprinckled wide;
At which the bushy Teade[2] a groome did light,
And sacred lamp in secret chamber hide,
Where it should not be quenched day nor night,
For feare of evill fates, but burnen ever bright.

38   Then gan they sprinckle all the posts with wine,
And made great feast to solemnize that day;
They all perfumde with frankincense divine,
And precious odours fetcht from far away,
That all the house did sweat[3] with great aray:
And all the while sweete Musicke did apply
Her curious[4] skill, the warbling notes to play,
To drive away the dull Melancholy;
The whiles one sung a song of love and jollity.

39   During the which there was an heavenly noise
Heard sownd through all the Pallace pleasantly,
Like as it had bene many an Angels voice,
Singing before th'eternall majesty,
In their trinall triplicities[5] on hye;
Yett wist no creature, whence that hevenly sweet[6]
Proceeded, yet eachone felt secretly
Himselfe thereby refte of his sences meet,
And ravished with rare impression in his sprite.

---

[1] **housling:** sacramental. Yet fire and water are only used in classical weddings, not Christian. See ACH and M&P notes. Another problem with this ritual is that it sounds more like an actual marriage than a betrothal. Spenser shows great interest in the betrothal period as a stage in a love affair. There was no separate ritual for betrothal in early modern England, aside from proclaiming the banns, which is really part of the wedding.

[2] **Teade:** torch.

[3] **all the house did sweat:** the state of a house that has been sprinkled with something—here, perfume.

[4] **curious:** in physical sense, elaborate, intricate.

[5] **trinall triplicities:** the nine orders of angels, a bit of traditional angelology mentioned chiefly for the sound of the words. The mysterious echo of the angels' song to God within the secular love song symbolizes the interpenetration of earthly married love with Christian love of God; see also Spenser, *Amoretti,* 68; and *Epithalamion,* 64–70. This beautiful image may represent an erotic analogue to the *Te Deum,* or so called Ambrosian Hymn, in both the Catholic Mass and the Anglican Holy Communion. There angels are stated to join their voices with the human singers, or vice versa, singing "Holy, holy, holy . . ." etc.

[6] **sweet:** sweet sound.

40   Great joy was made that day of young and old,
  And solemne feast proclaymd throughout the land,
  That their exceeding merth may not be told:
  Suffice it heare by signes to understand
  The usuall joyes at knitting of loves band.
  Thrise happy man the knight himselfe did hold,
  Possessed of his Ladies hart and hand,
  And ever, when his eie did her behold,
His heart did seeme to melt in pleasures manifold.

41   Her joyous presence and sweet company
  In full content he there did long enjoy,
  Ne wicked envy, ne vile gealosy
  His deare delights were hable to annoy:
  Yet swimming in that sea of blisfull joy,
  He nought forgott, how he whilome had sworne,
  In case he could that monstrous beast destroy,
  Unto his Faery Queene backe to retourne:
The which he shortly did, and *Una* left to mourne.

42   Now strike your sailes yee jolly Mariners,
  For we be come unto a quiet rode,
  Where we must land some of our passengers,
  And light this weary vessell of her lode.
  Here she a while may make her safe abode,
  Till she repaired have her tackles spent,
  And wants supplide. And then againe abroad
  On the long voiage whereto she is bent:
Well may she speede and fairely finish her intent.

Finis Lib. I.

THE LETTER TO RALEIGH

A
Letter of the Authors expounding his
whole intention in the course of this worke: which
for that it giueth great light to the Reader, for
the better vnderstanding is hereunto
annexed.

To the Right noble, and Valorous, Sir Walter Raleigh knight, Lo. Wardein of
the Stanneryes, and her Maiesties liefetenaunt of the County of
Cornewayll.[1]

Sir knowing how doubtfully all Allegories may be construed, and this booke of
mine, which I have entituled the Faery Queene, being a continued Allegory, or
darke conceit, I have thought good aswell for avoyding of gealous opinions and mis-
constructions, as also for your better light in reading thereof, (being so by you com-
manded,) to discover unto you the general intention and meaning, which in the
whole course thereof I have fashioned, without expressing of any particular purposes
or by accidents therein occasioned. The generall end therefore of all the booke is to
fashion a gentleman or noble person in vertuous and gentle discipline:[2] Which for
that I conceived shoulde be most plausible[3] and pleasing, being coloured with an
historicall fiction, the which the most part of men delight to read, rather for variety
of matter, then for profite of the ensample: I chose the historye of king Arthure, as
most fitte for the excellency of his person, being made famous by many mens former
workes, and also furthest from the daunger of envy, and suspition of present time.
In which I have followed all the antique Poets historicall, first Homere, who in the
Persons of Agamemnon and Ulysses hath ensampled a good governour and a ver-
tuous man, the one in his Ilias, the other in his Odysseis: then Virgil, whose like
intention was to doe in the person of Aeneas: after him Ariosto comprised them

---

[1] Appended to the 1590 edition of *The Faerie Queene,* Spenser's "Letter to Raleigh," also called "A Letter of the Authors," has been read as a preface, detailing both the larger plot and the poetics underlying the poem. It was not included in the 1596 edi- tion, and so only discusses the first three books directly.

[2] **discipline:** learning, training, orderly conduct, the system by which a church exercises control over its members.

[3] **plausible:** deserving applause, acceptable.

205

both in his *Orlando:*[1] and lately Tasso disseuered them againe, and formed both parts in two persons, namely that part which they in Philosophy call Ethice, or vertues of a private man, coloured in his *Rinaldo: The* other named Politice in his *Godfredo.*[2] By ensample of which excellente Poets, I labour to pourtraict in Arthure, before he was king, the image of a brave knight, perfected in the twelve private morall vertues, as Aristotle hath devised,[3] the which is the purpose of these first twelve bookes: which if I finde to be well accepted, I may be perhaps encoraged, to frame the other part of polliticke vertues in his person, after that hee came to be king.[4] To some I know this Methode will seeme displeasaunt, which had rather have good discipline delivered plainly in way of precepts, or sermoned at large, as they use, then thus clowdily enwrapped in Allegoricall devises. But such, me seeme, should be satisfide with the use of these dayes seeing all things accounted by their showes, and nothing esteemed of, that is not delightfull and pleasing to commune sence. For this cause is Xenophon preferred before Plato, for that the one in the exquisite depth of his judgement, formed a Commune welth such as it should be, but the other in the person of Cyrus and the Persians fashioned a government such as might best be: So much more profitable and gratious is doctrine by ensample, then by rule.[5] So have I laboured to doe in the person of Arthure: whome I conceive after his long education by Timon, to whom he was by Merlin delivered to be brought up, so soone as he was borne of the Lady Igrayne, to have seene in a dream or vision the Faery Queen, with whose excellent beauty ravished, he awaking resolved to seeke her out, and so being by Merlin armed, and by Timon throughly instructed, he went to seeke her forth in Faerye land. In that Faery Queene I meane glory in my generall intention, but in my particular I conceive the most excellent and glorious person of our soveraine the Queene, and her kingdome in Faery land. And yet in some places els, I doe otherwise shadow her. For considering she beareth two persons, the one of a most royall Queene or Empresse, the other of a most vertuous and beautifull Lady, this latter part in some places I doe expresse in Belphoebe, fashioning her name according to your owne excellent conceipt of Cynthia, (Phoebe and Cynthia being both names of Diana).[6] So in the person of

---

[1] Lodovico Ariosto, Italian author of *Orlando Furioso* (1532).

[2] Torquato Tasso, Italian author of *Rinaldo* (1562) and *Gerusalemme Liberata* (1581), in which the hero Godfredo embodies public or political virtues.

[3] Aristotle does not name twelve particular moral virtues in the *Nicomachaean Ethics*. There are, however, several Medieval and Renaissance commentaries on Aristotle from which twelve could be construed.

[4] Spenser indicates that he planned twelve books for *The Faerie Queene* and would willingly write twenty-four, the former matching Virgil, the latter Homer.

[5] Spenser says that Xenophon's *Cyropaedia*, celebrated for teaching by example, is commonly preferred to Plato's *Republic*, which taught by precepts.

[6] Belphoebe appears in Books Two, Three, and Four. Cynthia refers to Raleigh's poem of that name, which also celebrated Elizabeth. Spenser suggests that Gloriana, the Faerie Queen, represents Elizabeth's public role as monarch, while Belphoebe personifies her private, virginal life.

Prince Arthure I sette forth magnificence in particular, which vertue for that (according to Aristotle and the rest) it is the perfection of all the rest, and conteineth in it them all, therefore in the whole course I mention the deedes of Arthure applyable to that vertue, which I write of in that booke. But of the xii. other vertues, I make xii. other knights the patrones, for the more variety of the history: Of which these three bookes contayn three. The first of the knight of the Redcrosse, in whome I expresse Holynes: The seconde of Sir Guyon, in whome I sette forth Temperaunce: The third of Britomartis a Lady knight, in whome I picture Chastity. But because the beginning of the whole worke seemeth abrupte and as depending upon other antecedents, it needs that ye know the occasion of these three knights severall adventures. For the Methode of a Poet historical is not such, as of an Historiographer. For an Historiographer discourseth of affayres orderly as they were donne, accounting as well the times as the actions, but a Poet thrusteth into the middest,[1] even where it most concerneth him, and there recoursing to the thinges forepaste, and divining of thinges to come, maketh a pleasing Analysis of all. The beginning therefore of my history, if it were to be told by an Historiographer should be the twelfth booke, which is the last, where I devise that the Faery Queene kept her Annuall feaste xii. dayes, uppon which xii. severall dayes, the occasions of the xii. severall adventures hapned, which being undertaken by xii. severall knights, are in these xii. books severally handled and discoursed. The first was this. In the beginning of the feast, there presented him selfe a tall clownishe[2] younge man, who falling before the Queen of Faries desired a boone (as the manner then was) which during that feast she might not refuse: which was that hee might have the atchievement of any adventure, which during that feaste should happen, that being graunted, he rested him on the floore, unfitte through his rusticity for a better place. Soone after entred a faire Ladye in mourning weedes, riding on a white Asse, with a dwarfe behind her leading a warlike steed, that bore the Armes of a knight, and his speare in the dwarfes hand. Shee falling before the Queene of Faeries, complayned that her father and mother an ancient King and Queene, had bene by an huge dragon many years shut up in a brasen[3] Castle, who thence suffred them not to yssew: and therefore besought the Faery Queene to assygne her some one of her knights to take on him that exployt. Presently that clownish person upstarting, desired that adventure: whereat the Queene much wondering, and the Lady much gainesaying, yet he earnestly importuned his desire. In the end the Lady told him that unlesse that armour which she brought, would serve him (that is the armour of a Christian man specified by Saint Paul v. Ephes.[4]) that he could not succeed in that enterprise, which being forthwith put upon him with dewe furnitures[5] thereunto, he seemed

---

[1] See Horace, *Ars Poetica*, 146–52.

[2] **clownishe:** rustic.

[3] **brasen:** strong like brass.

[4] See Eph. 6.11–17.

[5] **dewe furnitures:** proper equipment.

the goodliest man in al that company, and was well liked of the Lady. And efte-soones[1] taking on him knighthood, and mounting on that straunge Courser, he went forth with her on that adventure: where beginneth the first booke, vz.

A gentle knight was pricking on the playne. &c.

The second day ther came in a Palmer bearing an Infant with bloody hands, whose Parents he complained to have bene slayn by an Enchaunteresse called Acrasia: and therfore craved of the Faery Queene, to appoint him some knight, to performe that adventure, which being assigned to Sir Guyon, he presently went forth with that same Palmer: which is the beginning of the second booke and the whole subject thereof.[2] The third day there came in, a Groome who complained before the Faery Queene, that a vile Enchaunter called Busirane had in hand a most faire Lady called Amoretta, whom he kept in most grievous torment, because she would not yield him the pleasure of her body. Whereupon Sir Scudamour the lover of that Lady presently tooke on him that adventure. But being unable to performe it by reason of the hard Enchauntments, after long sorrow, in the end met with Britomartis, who succoured him, and reskewed his love.

But by occasion hereof, many other adventures are intermedled, but rather as Accidents, then intendments.[3] As the love of Britomart, the overthrow of Marinell, the misery of Florimell, the vertuousnes of Belphoebe, the lasciviousnes of Hellenora, and many the like.[4]

Thus much Sir, I have briefly overronne to direct your understanding to the wel-head of the History, that from thence gathering the whole intention of the conceit, ye may as in a handfull gripe al the discourse, which otherwise may happily[5] seeme tedious and confused. So humbly craving the continuaunce of your honorable favour towards me, and th'eternall establishment of your happines, I humbly take leave.

23. January. 1589.[6]

Yours most humbly affectionate.
Ed. Spenser.

---

[1] **eftesoones:** immediately.

[2] This description is at variance with the beginning of Book Two at several points— e.g., the Palmer is already with Guyon when they encounter the bloody baby in Canto One.

[3] **intendments:** matters of central import.

[4] This description seems to make Scudamour the hero, rather than Britomart.

[5] **happily:** by chance.

[6] In the new calendar, 1590.

The Life of Edmund Spenser

Spenser (c. 1552–1599) was from a merchant family, possibly involved in the cloth trade and probably living in London. Although he may have been related to the noble family of Spencers, Spenser was not a gentleman. He was fortunate to attend the Merchant Taylors' School, an academy founded by the tailors' guild, and was registered there as a "poor scholar." The school, however, was excellent; in his eight years there, Spenser received a humanist education that was rich in classical scholarship and languages. In 1569 he entered Pembroke Hall, Cambridge. Again he was a scholarship student, called a sizar, earning room and board by performing servants' duties. In the same year that he arrived at Cambridge, Spenser was first published: several of his translations from Italian and French appeared in the Protestant miscellany *A Theatre for Worldlings.* Spenser completed a Bachelor of Arts degree in 1573, and then, in 1576, a Master of Arts (finishing 66th out of a class of 70). Spenser then began a career as secretary to high-ranking men, a position of some importance involving a broad array of duties that included much traveling and writing. Intermittent records show him serving as an emissary for the earl of Leicester, and in 1578 he was secretary to John Young, Bishop of Rochester. In 1579 he married Maccabaeus Chylde; we know little about the couple's family life other than the fact that they had two children. In 1580 he was appointed secretary to Lord Grey de Wilton, the new Lord Deputy of Ireland, and traveled there with him.

Spenser's career as a secretary and subsequent work as a civil servant in Ireland no doubt took up much of his time. But he was simultaneously establishing a second career as a poet. Probably while working for Leicester, Spenser met Philip Sidney and entered into his sophisticated literary circle. In 1579 Spenser published *The Shepheardes Calender,* his innovative and enormously influential collection of pastorals. It revealed Spenser not only as one of England's most skilled poets, but as a deeply interested and progressive Protestant thinker. He also cultivated his university friendship with the humanist scholar Gabriel Harvey, which in 1580 led to the publication of several of their letters. The Harvey letters mention several lost works, and suggest that by 1580 Spenser had begun working on *The Faerie Queene.*

Meanwhile, in Ireland with Lord Grey, Spenser participated in the complicated and exceedingly violent project of English colonialism. Grey was sent to govern a country that was struggling broadly against English domination, and he adopted a strategy of overwhelming force, including the notorious slaughter of 600 military prisoners at Smerwick, and policies aimed at subduing the population through famine. To what extent Spenser participated in Grey's governance, and to what extent he merely accompanied him and performed secretarial duties, is unclear. But it is clear that Spenser profited personally from empire building. Although Grey was recalled to England in 1582, Spenser made Ireland his permanent home, first in the New Abbey estate, and in 1589 in the three thousand acres of the Kilcolman estate. Throughout the 1580s, Spenser received a number of governmental appointments and established himself in Ireland as a well-off planter and gentleman. His complex relationship to Ireland is largely understood through *A View of the Present State of Ireland,* a prose dialogue that forthrightly defends Grey's violent tactics and advocates deeply repressive measures against the Irish. It has called forth both defenses of the poet and declarations of his complicity in the outrages of colonialism. The subtleties of *A View* cast a similarly complicated light on *The Faerie Queene,* which was written in Ireland, and reflects its beautiful and pitifully war-torn landscape.

In Ireland Spenser became friends with the explorer, author, and courtier Sir Walter Raleigh, who in 1589 traveled with him to England. Probably with the sponsorship of Raleigh, Spenser presented the first three books of *The Faerie Queene* to Elizabeth, who, by Spenser's report, was well pleased. Spenser secured the printer William Ponsonby in London, and Books One through Three of *The Faerie Queene* were published in 1590. The poem was a clear effort to win court favor, with a dedication to Elizabeth and as many as seventeen dedicatory sonnets to the major figures in court. As a reward, Spenser was granted a pension of £50 a year for life. Such a position in the patronage system of the day was not unusual, as poetry was commonly used as a means of preferment in court— for noblemen such as Sidney and Raleigh, it was one more personal accomplishment; for those like Spenser who were not noble, it was a way to win social and economic advantages. Spenser, however, maintained skepticism toward court life. In his pastoral "Colin Clouts Come Home Againe," which tells of his and Raleigh's journey to court, Colin declares that

> it is no sort of life,
> For shepheard fit to lead in that same place,
> Where each one seeks with malice and with strife,
> To thrust downe other into foule disgrace,
> Himselfe to raise.   (688–92)

Spenser returned to Ireland, where he lived, worked, and wrote throughout the 1590s. He published several important poems under the title of *Complaints* in 1591. In 1594 he married Elizabeth Boyle, resulting in at least one child, and in the following year he published *Amoretti* and *Epithalamion,* which celebrate their love and marriage. Throughout these years he continued work on *The Faerie Queene,* and in 1596 published the second edition. This extended the poem to six books; its final form was reached in the posthumous 1609 edition, with the inclusion of the fragment of a seventh book, the *Mutabilitie Cantos.* In 1596 he also published *Fowre Hymnes* and *Prothalamion.*

Spenser may have traveled to London to oversee the second printing of *The Faerie Queene.* If so, he returned to an Ireland wracked by rebellion. In 1598 the Tyrone Rebellion reached Munster, and Spenser and his family fled Kilcolman just before the estate was sacked and burned. Spenser carried letters from the President of Munster to the Privy Council in England, describing the military crisis. On January 13, 1599, while still in England, Spenser died. His life ended under the shadow cast by the destruction of his home and the scattering of his interests in Ireland, which Ben Jonson described, possibly hyperbolically, as dying "for lack of bread." Spenser's hearse was reportedly attended by poets, who threw their verses and pens into his tomb as he was buried in Poets' Corner at Westminster Abbey.

Textual Notes

This text is based upon the 1590 edition of *The Faerie Queene,* London: printed by John Wolfe for William Ponsonbie (STC 23081). It was edited from a reproduction of the original in the British Library by way of microfilm (UMI, Early English Books, 1475–1640). It has been checked against the *Faults Escaped* printed at the end of the 1590 edition (*F.E.*), and against the 1596 edition (STC 23082) and the 1609 edition (STC 23083). Quotation marks have been added; *i, j, s, u,* and *v* have been modernized; and abbreviations, ampersands, and diphthongs have been spelled out. Departures from the 1590 edition have been made with the aim of clarifying the text for modern readers. The table below lists substantive variants.

ii.Arg.3 stead] *F.E.,* 1596, 1609; steps, 1590.

ii.16.5. stand senceless] *F.E.,* 1596, 1609; stands fenceless, 1590.

ii.17.5 cruell spies] *F.E.;* cruelties, 1590, 1596, 1609.

ii.32.9 plaints] 1596, 1609; plants, 1590.

iv.22.8 corse] *F.E.,* 1596, 1609; course, 1590.

iv.45.5 of my new joy] *F.E.,* 1609; of new joy, 1590, 1596.

vi.26.5 fiers and fell] *F.E.,* 1596, 1609; swift and cruell, 1590.

vi.39.7 (quoth he)] 1596, 1609; (quoth she), 1590.

vi.44.1 fell] 1596, 1609; full, 1590.

viii.Arg.3 *the Gyaunt*] *F.E.; that Gyaunt,*1590, 1596, 1609.

ix.Arg 2 *hands*] 1590; *bands, F.E.,* 1596, 1609. In following 1590 here, in accordance with ix.1.8–9, I disagree with ACH.

ix.9.5. Timons] *F.E.,* 1596, 1609; Cleons, 1590.

ix.12.9 on] *F.E.,* 1609; at, 1590, 1596.

ix.52.1 saw] 1596, 1609; heard, 1590.

x.16.8 her] *F.E.;* be, 1590, 1596, 1609.

x.20.5 Dry-shod . . . tway;] 1609; not in 1590, 1596.

xi.3.1-9 And . . . misery.] 1596, 1609; not in 1590. This entire stanza appears for the first time in 1596.

xi.30.5 one] *F.E.;* it, 1590, 1596, 1609.

xi.41.4 Nor] 1609; For, 1590, 1596.

xii.34.2 vaine] *F.E.,* 1596, 1609; faine, 1590.

GLOSSARY

addressed/dressed: Directed, arranged, made ready for a purpose.

affray: Frighten.

amate/mate: Frustrate, frighten.

approved: Proved by testing and experience.

aread: Tell, explain, express; passive: aredd.

astownd: Confused, stunned; similar to astonied, astond.

balefull: In a passive sense: wretched, tormented; active: dire, fatal, bloodthirsty.

bewray: Manifest the presence of.

blent: Blemished or blinded.

borne: Carried off.

can: Did.

caytive: In a moral sense: base; physical sense: captive.

charet: Chariot, cart.

chaufed: Irritated, physically or mentally or both.

chear: Noun: disposition as manifested by external demeanor; intransitive verb: cheer up.

couch: Bring a spear down from its vertical position and lay it horizontally in the rest.

curious: In objective sense: elaborate.

despight: Insult or wrathful response thereto.

devise/devize: Talk.

dight: Dressed, arranged for a purpose.

dwell: Remain.

earst: Recently, a little while ago.

Eftsoones/eftesoones: Then; in consciously archaistic use: forthwith, immediately.

eke: Adv.: also.

embrewd/imbrewd: Steeped, soaked.

equal: Impartial.

errant: On a quest.

fain, faine, fayne: Adj. or adv.: eager, happy to do something (one possible meaning).

fell: Ruthless.

fitt: Mood.

forlore: Abandoned.

forwearied: Very wearied.

fray: Verb: make afraid.

Furies: Deities who see that crimes, especially murder, are avenged.

german: Relative.

girlonds: Garlands.

guerdon: Reward.

guise: Behavior.

habiliment: Attire.

hardly: With difficulty.

heben: Ebon, of ebony.

hight: Am called, designated; past tense: hot.

impe: Scion, offspring, with no sense of the modern impish.

implyes: Enfolds.

kind/unkind: In its older sense: natural/unnatural.

launch(ed): Pierce(ed).

light: Frivolous, sexually wanton; lightly: frivolously.

meed: Due reward or sometimes punishment.

mote: Past tense of verb, might.

mould: Structure, something made out of something.

noyous: Harmful.

or: Whether (one possible meaning).

ought: Owned.

payne: Care (as in painstaking), industry.

Paynim: Non-Christian, especially Saracen or Muslim.

pight: Securely placed, installed.

pine: Noun: emaciation; pine/pined, verb: starve, pine away, also cause somebody to do so.

priefe: Experiential test.

prov'd: Tested by experience, synomous with approved.

prowest: Superlative of prow, adj.: having prowess, or fighting ability.

purpose: Topic of conversation.

quite/quight: Requite, repay.

raught: Variant form of reached.

read: Figure out, tell.

reave: Snatch, take away violently; past tense: Reft.

rive/riven: Split open.

routes: Crowds.

rusty: Filthy or defiled, usually from use, not disuse.

ruth: Noun: pity; verb is rue/rew.

salvage: Spenser's unvarying spelling of savage; as adj.: wild; as noun: wild humanoid.

Sarazin: Saracen, Muslim from the Near East.

seely, silly: Innocent.

sithens/sithence: Since. As conjunctive adverb, synonymous with one meaning of "sith."

spright: Spirit, either an independent being with a body made of air, or the immaterial part of a human being.

stedd: Stead, place.

stownd: A short period of time, usually defined by the context as painful.

stowre: A time of turmoil, pain, and stress.

talaunts: Talons.

teene/tine: Sorrow, trouble.

tho: Then.

thrall: Prisoner.

thrill, thrild: Pierce, pierced.

trayne(s): Trickery.

trayne, traine: Of animals, tail; of humans, retinue.

uneath: Ill at ease, or with difficulty. Opposite of eath which means easy

unweeting: Unawares, not knowing; see weet.

wayne: Wagon, cart, or chariot.

weaker: Too weak; the "-er" ending on any adj. often denotes "too."

weedes: Clothes.

weet: Know.

wex, wexed, wox: Past tense of wax: grow, become; woxen: the perfect passive participle.

whylome: Formerly, some time ago.

wide: Off to one side.

wight: Human being.

wonne: Verb: remain, dwell; noun: dwelling.

wont: Verb: was accustomed; adj.: wonted accustomed; unwonted: unaccustomed.

wood: Crazy.

wot(e): Know; past tense of weet.

wot: Know.

wreak: Avenge.

ycled: Clad, clothed.

INDEX OF CHARACTERS

References to and appearances of major characters in Book One are listed by canto and stanza. In parentheses are references and appearances in other books, listed by book, canto, and stanza. This index is indebted to Shohachi Fukuda's "The Characters of *The Faerie Queene*" in ACH.

WORKS CITED AND SUGGESTIONS FOR FURTHER READING

Items marked with an asterisk are recommended for further reading.

Aeschylus. *The Eumenides*. Translated by Richmond Lattimore. *Greek Tragedies*, vol. 3. Edited by David Grene and Richmond Lattimore. 3 vols. Chicago, IL: University of Chicago Press, 1960.★

Alighieri, Dante. *The Divine Comedy of Dante Alighieri with Translation and Comment by John D. Sinclair.* 3 vols. New York: Oxford University Press, 1961.★

Auerbach, Erich. "Figura." Translated by Ralph Manheim. *Scenes from the Drama of European Literature: Six Essays.* New York: Meridien Books, 1959. 11–76.

Benson, Larry D. *Sir Thomas Malory.* Cambridge, MA: Harvard University Press, 1976.★

[Bible, Geneva] The Bible, that is, the Holy Scriptures conteined in the Olde and Newe Testament. London: Christopher Barker, 1594.

Bloomfield, Morton. "A Grammatical Approach to Personification-Allegory." *Essays and Explorations: Studies in Ideas, Language, and Literature.* Cambridge, MA: Harvard University Press, 1970. 243–60.

———. *The Seven Deadly Sins.* East Lansing, MI: Michigan State University Press, 1967.★

Chaucer, Geoffrey. *The Riverside Chaucer.* 3rd ed. Edited by Larry D. Benson. Boston: Houghton Mifflin, 1987.

Chew, Samuel Claggett. *The Pilgrimage of Life.* New Haven, CT: Yale University Press, 1962.

Chrétien de Troyes. *Yvain, or the Knight with the Lion.* Translated by Ruth Harwood Cline. Athens, GA: University of Georgia Press, 1975.★

Collinson, Patrick. *The Elizabethan Puritan Movement.* Berkeley, CA: University of California Press, 1967.

———. "The Elizabethan Church and the New Religion." *The Reign of Elizabeth I.* Edited by Christopher Haigh. Athens, GA: University of Georgia Press, 1985. 169–94.

Comes, Natalis. See: Lotspeich.

Cooper, Helen. *The English Romance in Time: Transforming Motifs from Geoffrey of Monmouth to the Death of Shakespeare.* Oxford: Oxford University Press, 2004.★

Cooper, Thomas. *Thesaurus Linguae Romanae et Britannicae. 1565.* Menston, England: Scolar Press, 1969.

Cullen, Patrick. *The Infernal Triad: The Flesh, the World, and the Devil in Spenser and Milton.* Princeton, NJ: Princeton University Press, 1974.

Davis, Walter R. *Sidney's Arcadia. A Map of Arcadia: Sidney's Romance in Its Tradition.* New Haven, CT: Yale University Press, 1965.

Frye, Northrop. *The Secular Scripture: A Study of the Structure of Romance.* Cambridge, MA: Harvard University Press, 1976.★

Gless, Darryl J. *Interpretation and Theology in Spenser.* Cambridge: Cambridge University Press, 1994.

Gower, John. *Confessio amantis.* Edited by Russell Peck. New York: Rinehart, 1968.

Greenlaw, Edwin, et al., eds. *The Works of Edmund Spenser, A Variorum Edition.* Eleven vols. Baltimore: The Johns Hopkins Press, 1932–1957.

Hadfield, Andrew, ed. *The Cambridge Companion to Spenser.* Cambridge: Cambridge University Press, 2001.★

Haigh, Christopher. "The Church of England, the Catholics and the People." *The Reign of Elizabeth I.* Edited by Christopher Haigh. Athens, GA: University of Georgia Press, 1985. 195–219.

Hamilton, A. C., ed. *Essential Articles for the Study of Edmund Spenser.* Hamden, CT: Archon Books, 1972.★

———. *The Structure of Allegory in* The Faerie Queene. Oxford: Clarendon Press, 1961.

Hamilton, A. C., et al., eds. *Spenser Encyclopedia.* Toronto: University of Toronto Press, 1990.★

Hankins, John E. *Source and Meaning in Spenser's Allegory.* Oxford: Clarendon Press, 1961.

Hawes, Stephen. *The Works of Stephen Hawes.* Introduction by Frank J. Spang. Delmar, NY: Scholars' Facsimiles & Reprints, 1975.

Heale, Elizabeth. The Faerie Queene: *A Reader's Guide.* 2nd ed. Cambridge: Cambridge University Press, 1987.★

Homer. *The Iliad of Homer.* Translated by Richmond Lattimore. Chicago, IL: University of Chicago Press, 1951.★

Homer. *The Odyssey.* Translated by E.V. Rieu. Baltimore: Penguin, 1951.★

Hooker, Richard. *The Works.* Arranged by John Keble; revised by R.W. Church and F.W. Paget. 3 vols. New York: Burt Franklin, 1970 [repr. of Oxford, 1888].

Hough, Graham. *A Preface to* The Faerie Queene. New York: Norton, 1963.

Jacobus de Voragine. *The Golden Legend; or, Lives of the Saints as Englished by William Caxton.* Edited by F[rederick] Ellis. 7 vols. London: J.M. Dent, 1900.★

Kaske, Carol V. "The Dragon's Spark and Sting and the Structure of Red Cross's Dragon-Fight: The Faerie Queene, I.xi–xii." In *Essential Articles for the Study of Edmund Spenser,* edited by A.C. Hamilton, 425–46. Hamden, CT: Archon Books, 1972.

————. "How Spenser Really Used Stephen Hawes." *Unfolded Tales: Essays on Renaissance Romance*. Edited by George M. Logan and Gordon Teskey. Ithaca, NY: Cornell University Press, 1989. 119–36.

————. *Spenser and Biblical Poetics*. Ithaca, NY: Cornell University Press, 1999.

————. "Spenser's Pluralistic Universe: The View from the Mount of Contemplation (Faerie Queene, I.x)." In *Contemporary Thought on Edmund Spenser*. Edited by Richard C. Frushell and Bernard J. Vondersmith, 121–49, 320–33. Carbondale, IL: Southern Illinois University Press, 1975.

Kennedy, William J. "Rhetoric, Allegory, and Dramatic Modality in Spenser's Fradubio Episode." *English Literary Renaissance* 3:351–68.

King, John N. *Spenser's Poetry and the Reformation Tradition*. Princeton, NJ: Princeton University Press, 1990.

Lake, Peter. *Anglicans and Puritans? Presbyterianism and English Conformist Thought from Whitgift to Hooker*. London, Boston: Unwin, Hyman, 1988.

Langland, William. *The Vision of Piers the Plowman: A Complete Edition of the B-Text*. Edited by A.V.C. Schmidt. London: Dent (Everyman), 1978.

Lewis, C.S. *The Allegory of Love: A Study in Medieval Tradition*. Oxford: Oxford University Press, 1938.★

Lorris, Guillaume de, and Jean de Meun. *The Romance of the Rose*. Translated into English Verse by Harry W. Robbins. Edited and with an Introduction by Charles W. Dunn. New York: Dutton, 1962.

Lotspeich, Henry Gibbons. *Classical Mythology in the Poetry of Edmund Spenser*. Princeton, NJ: Princeton University Press, 1990. [Translates all passages in Natalis Comes to which Spenser refers.]

Lovelace, Richard. "To Lucasta, Going to the Wars." Richard Aldington, ed. *The Viking Book of Poetry of the English-Speaking World*. New York: Viking Press, 1944. 446–7.

Low, Anthony. "Sin, Penance and Privatization in the Renaissance: Redcrosse and the True Church." *Ben Jonson Journal* 5 (1998): 1–35.

Luther, Martin. *Martin Luther: Selections from His Writings*. Edited by John Dillenberger. Garden City, NY: Anchor Books, 1961.

Malory, Sir Thomas. *Le Morte D'Arthur* [Caxton version]. Edited by Janet Cowen. Introduction by John Lawlor. 2 vols. Harmondsworth: Penguin Books, 1969.★

Marotti, Arthur. "Alienating Catholics in Early Modern England: Recusant Women, Jesuits, and Ideological Fantasies." *Catholicism and Anti-Catholicisn in Early Modern England*. Edited by Arthur Marotti. New York: St. Martin's, 1999. 1–34.

Miller, Jacqueline. "The Omission in Red Cross Knight's Story: Narrative Inconsistencies in *The Faerie Queene.*" *ELH: A Journal of Literary History* 53 (1986): 279–88.

Oram, William A. *Edmund Spenser.* New York: Twayne Publishers; London: Prentice Hall International, 1997.★

Ovid. *Metamorphoses.* Translated by Frank Justus Miller. 2 vols. London: Heinemann; Cambridge, MA: Harvard University Press, 1921–1922.★

Phillips, James E. "Spenser's Syncretistic Religious Imagery." *ELH: A Journal of Literary History* 36 (1969): 110–30.

Roche, Thomas P. *Edmund Spenser:* The Faerie Queene. New York: Penguin, 1978.

————. "Spenser's Muse." *Unfolded Tales: Essays on Renaissance Romance.* Edited by George M. Logan and Gordon Teskey. Ithaca, NY: Cornell University Press, 1989. 162–88.

Sidney, Sir Philip. *The Countess of Pembroke's Arcadia (the Old Arcadia).* Edited, with introduction and commentary, by Jean Robertson. Oxford: Clarendon Press, 1973.

————. *The Countess of Pembroke's Arcadia (The New Arcadia).* Edited by Victor Skretkowicz. Oxford: Clarendon Press, 1970.

Sophocles. *Oedipus the King.* Translated by David Grene. *Greek Tragedies,* v. 3. Edited by David Grene and Richmond Lattimore. 3 vols. Chicago: University of Chicago Press, 1960.★

Spenser, Edmund. *Edmund Spenser:* The Faerie Queene. Edited by Thomas P. Roche and C. Patrick O'Donnell. New York: Penguin, 1978.★

————. *Edmund Spenser's Poetry.* Selected and edited by Hugh Maclean and Anne Lake Prescott. 3rd ed. New York: Norton, 1993.★

————. *The Faerie Queene.* 1596 Facsimile. Introduction by Graham Hough. London: Scolar Press, 1977.

————. *The Faerie Queene.* Edited by A. C. Hamilton. Text edited by Hiroshi Yamashita and Toshiyuki Suzuki. New York: Longman, 2001.★

————. *Shorter Poems.* Edited by Richard McCabe. London: Penguin, 1999.★

————. *The Works of Edmund Spenser. A Variorum Edition.* Edited by Edwin Greenlaw et al. 11 vols. Baltimore: The Johns Hopkins Press, 1932–1957.

————. *The Yale Edition of the Shorter Poems of Edmund Spenser.* Edited by William A. Oram et al. New Haven, CT: Yale University Press, 1989.

Tasso, Torquato. *Jerusalem Delivered: Being a translation into English verse by Edward Fairfax of Tasso's Gerusalemme Liberata.* Introduction by John Charles Nelson. New York: Capricorn Books, 1963.

————. *Tasso's Allegory of Gerusalemme liberata.* Translated by Lawrence Rhu. In *The Genesis of Tasso's Narrative Theory,* by Lawrence Rhu, 155–62. Detroit: Wayne State University Press, 1993.

Torczon, Vern[on]. "On Spenser's Orgoglio and Despaire." *Texas Studies in Language and Literature* 3 (1991): 123–8.

Virgil. "Aeneid" in *Virgil*. Translated by H. R. Fairclough. 2 vols. London: Heinemann; Cambridge, MA: Harvard University Press, 1966–1967

Waters, D. Douglas. *Duessa as Theological Satire*. Columbia, MO: University of Missouri Press, 1970.

Watkins, John. "James I and Elizabethan Anti-Catholicism." *Catholicisim and Anti-Catholicism in Early Modern England*. Edited by Arthur Marotti. New York: St. Martin's, 1999. 116–36.

Weatherby, Harold. *Mirrors of Celestial Grace: Patristic Theology in Spenser's Allegory*. Toronto: University of Toronto Press, 1994.

Wells, Robin H. "Spenser's Christian Knight: Erasmian Theology in *The Faerie Queene*, Book I." *Anglia* 97 (1979): 350–66.★

Whitaker, Virgil K. *The Religious Basis of Spenser's Thought*. Stanford, CA: Stanford University Press, 1950.★

Williams, Arnold. "Medieval Allegory: An Operational Approach." *Poetic Theory/Poetic Practice: Papers of the Midwest Modern Language Association 1969, presented at the annual meeting for 1968. October 17, 18 and 19, in Cincinnati, Ohio.* Edited by Robert Scholes. Iowa City, IA: Midwest Modern Language Association, 1969. 77–84.★

Woodhouse, A.S.P. "Nature and Grace in *The Faerie Queene*." In *Essential Articles for the Study of Edmund Spenser,* edited by A. C. Hamilton, 58–83. Hamden, CT: Archon Books, 1972.

Yates, Frances. *Astraea: The Imperial Theme in the Sixteenth Century*. London: Routledge, 1975.